Ordo Salutis

BOOKS BY JAMES D. QUIGGLE

DOCTRINAL SERIES
Biblical History
Adam and Eve, a Biography and Theology
Angelology, a True History of Angels

Essays
Biblical Essays
Biblical Essays II
Biblical Essays III
Biblical Essays IV

Marriage And Family
Marriage and Family: A Biblical Perspective
Biblical Homosexuality
A Biblical Response to Same-gender Marriage

Doctrinal And Practical Christianity
First Steps, Becoming a Follower of Jesus Christ
A Christian Catechism (with Christopher McCuin)
Why and How to do Bible Study
Thirty-Six Essentials of the Christian Faith
The Literal Hermeneutic, Explained and Illustrated
The Old Ten In the New Covenant
Christian Living and Doctrine
Spiritual Gifts
Also Known As Tongues
Why Christians Should Not Tithe

Dispensational Theology
A Primer On Dispensationalism
Understanding Dispensational Theology
Covenants and Dispensations in the Scripture
Dispensational Soteriology
Dispensational Eschatology, An Explanation and Defense of the Doctrine
Rapture: A Bible Study on the Rapture of the New Testament Church
Antichrist, His Genealogy, Kingdom, and Religion

God And Man
Ordo Salutis: The Way of Salvation

God's Choices, Doctrines of Foreordination, Election, Predestination
God Became Incarnate
Life, Death, Eternity
Did Jesus Go To Hell?
Against Physicalism, Annihilationism, and Conditionalism

Small Group Bible Studies
Elementary Bible Principles (with Linda M. Quiggle)
Counted Worthy (with Linda M. Quiggle)

COMMENTARY SERIES
The Old Testament
A Private Commentary on the Bible: Judges
A Private Commentary on the Book of Ruth
A Private Commentary on the Bible: Esther
A Private Commentary on the Bible: Song of Solomon
A Private Commentary on the Bible: Daniel
A Private Commentary on the Bible: Jonah
A Private Commentary on the Bible: Habakkuk
A Private Commentary on the Bible: Haggai

The New Testament
James Quiggle Translation New Testament (JQTNT)

The Gospels And Acts
A Private Commentary on the Bible: Matthew's Gospel
A Private Commentary on the Bible: Mark's Gospel
A Private Commentary on the Bible: Luke 1–12
A Private Commentary on the Bible: Luke 13–24
A Private Commentary on the Bible: John 1–12
A Private Commentary on the Bible: John 13–21
A Private Commentary on the Bible: Acts 1–14
A Private Commentary on the Bible: Acts 15–28

Other Works On The Gospels
Four Voices, One Testimony (a Gospel Harmony)
Jesus Said "I Am"
The Parables and Miracles of Jesus Christ

The Passion and Resurrection of Jesus the Christ
The Christmas Story, As Told By God
Christmas Card Theology and the Bible

Pauline Letters
A Private Commentary on the Bible: 1 Corinthians
A Private Commentary on the Bible: Galatians
A Private Commentary on the Bible: Ephesians
A Private Commentary on the Bible: Philippians
A Private Commentary on the Bible: Colossians
A Private Commentary on the Bible: Thessalonians
A Private Commentary on the Bible: Pastoral Letters
A Private Commentary on the Bible: Philemon

General Letters
A Private Commentary on the Book of Hebrews
A Private Commentary on the Bible: James
A Private Commentary on the Bible: 1 Peter
A Private Commentary on the Bible: 2 Peter
A Private Commentary on the Bible: John's Epistles
A Private Commentary on the Bible: Jude

Revelation
A Private Commentary on the Bible: Revelation 1–7
A Private Commentary on the Bible: Revelation 8–16
A Private Commentary on the Bible: Revelation 17–22

REFERENCE SERIES
James Quiggle Translation New Testament (JQTNT)
Dictionary of Doctrinal Words
Old and New Testament Chronology (With David Hollingsworth)
(Also in individual volumes: Old Testament Chronology; New Testament Chronology)

TRACTS
A Human Person: Is the Unborn Life a Person?
Biblical Marriage
How Can I Know I am A Christian?
Now That I am A Christian

Thirty-Six Essentials of the Christian Faith

What is a Pastor? / Why is My Pastor Eating the Sheep?

Principles and Precepts of the Literal Hermeneutic

(All tracts are in digital format and cost $0.99)

Formats

Print, Digital, Epub, PDF. Search "James D. Quiggle" or book title.

Ordo Salutis

The Way of Salvation

James D. Quiggle

Table of Contents

Table of Contents

Introduction

The term "Ordo Salutis" is a Latin phrase meaning "the order of salvation." The Ordo Salutis is a theological construct of what is believed to be a logical sequence of events in God's work of saving a sinner and bringing that saved sinner to heaven.

There is nothing wrong with building a theological construct from biblical doctrines. God designed humankind with the ability to apply reason to knowledge. "Without reason there can be no religion: for in every step which we take, in examining the evidences of revelation, in interpreting its meaning, or in assenting to its doctrines, the exercise of this faculty is indispensable" [Alexander, 3–4]. The key to a proper biblical construct is to include all the biblical data.

There are two major Ordo Salutis, that of Reformed soteriology and that of Arminian soteriology. (Soteriology: the doctrine of salvation.)

> Reformed Ordo Salutis: election/predestination, followed by evangelism, regeneration, conversion, justification, sanctification, and glorification.

> Arminian Ordo Salutis: evangelism, followed by faith/election, repentance, regeneration, justification, perseverance, and glorification.

[Source: https://www.theopedia.com/ordo-salutis]

Naturally, the teaching of the Scripture as a whole must be sought. For example, an Ordo Salutis based on Romans 8:29–30, which is the basis of the Reformed Ordo Salutis, does not reflect the teaching of Scripture as a whole. By ignoring Romans 8:28 the Reformed Ordo Salutis does not include the theological basis for election/predestination, which is foreordination, expressed in Romans 8:28 as "being called according to his purpose."

As a consequence of over fifty years of Bible study, I have not been entirely satisfied with either the Reformed or the Arminian Ordo Salutis. Theologically, I am in agreement the Reformed view. But the Reformed view fails to interact with other aspects of salvation, e.g., perseverance. The Arminian view of faith-based election is hand-in-glove with Open Theism (God learns).

The way of salvation begins with God's purpose in creating, then

God's foreordination of events, continues throughout the Christian life, and ends with conscious active life endlessly in the presence of God. The focus of this book is an explanation of my view of all the elements of what I consider to be a scriptural Ordo Salutis. Each chapter discusses specific aspects of my view.

In the Table of Contents (TOC) I have given what I believe to be a scriptural Ordo Salutis, for all believers from Adam to end of this present heavens and earth. Here is the list from the TOC, with a few explanatory comments.

Foreordination, Election, Predestination
    An explanation of God's choices
Why All Are Sinners
    Conceived in sin, free will dominated by sin
Christ's Propitiation of God
    The legal satisfaction for the crime of sin
Hearing the Good News
    What is the Gospel?
Responding to the Good News
    How the unwilling and unable are made willing and able
Saving faith, Forgiveness, Eternal life, Regeneration
    The permanent change from sinner to saved
Positional Justification and Sanctification in Christ
    The believer's standing before God in Christ.
Adoption as a Consequence of Predestination
    The believer's position as one of the sons of God
Security and Assurance of Salvation
    The merit that secures and the testimony that assures
Perseverance and Experiential Sanctification
    The believer's state in the world
Physical Death, Soul Transformed, Intermediate State
    Conscious, active life after physical death
Transformation and Reanimation of the Body
    Resurrection
Endless Life Body and Soul in the Presence of God

The endless state of the believer after resurrection

My version of the Ordo Salutis is not as simple as the Reformed and Arminian views, but neither is the teaching of Scripture so simple.

In part, my version of the Ordo Salutis is based on my construct of six points of salvation.

Particular Redemption by God's Choice

Christ's All-sufficient Propitiation of God

Free Will Dominated by Sin

Enlivened by God's Efficacious Grace

Faith that Receives Salvation and Eternal Life

Perseverance in the Faith by Faith to the End of Life.

Some of the information in this book is from my previously published books. See Sources.

Foreordination, Election, Predestination

Introduction

Before creating the universe, Genesis 1:1, God made choices as to what kind of universe he would create. The Ordo Salutis properly begins with God's choices, which are collectively known as foreordination. Election and predestination are among God's foreordaining choices.

Definitions and Discussions

To understand the concepts of foreordination, election, and predestination, one must begin with God's sovereignty and God's omniscience.

Sovereignty

God's Sovereignty. God's omnipresent authority, omnipotent power, absolute holiness, and omniscient wisdom to govern himself and his creation and creatures as seems best to himself, in complete agreement with his essence and character as God, without experiencing effective opposition.

God's sovereignty means his choices incorporate all means to accomplish them, all consequences resulting from them, and all results—the end or goal—purposed in them. When man or angel makes a choice he wonders what will happen. When God makes a choice it includes everything that will happen and the outcome of those events. That is sovereignty.

God's sovereignty works in a specific manner with humankind. That manner is God's omnipotence, omniscience, omnipresence, holiness, justice, and love working together to infallibly accomplish God's purposes, plans, and processes through a person's choices to do right or wrong. Stated in practical terms, God's sovereignty works through man's responsibility and holds man accountable for his choices.

Omniscience

God's Omniscience. God has all knowledge and all understanding within himself without requiring knowledge or understanding outside himself. There are no exceptions to God's knowledge. There are no exclusions to God's understanding. Because God is all-knowing and all-understanding, God is all-wise.

Through the exercise of his omniscience God sovereignly determined a perfect purpose for his creation, and the perfect means and perfect ends to accomplish that perfect purpose. Those perfect means and perfect ends are encompassed in God's foreordaining decrees.

Omnisciently, God not only knows all things <u>actual</u>, but also knows all things <u>possible</u>. God does not know omnisciently because of his omnipresence in time and space, God knows omnisciently within himself; more simply, God does not learn anything, God knows everything without exception or exclusion.

In relationship to his sentient creatures (angels and human beings), God's omniscient knowledge and understanding includes all <u>possible</u> freely made choices that <u>could</u> be made by all his sentient creatures. By foreordination God has effectuated from possible to actual those possible freely made choices that actually <u>will be</u> made by all his sentient creatures. The freely made choices of the creature have been made certain (but not necessary, not fate, not determinism) by the sovereign Creator. Certain because foreordained, not necessary because freely made.

God's omniscience is opposed to the doctrine of Open Theism, which teaches God learns from experience and observation. In essence, Open Theism says God does not know by his omniscience what his creatures will do, God learns what his creatures will do by observation through his omnipresence.

God's omniscience is also opposed to the Arminian doctrine of foresight election, which closely resembles Open Theism. Foresight election states that God, as being omnipresent in time as well as space, discovered by observation who would believe and be saved, and on the basis of that experiential knowledge God elected those persons to salvation.

Omnipresence

God's Omnipresence: God is fully and immediately present in every possible aspect and dimension, spatial and temporal, in all created domains. God interpenetrates all created domains but his essence remains separate from all created domains and all that is in those domains. Simply put, all created domains have their existence within the one permanent domain that is God himself.

A domain is a sphere of existence. God is his own domain. God omnipotently created domains of existence other than himself, within the one permanent domain this is himself. There are no domains other than God himself and what God has created. God did not create other domains out of himself, but created *ex nihilo*. The two domains we know God created are the material domain and the spirit domain. Both the material and the spirit domains were created with the aspects of time and space.

God himself does not have time or space. God has spatial and temporal omnipresence in the time and space of all created domains, because those created domains exist within the increate domain that is God himself. Illustrations of God's spatial and temporal omnipresence in all created domains.

> Illustration, spatial omnipresence: imagine a sponge in the ocean. The ocean interpenetrates the sponge while remaining separate from it. God's spatial omnipresence is like the ocean, the sponge is like the created domains.

> Illustration temporal omnipresence: think of a person's existence. God is present simultaneously at every moment of the time and space of that person's existence.

God simultaneously experiences every place and moment of space-time because he thoroughly permeates the space and time he created without being a part of it. In simpler terms: God's omnipresence means he is present everywhere at once in the space and time of the material and spirit domains of the universe God created.

God himself is an eternal domain: increate, no beginning, no ending. The domains God created are temporary, 2 Peter 3:10; Revelation 20:11; 21:1.

God's Eternality And Infinitude

God's omnipresence must not be confused with God's eternality or infinity.

> God eternal. "I am he who exists," Exodus 3:14. God is increate, self-existent (John 5:26), without beginning and without end. Only God is eternal. All which is not God was created by God and continues in existence because maintained by God.

Time, therefore, and space, are not part of God's eternality, but time and space were created by God. Space is the material and spirit domains of the universe God created. Time is a mechanism God created to regulate and manage the universe God created.

God's infinitude must be viewed in relationship to himself and in relation to the universe he created.

> In relationship to himself. God is not infinite in the sense of space-time, but in that he is beyond any limitation of essence. God's essence has no space-time. God is beyond any limitation of being, substance, or essence.

> In relationship to the universe he created. God is immeasurable because he has no material or spiritual dimension, incomprehensible because he has no all-encompassing boundary, and everywhere because there is no place from which he is excluded and no place to which he is limited. [Ames, 86.]

THE DOCTRINE OF FOREORDINATION

Foreordination, An Overview

Many people, including believers, view foreordination in the sense of fate, or destiny, making human beings God's victims instead of participants in God's works. This chapter will clearly show foreordination is not fate or destiny. Human choices are certain, because foreordained, but not necessary (fate, destiny) because freely made.

In the simplest expression, foreordination is God deciding his purpose and works, before doing his works to accomplish his purpose.

In more detail. God, omnisciently knowing all possible agents, events, and outcomes that <u>might</u> occur in the universe he would create, including all <u>possible</u> choices that might be <u>freely made</u> by all the sentient creatures that would exist in the universe he would create, chose which possible agents, events, outcomes, and choices he would effectuate from possible to <u>actual</u> in the universe he created. Therefore, no freely made choice is necessary, because in the moment it is freely made by the sentient being, but all freely made choices are certain, because foreordained by God from possible to actual.

> Foreordination. The decree of God occurring between his decision to create and his act of creation as to which agents, events, and outcomes, out of all possible agents, events, and outcomes potential in the decision to create, would pass from possible to actual, in which the liberty or contingency of secondary causes is established, in which God is not the author of sin, and in which no violence is done to the free will of his creatures.

Prior to the act of creation, God omnisciently knew whatever might or could come to pass upon all supposed conditions. This was not the knowing of foresight, but God omnisciently understanding all possible agents, events, and outcomes (which outcomes included all possible freely made choices that might be made by all beings he would create and all possible consequences resulting from their choices) that could develop from the act of creation. God did not decree anything because he foresaw it as future, but because he determined all that was possible, and then chose which of all possible he would foreordain as actual.

Foreordination, A Discussion

To speak about God foreordaining is difficult because of the impossibility of the right terms and perspectives. For example, there is no exact term for when God decided to create, when God decided why he would create, and when God decided what he would create. There is no "when" in eternity; there is no "now" in eternity. There is only God's existence, which is neither when nor now, but simply is: "I am he who exists." A term has been invented for the when of God's foreordaining decisions: Aeviternity.

> Aeviternity. The state that logically lies between the timeless state of God and the temporal state of the things and creatures God created. God's pre-creation decisions as to what kind of universe to create were made in Aeviternity.

Scripture teaches God is increate, eternal, without space or time, Exodus 3:14, "I exist because I exist." Scripture teaches that within the space and time of the universe God created that God's works occur successively; otherwise God could not act within the time and space he created and to which his creation is subject.

Seen from God's perspective, because God is omnipresent at every moment in time and in every place in space, God is always working in the time and space he created, not successively, but omnipresently. Seen from his creature's perspective, as time in the universe progresses successively from past to present to future, God's works are occurring within the present time of his creatures, as his creatures progress successively from past to present to future.

Time is a tool, a mechanism God created to govern the universe he created. God is not subject to time, but he acts within time—he uses time as a tool for his interaction with his creation. God's works within the universe he created occur within the succession of moments and duration we define as "time."

What is time? Time is defined by duration and succession.

Duration: the continuing existence of a thing from beginning to end.

God himself does not have duration because he has no beginning and no end. The universe God created has duration because it had a beginning, Genesis 1:1, and has an end, 2 Peter 3:10; Revelation 20:10, 21:1.

Succession: the act or process of following in order or sequence.

God himself does not have succession. The universe God created has succession in its duration, a succession that God acts with and within. God acts with and within the succession of time because God is omnipresent at every moment of that succession.

We, being creatures subject to duration and succession, think of duration and succession as "time." Time is the succession of moments from past to present to future. Time is the duration of moments from beginning to end. A definition: time is the succession of moments from past to present to future occurring within a duration from beginning to end.

God exists without beginning or end: he has no beginning because he is increate, he has no end because he is eternal. Because God is increate and eternal God does not have duration: he has always existed and always will exist. There is no succession of moments in God's eternal existence: God possesses and experiences all of his eternity simultaneously. God does not have time and is not subject to time.

God knows time and all that happens in space-time the same way a clockmaker knows the time-keeping mechanism he created: he uses it, without being part of it or affected by it.

Isaiah 46:9–10 (LXX), I am God, and there is none other beside me, telling beforehand the latter events before they come to pass.

In trying to understand God's decisions in Aeviternity, we may propose a logical succession (not a time succession) in God's decisions before God created the universe.

God is eternally existing in his timeless decision in Aeviternity to create the universe.

22

God is eternally existing after he created the universe.

God is eternally existing when the moment of time arrives in the duration of the universe God un-makes the universe.

God acts within time but is outside of time.

Therefore, although we must speak in terms of Aeviternity and logical succession in God's decisions, God has no Aeviternity, God has no space-time, God has no succession of decisions. Space and time began with God's decree, "Let there be light." Aeviternity, succession, space, and time are terms human beings created to express what is to finite minds incomprehensible: a logical order to God's timeless pre-creation decision to create.

God's decision to create before he created time cannot be wholly understood. That one decision encompassed all we think of as individual choices and actions of what to create and how to create it. As creatures of time we rationally may think of God's decision as having a logical succession of parts and choices. The orthodox doctrines of the church assume this point of view, that there is a timelessness in God's decisions pre-creation, yet a logical succession of decisions by God pre-creation.

> On the one hand, God's decision to create, God's choices as to what kind of creation would be created, and God's act of creation are one and the same decision and action without time or succession.

> On the other hand, we may imagine a rational progression to those actions, e.g., the question "What kind of universe to create," rationally precedes the decree to create a universe. Recognizing that rational progression of decision and action in God is not a contradiction, but conforms to how Scripture explains God's works in the space-time of the universe, explanations that accommodate our finite capacity to understand.

Therefore, a logical succession of choices, decisions, and actions may be proposed.

God in Aeviternity (oversimplified):

Decided a purpose.

Decided to create a universe to accomplish that purpose.

Decided what kind of universe he would create to accomplish

23

that purpose.

Decided on plans to accomplish the purpose, and processes to fulfil the plans.

Created a universe with the processes to fulfill the plans to accomplish the purpose.

Just in case you are wondering where you come in, you—whether saved or not saved——are part of the processes that fulfill the plans that accomplish God's purpose in creating.

The Ordo Salutis

Salvation was not God's purpose in creating. Salvation is one process out of many processes in the plans to fulfill the purpose in creating. An Ordo Salutis attempts to explain parts of the plan and some of the processes that help fulfill the plans that accomplish the purpose God had when he chose to create the universe.

> Purpose, plans, and processes. This phrase, and these words, indicate the way in which God accomplishes his purpose in creating the universe. A purpose assumes a plan by which the purpose can be accomplished. A plan requires processes by which the plan is fulfilled.

For example, God's purpose to bring Israel into the Promised Land required a plan: free the Israelites from slavery in Egypt and bring them across the desert to the land promised to Abraham. The plan required processes, e.g., the leadership of Moses, the contest with Pharaoh, the Passover, the passage through the Red Sea, etc., by which the plan could be fulfilled and the purpose accomplished.

What was God's purpose in creating a universe? To manifest his glory to sentient creatures who could respond in appreciation of that manifested glory, and themselves be part of that manifestation. The salvation of sinners is one of many ways in which that purpose is accomplished; it is not the only way.

What is God's glory? To understand God's glory we must understand how the Scripture defines glory.

> The Old Testament Hebrew word is *kābēd* [Harris et al., s. v. 943 (*kābôd*, 943d, 943e)], which literally means "heavy," but a figurative use is more frequent in the Old Testament. A "weighty" person has worth, value, is honorable, is worthy of respect. Thus, *kābēd* is translated glory.

The New Testament Greek word is *doxa* [Zodhiates, s. v. 1391] from *dokéō* [Zodhiates, s. v. 1980]. The meaning is "a thought or opinion, especially when favorable" thus, reputation, praise, honor, to be of true value.

God's glory (*kābēd, doxa*) is who he is as God: his essential being and his intrinsic worth apart from any consideration of his works.

How is God's glory manifested? In revealing his nature, character, and attributes: in his essential Person, e.g., Revelation 4:3; 5; his intrinsic worth, e.g., Revelation 4:11; and his attributes as seen in through his works, e.g., Revelation 5:12.

God's glory is the demonstration of who God is and what God has done. God's glory is the manifestation of his intrinsic worth as God, not merely as the Creator, Sustainer, Governor, Redeemer, and Judge of his creation, but simply due to his essential being as God.

God's glory is perfect and complete. Nothing is able to add to God's glory and nothing is able to subtract from God's glory. All God's works, whether in the grace and love of an endless salvation or in the just wrath of endless conscience punishment, manifest God's perfect and complete glory. To "give God the glory," as is sometimes said, means to manifest God's perfect and complete glory in word, deed, worship, praise, fellowship, service, obedience—in all the works of life and living.

Think on this: you were created to manifest God's perfect and complete glory. Whether you manifest God's glory in his grace or in his wrath depends on your choices. Choose wisely.

God's Foreknowledge

We are almost ready to discuss foreordination. But first, foreknowledge. God's foreknowledge is God's knowledge of all that will happen in the universe from its beginning to its end.

However, God does not know what will happen because he foresaw what would happen as an act of omnipresent observation of all space and time. God knows what will happen, foreknowledge, because before God created space and time God foreordained (chose) what would happen, an act of sovereignty based on God's omniscience.

Omniscience: God has all knowledge and all understanding within himself without requiring knowledge or understanding outside himself. God does not learn, God knows.

Therefore, God's foreknowledge encompasses all agents, events, and outcomes, because God sovereignly chose which agents, events, and outcomes would happen in the universe, based on his omniscient knowledge and understanding of all agents, events, and outcomes that could develop (were possible) as a consequence of his decision to create the universe. Out of all things possible (what could happen) God chose to effectuate some from possible to actual (what would happen). Those omniscient, sovereign choices are the sole basis for God's foreknowledge.

There is an aspect of foreknowledge that encompasses God's knowledge of all that is possible, which (foreknowledge) is based solely on God's omniscience. However, foreknowledge is usually defined on the basis of God knowing what will happen. Remembering that foreordination is God's choices of all that will happen, we may properly define foreknowledge as "God's pre-creation omniscient understanding of all that will happen because of his foreordination of all agents, events, and outcomes." Perhaps more simply, God's choices create God's foreknowledge.

God's foreknowledge is always a subset of God's omniscience, not God's omnipresence. If foreknowledge was a subset of God's omnipresence, then God would know because of what he saw occurring in events yet future—God would learn experientially. Foreknowledge is not a subset of omnipresence: God does not learn.

God's foreknowledge is based solely on what God knows within himself (omniscience) without requiring a source outside himself (observation by omnipresence). Foreknowledge is never an act of omnipresence but is always the consequence of omniscience. When Romans 8:29 states, "those whom he foreknew," he foreknew them because he had previously "called [them] according to his purpose," Romans 8:28, indicating God's foreordination of certain plans and processes necessary to accomplish his purpose in creating the universe.

God's Foreordination In The Ordo Salutis

As stated above, foreordination is the decree of God occurring between his decision to create and his act of creation, as to which agents, events, and outcomes, out of all possible agents, events, and outcomes potential in the decision to create, would pass from possible to actual, in which the liberty or contingency of secondary causes is established, in which God is not the author of sin, and in which no violence is done to the free will of his creatures.

A little more in depth.

Prior to the act of creation, God omnisciently knew whatever might or could come to pass upon all supposed conditions: every possible agent, every possible event, and every possible outcome. This was not the knowing of foresight, but God omnisciently understanding all possible agents, events, and outcomes that could develop from the act of creation—including all possible freely made choices (events) that might be made by all beings (agents) he would create and all possible consequences (outcomes) resulting from their choices. God did not decree anything because he foresaw it as future, but because he determined all that was possible, and then chose which out of all possible he would foreordain as actual. God's choices were the consequence of his purpose in creating (to manifest his glory).

In an illustration, we might say God omnisciently understood that from cause A, events 1, 2, 3, a, b, c were possible, and then God chose which possible events to make actual. Not because he foresaw the events, but because he omnisciently understood all that might be possible from his decision to create, and then decided which of the possible to make actual to fulfill his purpose for creating. God then created the universe his choices effectuated. God effectuated those choices because those particular choices were the choices made by God and all sentient beings that accomplished his purpose in creating.

Foreordination is not fate or determinism. Foreordination makes choices certain but not necessary. The choices we make during our lifetime are certain because foreordained, but not necessary because those choices are freely made by us in response to agents, events, and outcomes occurring within our space and our time.

Excursus: Foreordination is not Molinism.

The above explanations are not Molinism. The doctrine of Molinism is its own peculiar Ordo Salutis. Creation in Molinism is this: God omnipresently (not omnisciently) foresaw all possible worlds he might create, and then chose to create one of those worlds he foresaw that fit his purposes in creating.

In biblical foreordination, God omnisciently understood, not omnipresently foresaw, all possibilities, and then decided which possibilities to effect from possible to actual, thereby creating a universe according to his choices of every agent, event, and outcome.

Salvation in Molinism is this. God omnipresently foresaw in all possible worlds he might create who would or who would not believe and be saved, and then chose which of those possible worlds to create. Molinism, like Arminianism, is foresight election.

In biblical foreordination, God omnisciently understood all human beings were sinners (I will explain later), and then God chose whom he would rescue from sin by giving those persons his gift of grace-faith-salvation (Ephesians 2:8), thereby guaranteeing their salvation. God giving his gift of grace-faith-salvation is election, which I will explain later.

More On Foreordination

Foreordination is difficult to understand, because we are so severely limited by our finiteness, that we cannot comprehend all possible agents, events, and outcomes, and we lack the sovereignty, omniscience, and omnipotence to choose and effectuate the actual from the possible.

We may use the game of chess as an illustration to help us understand our limitations. A grandmaster is able to see up to 20 likely moves ahead at any point in the game. For example, if in the opening move, you move one of your eight pawns, one or two spaces forward, your opponent has sixteen possible responses with his eight pawns, and two possible knight moves, for a total of eighteen possible responses to your one first move; twenty possible game piece positions in the two opening moves of the game by you and your opponent. Whatever moves you might make during a game, a chess grandmaster is able to see up to 20 likely moves ahead—his moves and your responses.

However, no human being is able to foresee all the possible combinations of game pieces that could occur in 20 moves at any stage of the game. In 20 moves all possible combinations are 20 to the 60th power:

1,152,921,504,606,846,976,000,000,000,000,000,000,000,000
,000,000,000,000,000,000,000,000,000,000,000,000,000   possible game piece positions.

But God omnisciently knows every possible move, and every possible combination, in every game of chess that might be played from the beginning to the end of the universe, before the game was invented, before the first game piece was moved.

God   sovereignly   decides   which   moves   out   of   all

1,152,921,504,606,846,976,000,000,000,000,000,000,000,000,000,00 0,000,000,000,000,000,000,000,000,000 possible combinations in 20 moves, which combinations will be the moves actually made by the players—by every chess player of every chess game. From the first game of chess ever played to the last game of chess that will be played, God foreordained from possible to actual which possible freely chosen moves would actually be made by each player.

God not only foreordained the moves, but foreordained the agents (the players) that make the moves, foreordained the event (each game that will ever be played), and foreordained the outcomes (who wins, who loses). God foreordained all those actual things out of all things possible concerning the game of chess.

Whether God plays chess is not the point. Expand your mind to think of every possible choice every sentient creature might possibly make during his or her mortal lifetime, and beyond into the endlessness of heaven for the saved and the endlessness of hell for the unsaved.

For example, when driving a car, or riding a bike, or walking, at every intersection where two paths cross there are four choices: straight, left, right, reverse. Now, multiply those four choices by all the intersections in your city; now multiply that number by all the drivers, bikers, and walkers in your city at any one moment in time. God omnisciently knows all the possible agents (drivers, bikers, walkers) and all the intersections, and all the possible choices, and from that omniscient knowledge God omnipotently made choices as to which freely made choices he will effectuate from possible to actual.

Before God created the universe, God omnisciently understood all things possible. Before God created the universe, God effectuated certain agents, events, and outcomes from possible to actual. Before God created the universe, God effectuated certain freely made choices from possible to actual. What God effectuated is the universe that God chose to create. That is foreordination.

God did not make your choices necessary—they are not fate or destiny—because they are freely made by you in a moment of your time in the world. God made your choices certain, because the freely made choices you do make were foreordained as your actual choices. Thus the definition of foreordination encompassing God's choices and your choices, consistent with God's sovereignty and omniscience, and your responsibility.

Foreordination And God's Choices In Salvation.

Some information in this section and following is from my book *God's Choices, the Doctrines of Foreordination, Election, and Predestination.*

Very early in the history of the New Testament church, an Ordo Salutis began to be developed. The focus was on a logical sequence of events concerning God's pre-creation choices leading to the moment of salvation. Three views developed during the centuries—views that preceded the origins of Calvinism (which was a revival of Augustinian theology) and Arminianism (the Arminian Ordo Salutis was a response to one of those views, the supralapsarian view of the order of God's pre-creation foreordaining decrees).

The three views came to be known by the names supralapsarianism, infralapsarianism, and sublapsarianism. The suffix -lapsarian refers to the "lapse" in man's holiness, i.e., Adam's sin. Adam was both legal head of the human race (his sin is our sin) and seminal head of the human race (we inherit the consequences of his sin): so Genesis 5:3; Romans 5:12; 1 Corinthians 15:22.

The purpose of the three views began as an Ordo Salutis. But over time disputes about the three views led to this question,

> "Were the objects [human beings] of the divine decree [of election] contemplated as fallen creatures? or were they contemplated merely as men whom God would create, all being equal?" [Harrison, *Dictionary*, s. v. "Predestination."]

(Harrison addresses the issue under the word "predestination," but is actually speaking of election. As I explain below, Reformed theology views predestination as one of four parts of election, and by a metonymy misnames election as predestination.)

The three views divide on that question: were the objects of election viewed as sinners, or not sinners? The supralapsarian view says all persons yet to be created were contemplated as equally sinless when some were elected to salvation and others elected to reprobation (damnation). The infralapsarianism and sublapsarianism views say all persons yet to be created were contemplated as equally sinful when some were elected to salvation, and all others were left as they were, sinners.

Before taking a closer look at the lapsarian views, I must correct the common confusion between election and predestination. That confusion exists today because in Reformed theology the word "predestination" smashes together four distinct doctrines and actions by God. In Reformed theology the term "predestination" means "foreordination + election + predestination + providence." In the Scripture each is a separate doctrine, a separate action by God. Election is not predestination, so when I refer to election I do not mean predestination. Definitions.

I defined foreordination above.

Election is the choice of a sovereign God (Ephesians 1:4), (1) to give the gift of grace-faith-salvation to effect the salvation of some sinners (Ephesians 2:8), and (2) to take no action, positive or negative, to either effect or deny salvation to other sinners (Romans 10:13; Revelation 22:17). The decree of election includes all means necessary to effectuate salvation in those elected.

Predestination is God's decree to conform the believer to be like Christ according to certain aspects of Christ's spiritual character and physical form (Romans 8:29–30; 1 John 3:2), and to place the believer in the legal position of God's son and heir (adoption) (Ephesians 1:5, 11), so that the believer has an inheritance from God and is God's heritage.

Providence is God's unceasing works by which he maintains and preserves the universe and all his creatures, and governs its operations and their actions, so as to accomplish his plans and eternal purpose. That which God's foreordination effectuated in eternity-past, God's providence accomplishes in historical-present.

I will discuss election and predestination at a later time. Here and now I will discuss election in relation to foreordination, as supposed in the three lapsarian views.

The Three Lapsarian Views Of God's Pre-Creation Decrees

"In the standard lapsarian frameworks, supralapsarianism places election before creation and the fall, emphasizing God's sovereignty but implying a decree of reprobation. Infralapsarianism sees election occurring after the fall, highlighting God's response to human sinfulness. Sublapsarianism orders the decrees similarly to infralapsarianism but emphasizes the provision of a Redeemer before election" (theologian J. Neil Lipscomb, in a letter to the author).

31

In more detail (as an overview), the supralapsarian order says the first decree God made concerning salvation was election, then to create, then to permit the fall into sin. The infralapsarian order says the first decree God made concerning salvation was to create, then permit the fall, then election. The sublapsarian order says the first decree God made concerning salvation was to create, then to permit the fall, then to provide a redeemer, then election.

I will discuss the significance of each lapsarian order below. Then I will present my view of God's pre-creation decrees which, "in contrast [to the standard lapsarian frameworks], begins with the overarching purpose of manifesting God's glory, which sets the stage for all subsequent decrees" (J. Neil Lipscomb, in a letter to the author).

Bear constantly in mind these views are theological constructs designed to describe God's choices during Aeviternity before the universe was created. They are a succession of logical choices proposed as a means of understanding what God has done in relation to the Ordo Salutis. The test for these proposed choices is this, do they conform to what the Scripture as a whole teaches about God and his works?

Supralapsarian

The supralapsarian view of God's pre-creation foreordaining decree began ca. 560 BC with Isidor of Seville's doctrine that an election to salvation logically required a corresponding election to reprobation (damnation) [Lipscomb, 25, n. 13]. About 250 years later, Gottschalk of Orbais (ca. 800–867) developed the supralapsarian order incorporating Isidor of Seville's reprobation doctrine [Lipscomb, 25]. Every subsequent synod that examined Gottschalk's supralapsarian order rejected the supralapsarian view.

Seven hundred years after Gottschalk, the Reformer Theodore Beza (1519–1605) renewed and reenergized supralapsarianism with a new purpose: to securely establish monergism and prevent any possibility of synergism in man's salvation.

Monergism means God alone is the origin, source, initiator, and completer of man's salvation. Synergism means both God and man contribute something to man's salvation. Let us remember that in 1517 Luther posted his Ninety-five Thesis, and the Roman Catholic Church Council of Trent occurred during Beza's lifetime, 1545–1563. In Roman Catholic Church soteriology grace alone saves, but grace is activated to save by man's good works, thus a synergistic view of salvation.

In relation to Reformed soteriology, Beza argued against a foresight view God's reprobation of certain human beings (reprobated because foreseen to be unbelieving), because he thought that required a foresight view of election (elected because foreseen to be believing), which logically led to man's free will contributing to his salvation; hence Arminian soteriology developed foresight election after Beza's death (in part) to oppose Beza's election to reprobation.

(Calvin, 1509–1564, usually comes up on this issue, but it was Beza who developed the supralapsarian view, not Calvin. Calvin thought an election to salvation logically required an election to reprobation. However, Calvin viewed an election to reprobation not as a positive decree, but as the logical consequence of not being elected to salvation; if not saved, then reprobated. Calvin never developed the concept of a positive decree of reprobation, as did Beza, and in many places in his works there are differing, and even opposing, views. The most consistent view is that a person is reprobated because of unbelief caused by sin, not by decree. Calvin's initial works should be compared with the more mature works. This book will address Beza's supralapsarianism.)

Beza's concern was to eliminate any possibility of man's free will (and therefore merit) in salvation [Thomas, 43]. He was logical and methodical but not necessarily scriptural, because an election to reprobation is a logical construct unsupported by any scripture.

The supralapsarian view of God's pre-creation foreordaining decree says God decided to elect to salvation some human beings he would create, and elect to reprobation (endless damnation) other human beings he would create, at a moment in Aeviternity when God viewed all human beings as equally sinless. In this view God chose:

> To elect to eternal life some of the persons who were to be created, and to elect (condemn) to destruction the other persons who were to be created.
>
> To create.
>
> To decree the fall of mankind into sin.
>
> To send Christ to redeem the elect.
>
> To send the Holy Spirit to apply this redemption to the elect.

The first decree in supralapsarianism is also known in Reformed theology as double predestination: an election to salvation and a corresponding election to reprobation.

According to the supralapsarian order, election precedes ("supra") the lapse into sin. The problem with this view is that men who are not contemplated as sinners are ordained to eternal punishment. Since, in this view, God decided the eternal fate of all human beings before the decree concerning the lapse into sin, then God specifically created some human beings for eternal damnation.

Let me make sure you understand: in supralapsarianism God condemned to endless punishment in the lake of fire human beings who at the time of the decree were viewed as righteous, because the decree concerning sin had not yet occurred.

Moreover, in this view, God decreed—not allowed a freely made choice, not permitted a freely made choice—but God decreed Adam must commit his act rebellion, disobedience, and sinning. The supralapsarian doctrine makes God the culpable (criminally responsible) author of man's sin because in the supra view God decreed Adam must sin, without regard to the free will God designed into Adam's human nature.

The supralapsarian view makes God an arbitrary unrighteous monster. The intent of the supralapsarian view was good: to deny any possibility of any act by the sinner that would merit or contribute to his or her salvation. The method was evil: God deliberately and arbitrarily first condemned some sinless human beings, and then created all human beings, and then forced all human beings to become sinners as a reason to save those elected to salvation and damn those elected to reprobation.

The supralapsarian view is opposed by scriptural concepts of God as just, e.g., Genesis 18:25, "Shall not the Judge of all the earth do right?" The supralapsarianism view sees God as electing righteous persons to eternal condemnation—righteous because not yet fallen in the order of God's decrees according to the supralapsarian view. This view also contradicts scriptural ideas concerning the treatment of the innocent (as a concordance search on the word "innocent" will clearly demonstrate).

Supralapsarianism was rejected by the Synod of Dort (1618–1619), who developed an infralapsarian view (see below).

The supralapsarian view had a resurgence in the last century due to the popularity of John Owen's (AD 1616–1683) works, and the AD 1905 TULIP (see Stewart, *Ten Myths*, Appendix), and Boettner's AD

1934 work, *The Reformed Doctrine of Predestination*. Few holding the supralapsarian view understand it condemns the righteous and makes God the culpable (criminally responsible) author of Adam's sin. Nor do they understand the supralapsarian view been consistently condemned or rejected by multiple synods of the New Testament church. Modern supralapsarianism persists as the "Christ died only for the elect" view popularized by Owen.

Infralapsarian

The infralapsarian order of God's precreation decrees began with the belief that God's decree to permit the lapse into sin must come after the decree to create, before election and reprobation. Thomas [90] first mentions infralapsarianism in his discussion of Girolamo Zanchi (1516–1590), although the concept had probably been around for a long time.

Zanchi supported the supralapsarian order, but saw the supralapsarian order as God's intention and the infralapsarian order as the execution of God's intent. (Many Reformers in those times championed a revealed and secret will of God that did not always agree.) The Synod of Dort rejected the supralapsarian order to champion the infralapsarian order. Whereas supra says Christ's atonement is sufficient and efficient only for the salvation of the elect, the Synod said Christ's atonement is sufficient for all sins, but efficient only for the salvation of the elect.

The prefix "infra" means "after," so named because election follows after the decree to allow Adam's sin (not "must sin" but allowed to freely choose to sin). The infralapsarian view of the Synod of Dort understands the order of God's foreordaining decrees to be the following. In this view God chose:

To create.

To permit the fall.

To elect some out of this fallen mass to be saved, and to leave the others as they were.

To provide a redeemer for the elect.

To send the Holy Spirit to apply this redemption to the elect.

According to the infralapsarian view the decree of election followed the decree permitting the fall. That means God saw all human beings as sinners before electing some to salvation. The fall into sin was Adam's choice not God's decree, so Adam is criminally responsible for human sin. Sin was the background in which God viewed all human beings, and from which he chose to save some. None were innocent because the fall was permitted before the election; in deciding who to elect God contemplated all as sinners. God chose to rescue some from sin by electing them to salvation. God chose to take no action to help or hinder those he had not elected to salvation (no election to reprobation).

In this view man is the author of his sin and eternal punishment, God is the author of eternal salvation. Let's take a moment and discuss God's foreordination and Adam's freely made choice to commit an act of sinning.

In relation to humankind, God's foreordination is God choosing out of all possible freely made choices which possible choices to make the actual choice. Therefore, out of all possible choices Adam might have made, does God's foreordaining the choice to sin mean God is the author of Adam's sin? No, for three reasons.

> One, in the process of living his life Adam freely choose to disobey God.

> Two, foreordination does not create a person's choices, it effectuates freely made choices. Perhaps all of Adam's <u>possible</u> freely made choices may have been to sin; we cannot know.

> Three, God cannot create what he does not have. God has no sin, and therefore God did not choose to make Adam sin. God choose to effectuate Adam's freely made choice from possible to actual.

As a result of Adam's freely made choice, all his descendants were made sinners. I will explain later how Adam's sinful human nature was passed along to his descendants. For now, Adam was both legal head of the human race (his sin is our sin) and seminal head of the human race (we inherit the consequences of his sin): so Genesis 5:3; Romans 5:12; 1 Corinthians 15:22.

The infralapsarian view agrees with Scripture in that those who were elected to be saved from sin were chosen in the logical succession of God's decrees after the decree to allow sin. All men are made of the same lump of sinful clay, Romans 9:21, out of which God took some of the sinful clay and fashioned the lumps into vessels of honor.

The Canons of the Synod of Dort reflect the Synod's doctrine that Christ's propitiation of God for human sin was "sufficient for all, efficient for the elect." By that phrase the Synod meant the merit of Christ's propitiation was limitless in its sufficiency to save all sinners, contra the supralapsarian view, but limited in its efficacy to God's election of some to salvation—in relation to God's foreordination, limited to those sinners whom God chose to give his gift of grace-faith-salvation, Ephesians 2:8 (that is election), that inevitably results in salvation.

Sublapsarian

I was unable to find the origin of the sublapsarian order, but suspect it developed alongside infralapsarianism.

The sublapsarian view is similar to the infralapsarian view. The prefix "sub" means "below" or "under." The difference between infralapsarian and sublapsarian is the order of "provide a redeemer" and "election" are reversed. In this view God chose:

To create.

To permit the fall.

To provide a redeemer

To elect some out of this fallen mass to be saved, and to leave the others as they were.

To send the Holy Spirit to apply this redemption to the elect.

The key difference between the infra and sub views is the infralapsarian view—election then a Redeemer—focuses the benefits of the Christ's death on the elect alone. The sublapsarian view—a Redeemer then election—means the elect will be saved, but a non-elect person could be saved, if he or she, on their own, without the aid of God's gift (Ephesians 2:8), met the condition for salvation: faith in God and God's testimony as to the way of salvation. The decree of a redeemer before the decree of election also allows for temporal benefits for all humankind, as well as securing eternal benefits (salvation) for the elect.

My Lapsarian Doctrine

My view of the Ordo Salutis begins where soteriology must begin, with God's decisions before any choices were made concerning human beings. One must reasonably ask why God would create anything? As a Trinity of persons God is perfectly self-sufficient, needing no one or nothing, having perfect communion and fellowship within and among the three persons of himself. The true beginning of the Ordo Salutis is to answer the question "Why did God create the universe with all its

37

things and beings, including sentient beings.

The three lapsarian views discussed above do not consider that question. All three focus on man's salvation. Supralapsarianism, in its effort to create a perfect monergism, says salvation is all of God man has no part; but it ignores that essential part of the salvation principle that says "by faith," indicating the sinner must at some point make a choice to "believe" as commanded by the Good News.

However, before there could be a universe, there must be a reason for creating a universe. This falls under the category of God's glory.

There must also be a reason for creating this particular universe. For undoubtedly God could have created any kind of universe, so why this particular universe, with its particular events, and agents, and outcomes and people? A particular kind of universe falls under the category of foreordination.

The decree of foreordination incorporates all the righteous and sinful choices each person will make during their lifetime, and sovereignly causes all choices, holy or sinful, to accomplish the purpose God had in mind when he created the universe.

In my lapsarian view, the order of God's foreordaining and electing decrees (including the subsequent decree of predestination) is proposed to be:

God's decision to manifest his glory.

God's decision to manifest his glory in a particular manner by creating a universe populated with sentient creatures.

God's exercise of his omniscient knowledge and wisdom to understand all <u>possible</u> agents, events, and outcomes in the proposed universe that <u>could</u> fulfill his purpose.

God's decree of foreordination: to create a particular universe by choosing to effectuate certain agents, events, and outcomes (out of all possible) that <u>would</u> fulfill his purpose.

God's foreordaining decision to permit the fall of humankind into sin.

God's decree to satisfy his justice and holiness against sin through a propitiation for sin.

God's decree to give both temporal and eternal benefits to humankind out of Christ's propitiation.

God's decree to justly leave some sinful persons as they

were (the non-elect), taking no action to either hinder or aid in their salvation.

God's decree of mercy to give some sinful persons the gift of grace-faith-salvation (election) to be saved.

God's decree to send the Holy Spirit to effect the redemption of the elect.

God's decree of predestination to conform the saved person to the image of Christ, and to adopt him or her as a son of God and joint-heir with Christ.

God's omnipotent act of creating the universe.

After the universe came into existence, then God's providence worked and is working to effect his pre-creation decrees, according to his purpose in creating.

There are therefore two reasons my lapsarian view is different from supra, infra, and sub. My lapsarian view begins where God began: why create anything. God's glory, not man's salvation, is the focus on my lapsarian view.

The second reason my view is different is because the Scripture teaches atonement/propitiation is not in itself redemption. Atonement is the propitiation, the legal satisfaction, of God's justice for the crime of sin through a suitable vicarious sacrifice suffering the judicial penalty against sin, 2 Corinthians 5:21. Because of that legal satisfaction made by Christ on the cross, both temporal and eternal benefits are justly given by God, according to God's choices.

One must always keep in mind God's pre-creation foreordaining decrees were designed to accomplish God's purpose in creating: to manifest his glory to sentient creatures who could respond in appreciation of that manifested glory, and themselves be part of that manifestation. Both salvation and reprobation conform to that purpose.

Definition, reprobation: those dying without forgiveness of sins are condemned to endless punishment. Every human being is from birth conditionally reprobate until their spiritual state is changed from sinner to saved by salvation, or confirmed as unsaved by physical death, Hebrews 9:27. There is no such thing in the Scripture as an election to reprobation.

No list, of course, can fully capture, nor accurately define, exactly what God thought and did in eternity-past. However, based on what

God has recorded in Scripture about his decisions and subsequent events, and applying reason and logic to what the Scripture says, my lapsarian view proposed above seems a rational view of God's decisions, decrees, and actions concerning foreordination, election, and predestination.

Foreordination and Mercy

Yes, God foreordained every choice, but every choice is a freely made choice, freely made by the person in the moment during the course of his or her lifetime. All were sinners before God chose to give his gift of grace-faith-salvation. That some are saved is mercy, that some are not saved is justice. God is the author of salvation. Human beings are the author of condemnation because God does not prevent any from believing; that is what sin does.

Justice is the righteous response to punish criminal acts; sin and acts of sinning are criminal acts against God and his laws. God, however, may choose to act in mercy.

Mercy has two aspects. The first aspect is the delay of deserved justice. The second aspect is relieving misery.

> God has been made willing by Christ's propitiation, in mercy to relieve the temporal suffering of unsaved and saved, making his rain to fall on the evil as well as the good.

> God has been made willing by Christ's propitiation, in mercy to delay the judgment against sin so all have the opportunity during this mortal life to believe.

> God has been made willing by Christ's propitiation, in mercy to give eternal benefits to all who believe in God and his testimony as to the way of salvation.

"... but God being rich in mercy, because of his great love with which he loved us, 5 even we being dead in trespasses, made us alive together with Christ ..." Ephesians 2:4.

The choice of disbelief is the natural choice of the sinner; hence the necessity of God's gift of grace-faith-salvation. God foreordained all are sinners, through the decree to permit Adam's sin, so the promise of salvation might be given to those who believe. Some will believe, that is the guarantee of election; any may believe, that is the promise of God in the gospel (Romans 10:13; Revelation 22:17). To repeat from above, God would have all persons to be saved (1 Timothy 2:4), but he wills for certain persons to believe (Ephesians 1:4; 2 Thessalonians

2:13), thereby guaranteeing the elect will believe, without any kind of decree preventing any from believing (disbelief is what sin does).

Even the choice of the elect to believe is a freely made choice, foreordained by God, through his gift, because the gift of God efficaciously changes the moral boundaries of human nature, changing the unable and unwilling sinner to able and willing (see chapter 2). But even the elect would not choose to believe if God had not foreordained to give them his gift. Therefore all are free to make the choice to believe, but the elect are guaranteed to make that choice, because God foreordained those he elected to receive his gift.

Foreordination Is Comprehensive

In God's decree of foreordination, God omnisciently knowing all things possible, sovereignly decided all agents, events, and outcomes that would actually occur in the universe he created, from Genesis 1:1 to Revelation 20:11; 2 Peter 3:10—from the creation of the universe to its destruction. One may rightly suppose foreordaining decrees for the new heavens and earth, Revelation 21:1.

God's decree of foreordination includes all the righteous choices and all the sinful choices all persons will make, and God sovereignly causes all choices, righteous or sinful, to accomplish the purpose God had in mind when he created the universe. (Sinful choices are allowed because of free will, see chapter "Why Are All Sinners.")

THE DOCTRINE OF ELECTION

From its beginning Reformed theology has used the term "predestination" to mean "foreordination + election + predestination + providence." In the Scripture each is a separate doctrine, a separate action by God. Election is not predestination, so when I refer to election I do not mean predestination. I will define predestination in a later section.

Some of these discussions are from my work, *Dispensational Soteriology*, lightly edited to the present purpose.

Statement of the doctrine.

> Election. The choice of a sovereign God (Ephesians 1:4), to give the gift of grace-faith-salvation to effect the salvation of some sinners (Ephesians 2:8), and to take no action, positive or negative, to either effect or deny salvation to other sinners (Romans 10:13; Revelation 22:17).

The decree of election includes all means necessary to effectuate salvation in those elected. God's decree of election ensures the salvation of the elect, but does not prevent any non-elect sinner from coming or willing to be saved. God will act savingly toward any who choose to seek him and come to him for salvation (Romans 10:13; Ephesians 1:4; Revelation 22:17).

An illustration. The river of sinful humankind is justly racing toward the waterfall of death emptying into the lake of eternal fire; God reaches into the river and saves many; he prevents no one from swimming to the safety of the heavenly shore; he puts his saved people on the shore encouraging all others to believe on God and his testimony of salvation and be saved; he saves all who will come to him by faith in God and his testimony.

An Introduction

God would have all persons to be saved (1 Timothy 2:4), but he wills for certain persons to believe (Ephesians 1:4; 2 Thessalonians 2:13), thereby guaranteeing the elect will believe, without any kind of decree preventing any from believing (disbelief is what sin does).

What is election? Election is God's foreordaining choice to give to certain persons his gift of grace-faith-salvation (Ephesians 2:8), so that they will infallibly choose to believe. Election is not specifically redemption, but the decree effecting redemption. Election is God's gift of grace-faith-salvation.

Because God would have all persons to be saved (1 Timothy 2:4), God does not will (elect) any person to reprobation, but permits any person not elected to choose to believe, if they will (but their love of their sin prevents that choice).

All persons begin life as reprobate, Romans 3:23. All persons believing are saved from reprobation and have eternal life, John 3:15; 17:2. All persons not believing remain reprobate and will endlessly experience God's just wrath against their sins, Revelation 20:15.

God's wrath is his justice in action against the impenitent.

God's wrath against the sinner who dies unforgiven and thus unsaved is expressed as endless punishment.

God's wrath against the unrepentant believer who has committed an act of sinning is expressed as chastisement.

God's wrath against the unforgiven sinner is of a different order than God's wrath against the sinning believer. Why? Propitiation. Jesus Christ on the cross suffered the wrath of God justly due the unsaved sinner, through the imputation of the sinner's judicial guilt to Christ, 2 Corinthians 5:21, wherein by God's grace through the sinner's faith and Christ's limitless merit the unsaved sinner becomes saved. When a believer responds to temptation and chooses to commit an act of sinning, that same limitless merit that saved from condemnation (Romans 8:1) is the limitless merit that causes forgiveness of the believer's act of sinning, 1 John 2:1–2.

Discussion of Election

All human beings are conceived as sinners, and unless saved during this mortal life will die as unforgiven sinners justly deserving God's wrath against the crime of sin.

(One of the more troubling issues—and highly charged emotionally–is the relationship God's election has toward those who either have not developed, or never will develop, the moral capacity to decide for faith or no faith. I will defer this discussion to the next chapter, "Why All Are Sinners.")

As I previously discussed, there are three views (lapsarian) of God's foreordination. But those views give the fact of election but not the process of election. Election was a choice made by God, but how was that choice effectuated? How are those sinners who were to be elected identified by God as those whom God would chose to elect? The answer is twofold.

First, God never tells us the basis on which one was elected and another was not. All we know is the choice was not based on foreseeable merit. In the proper order of God's foreordaining decrees, the decree to permit sin came before the decree of election. Therefore, all human beings were viewed as sinners, and therefore none had merit when God decreed to give some his gift, Ephesians 2:8, and by that gift effect their salvation.

God looked inside himself (omniscience), and thereby knowing (1) all human beings he would create, and (2) that all human beings would be sinners because of Adam's sin, (3) decided which of those sinful human beings he would give prevenient grace for salvation (Ephesians 2:8). Those individuals whom God decided to give prevenient grace are identified as elected to salvation, because of the infallible efficacy of the gift of God to effect salvation.

(Prevenient grace: the theological and biblical concept that God must give grace to bring the sinner to saving faith. All biblically-based soteriologies, including Reformed, Dispensational, and Arminian, teach the necessity of prevenient grace. However, Arminian soteriology differs from Reformed and Dispensational soteriologies on how and when God applies his prevenient grace. In Arminian soteriology all human beings receive prevenient grace, but that grace is not infallibly efficient to save all.)

That brings us to the process of election: God foreordaining to give to certain sinners his prevenient grace; or as it is otherwise known, God's gift of grace-faith-salvation, Ephesians 2:8. God's decree that a particular person will receive God's gift, at some point during the course of that person's lifetime, is the foreordaining act of electing that person to salvation, an act that occurred before God created the universe.

Therefore election is "the choice of a sovereign God (Ephesians 1:4), to give the gift of grace-faith-salvation (Ephesians 2:8) to effect the salvation of some sinners."

In the Arminian system, election is based on God's omnipresence that foresees a person's faith. In the Arminian system, God gives prevenient grace to all human beings, thereby overcoming the dominion of sin, so that when a human being is confronted by the gospel, he or she is unhindered by sin to freely make a decision to believe and be saved, or not. In Arminian soteriology election has zero to do with salvation, it is only a foreseen recognition of faith.

Therefore, in the Arminian system, all hearing the gospel are able to choose to believe, but some hearing the gospel choose not to believe. So in Arminian soteriology, God permits sin, God gives all sinners prevenient grace, God omnipresently foresees all who will choose to believe, God decrees those who will choose to believe are elected to salvation.

No, it does not make logical sense to elect to faith someone who is foreseen to have chosen faith. In the Arminian system election is because of faith, not to faith. But certainly if one is chosen in Christ, Ephesians 1:4, then faith is the very thing to which one has been elected.

In the Reformed system, to which many Dispensationalists will agree, God has a secret will and a revealed will. The revealed will calls all to believe, knowing the secret will says only some can believe, because only those elected to believe can believe. In this view, God's secret will conflicts with God's revealed will.

A conflict within God is impossible, therefore I disagree. None can know the secret will of God, Deuteronomy 29:29, but we do know what has been revealed to us cannot contradict what has not been revealed to us. Therefore the call of God to "whosoever will" cannot contradict an unknown and unknowable "secret will," if such a things exists. Therefore, God has one will for salvation: election is a guarantee of salvation, election does not prevent any non-elect person from being saved.

God is not deceitful. If all are called upon to believe (1 Timothy 2:4), then none are prevented by some secret will of God from believing. Sin is what effects unbelief, not God. Therefore a decree of election guarantees the salvation of those of the all (1 Timothy 2:4) who were elected to salvation (1 Ephesians 1:4; 2 Thessalonians 2:13), but a decree of election does not prevent belief in any of the all (1 Timothy 2:4) who were not elected. God does not prevent belief, sin is what prevents belief.

The supralapsarian view gets around this logical reasoning by redefining "all" as "only the elect." No. The call to come and be saved is universal.

> Romans 10:13, For all that may call upon the Lord's name will be saved.
>
> Revelation 22:17, And the Spirit and the bride say, 'Come.' And the one hearing let him say 'Come.' And the one thirsting—the one desiring—let him come, let him take freely the water of life.

None are prevented by God and his election from calling on the Lord's name for salvation. None are prevented by God and his election from coming and taking freely the water of life. All that is required is faith in response to grace. The call to come and be saved is legitimately offered to all. Why are not all saved? The Scripture teaches salvation is conditioned upon faith in God and God's testimony as to the way of salvation. Not all (1 Timothy 2:4) are willing to turn from sin and believe.

What prevents salvation is the freely made choice to rebel against God. All are infected with this spiritual condition, from conception. God chose to give some his gift of grace-faith-salvation to effect their salvation through his gift. God leaves the others as he found them, unsaved sinners, which also means he leaves them to their own freely made choices. God never prevents the choice to believe and be saved, the sinful human nature makes the choice to reject God and his salvation the natural choice. God's foreordaining choices allow that choice.

An Appeal To Reason

Yes, I know I am repeating, but I am teaching an Ordo Salutis that is contrary to today's dominant supralapsarian view. That view says God foreordained damnation, by condemning those who were not yet contemplated as sinners. That view makes God an unrighteous arbitrary monster. I will repeatedly stab the supralapsarian monster in the heart until I kill it. There is no such thing in Scripture as an election of reprobation to damnation, there is no such thing in Scripture as "double predestination" (an election to salvation and an election to damnation).

Excursus: A Biblical Illustration of Election: Lumps of Sinful Clay

Above I mentioned Romans 9:21, "Or does the potter not have authority over the clay, out of the same lump to make one truly a vessel unto honor, but one unto dishonor?" How does this scripture interact with the doctrines of foreordination and election?

Here is the heart of God's sovereignty, and the world's disagreement. The Creator has made his creatures according to his choices, to serve his purpose in creating. Some to honor, some to dishonor. But there is another choice by God, which seems hidden— but the Scripture reveals—that God's sovereignty includes the choice to give grace, or not, to whichever lumps he chooses.

For the clay is the same in each lump, each human being is made from the same stuff. The original creature, Adam, was created as sinless clay, but sinned, thereby making all the lumps of clay formed from Adam sinful. So then all the lumps formed from Adam are conceived and born as vessels unto dishonor.

The lumps of clay formed from sinful Adam act according to their nature: they choose to sin. God designed the original clay, Adam, with the capacity to freely make moral choices, and the capability to change. That capacity to choose and capability to change continues in all the lumps of clay that are "in Adam," i.e., that are formed from the clay that was Adam; like Adam each freely chooses to sin. Indeed, because

46

the nature of the clay was changed by Adam to be sinful, the freely made choice to sin is the natural consequence of the sinful clay all are formed from. For the clay must act according to its nature, unless that nature is changed.

So Adam's choice made all the lumps of clay formed from him to be sinful, therefore all in Adam are born as vessels unto dishonor. But God. Oh blessed words! God made a choice to give grace to some of the vessels of dishonor. That grace changes the nature of the lump of clay. The nature having been changed, the lump of clay naturally and inevitably acts according to its new nature to freely choose God over sin, eternal life over death. Because it is in the nature of the clay to be capable of change, God's grace is able to change the lump from dishonor to honor.

God's choice to leave the other lumps of clay as they are, their nature sinful, is not unjust, because potter does have authority over the clay, the clay does not have authority over the potter. The clay cannot complain, "Why did you make me thus," because the original lump, Adam, was made sinless, and freely chose to sin, thereby making all the lumps of clay made from Adam to be sinful lumps. But the capacity for choice and the capability of change remain intact and functioning in every sinful lump of clay.

Sinless Adam chose to sin. His free will and capacity for change (mutability) allowed that unlikely choice. Why an unlikely choice? There was nothing in sinless Adam's sinless human nature that might have led to an act of sinning. Everything God created in Adam was good, sinless, righteous. God cannot create something contradicting himself. Therefore all that Adam was in soul and body was in complete harmony with God and his commandments. Sinless Adam exercised his free will contrary to his sinless human nature and chose to sin; his capacity for change allowed that choice. Therefore it is possible, however unlikely (a sinner is both unable and unwilling), that some sinful Adams might exercise their free will contrary to their sinful human nature and chose to believe.

God does not prevent a sinner from choosing faith, that is what sin does. Even so, God was not unjust to allow Adam's choice to sin. God designed Adam with the moral capacity to make choices. Will we lumps of clay require the Potter to prevent the clay that was Adam from acting according to its design? That is unreasonable, the Potter chooses what he will do with the clay, and he choose to allow Adam to make the choice to sin.

So also the lump of sinful clay not receiving grace is just as free to choose God as to choose sin, because the moral capacity to make choices is an essential part of its design. Just as God did not prevent Adam from freely making a choice, so also all the lumps of clay in Adam are designed to make choices, each lump according to its nature as formed from Adam, or as changed by God.

God makes choices. One choice is to let the nature of the clay to take its natural course. The nature of the lumps of clay not receiving grace is to choose sin, but that is not because God made him that way, but because God allows him to act according to his design: to make choices according to his nature. Another choice by God is to change the nature of some of the lumps of clay with his gift of grace. Would we deny God the authority to make choices because we don't like the choices he made? "Should the thing formed say to the one molding, 'Why have you made me like this?'"

God did not make the clay, or the lumps, sinful. God chooses to make one vessel of dishonor to be honorable and chooses to leave others in their dishonorable state. Does not the Potter have authority over the clay? Is God, having given the clay the right to choose, not allowed to make choices concerning the clay? The Potter has authority over the clay, to choose which vessels of dishonor to make honorable.

Paul's example of the Pharaoh illustrates the authority of the Potter. Pharaoh freely choose to reject God; God freely choose not to change the sinful nature of that lump of clay. God choose to give the Pharaoh many opportunities to make different choices, the lump of clay choose to reject those opportunities. The Pharaoh was and remained a vessel of dishonor, by his choice confirmed by God's choices.

What is Paul saying? God is not required to act to save every person, but makes choices as to whom he will act to save. That is the authority of the Potter over the lumps of clay.

God as the creator of the clay that was Adam has the intrinsic authority to choose to give grace to some of the lumps formed from Adam in order to make them vessels of honor. God as the creator of the clay has the intrinsic authority to choose not to give grace to other lumps, to leave them vessels of dishonor. But let us not forget that God in grace has given all the lumps of Adam's clay the capability to make choices, and the capacity to change. God makes choices, and one of those choices is not to prevent any lump of sinful clay from believing; that is what sin does.

Discussion of Predestination

In my lapsarian view (above) of God's foreordaining decrees, the last decree mentioned is, "The decree of predestination to conform the saved person to the image of Christ, and to adopt him or her as a son of God and joint-heir with Christ." As I mentioned earlier in the chapter, election is often misidentified as predestination.

What is the biblical view of predestination?

> Romans 8:29–30, For those whom he foreknew, also he decreed beforehand [predestined] to conform to the image of his Son, for him to be firstborn among many brethren. 30 Now those he decreed beforehand [predestined], these also he called; and whom he called, these also he justified. Now whom he justified, these also he glorified.

> Ephesians 1:5, he predestined us for sonship to himself through Jesus Christ, according to the good pleasure of his will

> Ephesians 1:11, In whom also we were made his heirs and his inheritance, having been predestined according to the purpose of the One, all things working according to the counsel of his will.

> 1 John 3:2, Beloved ones, we now are God's children, and what we will be has not yet been revealed. We certainly know that when he is made visible we will be like him, because we will see him just as he is.

Definition, predestination. God's decree to conform the believer to be like Christ according to certain aspects of Christ's spiritual character and physical form (Romans 8:29–30; 1 John 3:2), and to place the believer in the legal position of God's son and heir (adoption) (Ephesians 1:5, 11), so that the believer has an inheritance from God and is God's heritage.

Election is God's decree concerning the unsaved. Predestination is God's decree concerning the saved. The decree of election gets sinner's saved. The decree of predestination conforms the saved to be like Christ, gives the saved an inheritance, and makes the saved God's heritage out of a sinful world.

Chapter Summary

An Ordo Salutis begins with God's choices and God's actions in Aeviternity before God created. To prepare the reader for that discussion the chapter began with who God is: his sovereignty, omniscience, omnipresence, eternality and infinitude. God existed before he created, he is increate and eternal. God has no boundaries in time and space, his infinitude. God does not learn from what he observes through his omnipresence, God knows all within himself, his omniscience. The universe was created according to God's omniscience and sovereignty.

Aeviternity was defined: that timeless moment between God's decision to create and God's act of creation, when time began. A simplified list of God's choices in Aeviternity was suggested.

Certain choices were required before God made the choice of whom and how he would save, beginning with God's choice to create and God's purpose in creating. Salvation was not God's purpose in creating. Salvation is one process out of many processes in God's plans to fulfill his purpose in creating: the manifestation of God's glory and its appreciation by the sentient creatures God would create. This led to an extended discussion of God's glory and how his glory is manifested in his works.

Foreordination was explained. The basis of foreordination is God's omniscient understanding of all possible agents, events, and outcomes that might occur in the universe he would create, including all possible choices that might be freely made by all the sentient creatures that would exist in the universe he would create. God then chose (foreordination) which possible agents, events, outcomes, and freely made choices he would effectuate from possible to actual in the universe he created. (A discussion of free will was deferred to chapter 2.)

A discussion of foreknowledge followed, and its relationship to the Ordo Salutis. God's foreknowledge is based on his omniscient knowledge, understanding, and his foreordaining choices. In effect, God's foreknowledge is a subset of God's omniscience, not God's omnipresence: what God knows within himself (omniscience) without requiring a source outside himself (observation by omnipresence).

Illustrations—a chess game and choices at a road intersection—were presented to clarify the relationship between God's omniscience, sovereignty, omnipotence, man's free will, and the foreordination of all agents, events, and outcomes. God omnisciently knows all the possible agents and all the possible choices, and from that omniscient knowledge God omnipotently made choices as to which freely made choices he will effectuate from possible to actual in the creation of the universe, to accomplish his purpose in creating.

The chapter then turned to an extended discussion of the lapsarian views of God's precreation choices concerning salvation. (An appendix on the lapsarian views continues the discussion.) This discussion was followed by my lapsarian view and an exploration of why my view is preferable and how it addresses the shortcomings in other views. My lapsarian order does not begin with man's salvation but God's purpose in creating, which is the guiding principle in God's choices concerning salvation.

The section of foreordination comes to a conclusion with a discussion of foreordination and its relationship to mercy.

The chapter concludes with a lengthy discussion of the doctrine of election. Contra the supralapsarian view, there is no such thing as an election to reprobation. The basis for election is all are sinners. Election is understood as God giving his gift of grace-faith-salvation (Ephesians 2:8) to certain sinners. Election guarantees the salvation of those whom God choose to give his gift; election says nothing pro or con about those not elected.

Then, having previously explained why predestination is not election, the chapter ends with a brief discussion of predestination as defined by the Scripture: to conform the believer to be like Christ and to place the believer in the legal position of God's son and heir.

Why All Are Sinners
and
Free Will Dominated by Sin

Why All Are Sinners

Does sin begin with a choice, an attitude, or an action? Is sin innate to human nature? Do acts of sinning make a person a sinner, or does a person commit acts of sinning because he or she is a sinner by nature? The apostle John provides an answer.

> 1 John 1:8, If we should say that we have no sin, we deceive ourselves and the truth is not in us.

> 1 John 1:10, If we should say that we have not sinned, and as a result are not now sinning, we make him a liar, and his word is not in us.

The difference between "no sin" in 1:8 and "not sinned" in 1:10 is two different Greek words. In 1:8 the word is *hamartía*, [Zodhiates, s. v. 266], the sin attribute resident in human nature. In 1:9, 10, the word is *hamartánō* [Zodhiates, s. v. 264], acts of sinning. Human beings commits acts of sinning, 1:9–10, because human beings are by nature sinners, 1:8, i.e., the sin attribute, *hamartía*, is resident in human nature.

We see, then, the Scripture uses the word "sin" in two senses. One, the principle of rebellion (aka: sin) as an attribute in human nature. Two, to describe an act of rebellion (aka: sinning). A person sins, because the person is a sinner.

Three questions: what is an attribute in human nature; what is the sin attribute; how did sin become an attribute in human nature?

> What is an attribute in human nature? An attribute is a characteristic or life-principle of human nature that influences a person's behavior and choices. Human attributes are principles of behavior such as love, hope, desire, patience, initiative, etc. Sometimes attributes are known as personality traits.

> What is the sin attribute? An evil life-principle (attribute) that is part of fallen human nature which, through constructive interaction with other life-principles (attributes) in one's human nature, influences a person to self-determine his or her course

in the world in opposition to God's holy character and revealed will, whether that will of God is discovered in Scripture, or in that revelation of himself God has made in human conscience. Sin is accomplished in acts of rebellion against God and disobedience to his commandments.

How did sin become an attribute in human nature? In two ways: by Adam's act of rebellion and disobedience against God; by God's Law of Biological Reproduction.

Let us examine each of these answers.

Human Attributes

Human nature was designed by God with moral, spiritual, and intellectual attributes based on God's communicable attributes, Genesis 1:26, 27, the image and likeness of God. God's communicable attributes are: holiness, love, faithfulness, intellect, wisdom, righteousness, mercy, goodness, kindness, personality, will, volition, veracity. "The communicable attributes are those which are possessed in a finite degree, more or less, by men and angels." [W.G.T. Shedd, *Dogmatic Theology*, 1:334.]

To maintain the balance of what Scripture teaches we should know God's has incommunicable attributes. "The incommunicable attributes are those that belong to God exclusively, so that there is nothing resembling them in a created spirit." [W.G.T. Shedd, *Dogmatic Theology*, 1:334.] God's incommunicable attributes are: omnipresence, omniscience, omnipotence, self-existence, eternity, immutability, simplicity, infinity, sovereignty, unity, glory.

What then are the attributes of human nature? Human nature was designed by God with moral, spiritual, and intellectual attributes based on God's communicable attributes, Genesis 1:26, 27, (the image and likeness of God).

Moral attributes: Holiness; Sanctification; Righteousness; Justice; Mercy; Faithfulness

Intellectual attributes: Personality; Will; Volition; Veracity; Knowledge; Wisdom

Spiritual attributes: Love; Compassion; Goodness; Kindness; Longsuffering; Mercy

Man in God's image is man's soul fashioned according to God's communicable attributes in finite measure, in a greater or lesser degree, depending on the attribute in question. Stated a little differently, the pattern God used to create man's soul were his communicable attributes in a measure suitable to a finite creature.

Adam's disobedience added a principle of evil, the sin attribute, to human nature. The sin attribute, and all its consequences (greed, immoral lust, pride, etc.) is the principle of rebellion against God. Whatever is of God, the sin attribute is opposed to it. Sin is the principle of "Me, Me, Me; I, I, I," in thought, word, and deed.

> Sin is alienation from God. Sin is the absence of righteousness. Sin is the opposite of holiness. Sin is the lack of desire to conform to God's will, the inclination to act in opposition to God's will, and the unwillingness to be holy as God is holy. Sin is not passive opposition, sin is active rebellion against God, expressing that rebellion in acts of deliberate, intentional disobedience to God's revealed will (revealed in Scripture and in the conscience).

> At its most basic, sin is the failure to conform fully to God's image and likeness. In the final analysis, sin is any thought or action that does not conform to the essence, personality, character, attributes, or purpose of God.

Historically, sin has been defined as moral evil and legal disobedience. The Westminster Shorter Catechism gives the legal view.

> Question 14 asks, "What is sin? The answer is, "Sin is any want of conformity unto, or transgression of, the law of God," based on Leviticus 5:17; James 4:17; 1 John 3:4.

The law of God is the expression of God's will, so sin is the violation of God's will: rebellion against and disobedience of God's commandments and God's "Do this, Don't do that" rules for godly living.

The moral view defines sin as "anything in the creature which does not express, or which is contrary to, the holy character of the Creator" [Buswell, 1:263–264], because the Bible also views sin as a violation of the expression of God's holy character (e.g., Leviticus 19:2). Sin, in fact, violates both God's law and his Person; therefore sin is a violation of God's character and revealed will.

Sin is not only doing evil, but is also not doing good.

> Now the law not only forbids the doing of evil, whether by thought, word, or deed, but also commands the doing of good. So to omit the good commanded is sin, as well (or ill) as is the

doing of the evil that is forbidden. [Venning, 25.]

The essence of sin is I. "I don't need God"; "I don't want God"; "I will not submit to God"; "I will not have God rule over me"; "I don't need God to manage my life"; "Who is God to tell me what to do"; "God can just leave me alone and I will leave him alone." The last denial was the author's personal declaration of autonomy before his salvation.

How did sin become an attribute in human nature? Here is how the Scripture answers the question of the origin of sin in humankind, and how every human being is sinful from the moment of conception, liable for sin's judicial guilt, and liable to sin's judicial punishment. There are two reasons all human beings have the sin attribute: Adam's disobedience; God's Law of Biological Reproduction.

We have already looked at Adam's disobedience: he committed an act of sinning. God's Law of Biological Reproduction is the biblical teaching and observable truth that "each kind of being reproduces its own kind of being and no other kind of being." This law may be observed in Genesis 1:11–12, 21, 24–25, 28; 5:3. This law has been seen by every observer in each and every act of reproduction—plant, animal, human—since the beginning of the world.

Whatever a "kind" of being might be (opinions vary), each kind of being reproduces its own kind and no other kind. For example, there are all manner of species of birds, or cats, or rodents, but all birds are of the kind "bird," and all cats of the kind "cat" and each of the 2,052 species of rodents are all of the kind "rodent," whether mouse, hamster, squirrel, capybara, beaver or any other of the 2,052 species of rodents. Individual speciation in response to environmental conditions may momentarily obscure that fact—e.g., penguins "fly" in the water, not the air; some lizards are legless and superficially resemble snakes—but any examination of any species will place that species within a certain kind. Penguins are of the kind bird; legless lizards are of the kind reptile (as are snakes, turtles, lizards, alligators, and crocodiles).

All human beings are of the kind "human." Human beings agree, having named themselves "humankind" to distinguish humanity from all other kinds.

Adam was the first human being. Adam is in fact the source of the kind "human." All other human beings are Adam individualized, into two genders, through Adam's propagation. When God created Adam, he designed into Adam's body and soul all that was necessary for a race of two genders, Genesis 1:27. The woman was formed from Adam, body and soul, Genesis 2:22. The person Adam is the only original, all others, including the Woman, are Adam individualized as a substantive entity of the male or female gender. Not clones or copies, but procreated through the propagation of Adam and Eve: "For just as the woman is of the man [Genesis 2:21–23], so also the man is through the woman [Genesis 3:20]," 1 Corinthians 11:12.

Adam was not only body, but soul, Genesis 2:7. We might think of the soul as a container in which are the human essence, the animating principle life, and the human nature with all its attributes. Adam would procreate with the Woman (Eve) and propagate himself body and soul, because each kind of being reproduces its own kind of being and no other kind of being.

We have now come to the place where human beings gained a new attribute, the sin attribute.

God formed Adam's material being, his body, from existing elements of the earth, Genesis 2:7, "the dust of the ground." The human body is composed of about seventy elements. God created the person Adam as an immaterial being—in a word, his soul—*ex nihilo*, from nothing, Genesis 2:7, and placed that living soul, Adam, into the lifeless material body to make Adam a physically living being, a person in body and soul.

As I said above, we may think of the soul as a container in which are the human essence, the animating principle life, and the human nature with all its attributes. The immaterial human essence is what makes a human being human versus another kind of being, such as an angel. Life, also an immaterial essence, comes from God, who is self-existent, Exodus 3:14, having life-in-himself, John 5:26. God is the origin and source of all life. Because the life in human beings is an immaterial essence from God, it cannot be destroyed, it makes the person (the soul) immortal.

The human nature is composed of multiple principles (attributes) regulating human behavior. God designed Adam's human nature to be sinless. Adam's sinless human nature was in complete agreement and harmony with God's moral values and precepts (commandments, rules). Nothing in Adam's nature resisted God, everything in Adam's nature embraced God. So also the Woman (Eve, Genesis 3:20) was formed sinless in body and soul from Adam's sinless soul and body,

Genesis 2:21–22.

If, as is the case, both Adam and the Woman were in total agreement and complete harmony with God's principles, moral values, and precepts, how could Adam and Woman commit an act of rebellion and disobedience to God? The Woman, "having been deceived," (1 Timothy 2:14), chose to disobey God's commandment; Adam, not deceived, chose to disobey God's commandment; see Genesis 2:6–7.

There are two reasons, synergistically working together, the Woman and Adam could act against their sinless nature. The first reason is their mutability: their capacity for change. God made them capable of change so they might grow in their stewardship responsibilities, Genesis 1:28, and might grow in their spiritual relationship with God.

The second reason was the moral authority (free will) to make decisions, that God designed into human nature. Though having neither the disposition, inclination, or tendency to sin, because they were capable of change, they had the possibility of sin; they were capable of exercising their free will to make a wrong choice. The choice to commit an act of sinning, it must be emphasized, was wholly contrary to their sinless human nature. Adam originated his act of sinning through the misuse of his free will, allowable because of his mutability—there was nothing in his sinless nature as created by God to give him the inclination, the disposition, or the tendency to sin.

God gave Adam and the Woman the moral authority to make decisions: free will. I explain free will in another section, below. What we need to understand here is their capacity for change and their moral authority to make decisions allowed a wrong decision to be made. Adam and the Woman misused their moral authority to choose to disobey God's commandments.

The Woman was deceived into thinking she would become better than God had made her. That deception led to her disobedience; she valued what the serpent said over what God had commanded.

Adam was not deceived but chose to be autonomous rather than in submission to God. Adam's stewardship responsibilities were to be accomplished in submission to and dependence upon God. All Adam's authority was delegated. Adam chose autonomy over dependence, desiring his authority to be innate, not delegated.

They both thought they could be like God, but in their sinless state they were as much like God as a created being might be. In their rebellion they became less like God. (See my book, *Adam and Eve, A Biography and Theology* for further discussion).

Having rebelled and disobeyed God, their mutability added the principles of rebellion and disobedience to their human nature; in a word, sin. They became sinful creatures. How then did Adam's descendants become sinful creatures? The answer is God's immutable law of biological reproduction: each kind reproduces its own kind and no other kind..

God's Law Of Biological Reproduction In Action.

Genesis 5:3 states Adam propagated children who were "after his own form, and after his own image" (LXX). These words deliberately echo Genesis 1:26 (LXX), "And God said, Let us make man according to our image and likeness." After his act of sinning, Adam's human nature (and that of Eve) was sinful, possessing the sin attribute as a part of his human nature. Adam's children were formed (procreated) in his sinful image and sinful likeness and therefore also possessed the sin attribute.

The truth expressed in Genesis 5:3, concerning Seth and Adam's other "sons and daughters," was as true of Cain and Abel as it was of Seth.

> Adam and Eve were sinful when Cain was conceived; God's Law of Biological Reproduction says Cain was as sinful as his parents.

> Adam and Eve were sinful when Abel was conceived; God's Law of Biological Reproduction says Abel was as sinful as his parents.

> Adam and Eve were sinful when Seth was conceived; God's Law of Biological Reproduction says Seth was as sinful as his parents.

> Adam and Eve were sinful when sons and daughters were conceived; God's Law of Biological Reproduction says every one of those sons and daughters were as sinful as their parents.

And so every human being is sinful, because descended from sinful Adam and Eve, and every human being reproduces sinful offspring, because they themselves are sinful. Thus the truth of 1 Corinthians 15:22, all that are in Adam—the entire human race—die because all are sinful, Romans 3:9, 23; 5:12; Galatians 3:22.

Adam and the Woman (Eve) misused their moral authority, allowed by their mutability, resulting in the penalty of sin being applied to all who are of Adam, because all who are in Adam are naturally sinful. We must also understand that God made this perfect, sinless human being the legal representative of all his descendants, and thereby legally, as well as seminally (biologically), all Adam's descendants are sinful.

Praise God that although sin earns death, faith in Christ is eternal life, Romans 6:23. Praise God for the mutability of human nature, for without that mutability our sinful human nature could not be saved and born-again. Praise God for the moral authority to make decisions, which God uses in the sinner's salvation and subsequent Christian life.

Election And The Morally Undeveloped

Now that I have shown all human beings are propagated by sinful parents, thereby inheriting their sinful human nature, I can rationally assert that all human beings are sinful from conception. So also the Scripture. Psalm 51:6, "See now, in iniquity I was born, in sin she conceived me"; Romans 3:10, "none is righteous, not one"; Romans 3:23, "all have sinned and come short of God's glory."

One of the more troubling issues—and highly charged emotionally—is the relationship God's election has toward those who either have not developed, or never will develop, the moral capacity to decide for faith or no faith. Usually these are defined as babies or infants. But the reality is as a group those with an undeveloped moral capacity include human beings from conception to birth; babies, infants, and small children; adults who never developed the moral capacity to decide for faith or no faith.

From an observational point of view, we cannot know if the persons in that class of people—the morally undeveloped—have believed unto salvation. Let us be honest: we become aware of whom we believe is saved through a credible profession of saving faith, which includes both verbal testimony and a changed life. Neither criteria is available to us in the morally undeveloped group of persons. Because we cannot observe the choice for faith or no faith in persons of that group, we are emotionally distressed that the "innocent" (none are innocent, all are sinful) may be unfairly condemned (but the wages of sin is death). The usual solution is to manipulate Scripture to say, "babies and infants are automatically saved," disregarding all others in that morally undeveloped group.

Some who understand that all are sinners from conception forward (as being conceived in Adam's sinful likeness and image), have a slightly different solution: the intrinsically sinful nature is not counted against the morally undeveloped until they commit an act of sinning. This view admits all are sinners by nature (through God's Law of Biological Reproduction), but make this group a special class of sinners, whose sinful condition is not counted against them until expressed in an act of sinning. They redefine the "none" in Romans 3:10, 11, and the "all" in Romans 3:23 to exclude this one group of persons.

But that is a slippery slope. Is the infant who won't nurse at his mother's breast, or occasionally refuses a bottle, or sometimes won't eat his pureed baby food, sinning? In some cases that refusal is a denial of parental authority, a sin. When does the Scripture say a person is a sinner? From conception, because in possessing the sin attribute, those persons are not in the image in which God created humankind. All without exception are sinners by nature, and therefore are accountable and liable for their sinfulness.

This "saved until sinning" solution is unscriptural. For one thing it teaches salvation may be lost. The "saved until sinning" solution also manipulates Scripture to create a standard of moral accountability (an "age" of accountability) that begins with the moral choice to commit an act of sinning. This is similar to that aspect of Arminian soteriology that says moral inability absolves moral responsibility. This view creates a class of persons not susceptible to the testimony of the Scripture that all are sinful.

This "saved until sinning" solution also denies the cause of physical death. Physical death is the calling card of sin, the indisputable sign a person is sinful. All who die, at any age from conception forward, suffer physical death because they are sinners accountable to God for their sin, Romans 5:12; 6:23. That accountability is resolved only by salvation, or by endless judgment.

What says the Scripture? The following is drawn in part from my book, *Adam and Eve, A Biography and Theology*.

Culpability For Sin From Conception

If, as Scripture teaches, all persons are culpable (criminally liable) for the moral guilt of sin from the moment of conception—which we know is true because physical death, the observable consequence of sin's judicial guilt (Romans 5:12–14), may occur at any moment from conception forward—then how are those persons who are morally undeveloped able to make a faith-based decision required to be saved? The unborn (a human being from conception to birth), infants, small children, adults who never became mentally or morally competent, how are they able to make a faith-based decision and be saved from their sin?

The answer, as far as can be known by observation, is that they cannot. I am not saying that a person must verbalize his or her faith in order to be saved. The exercise of saving faith is not necessarily verbal. Saving faith is the positive response of the soul to God's gift of grace-faith-salvation. However, the way a person's saving faith can be known to others (other than God) is when it is verbalized or actualized.

The morally undeveloped group of persons under discussion cannot verbalize faith and they cannot demonstrate their faith by their works (a changed life). Therefore, we cannot know if this class of persons are saved, because they are not capable of making their salvation (or lack of salvation) known. Since they are culpable for their sin, but as much as we can observe are morally undeveloped to make a faith-based decision, can they be saved? Let me firmly answer that the question is not, "can these persons be saved," because they can.

The question that disturbs all believers is this: "how can we know if these persons can be saved?" The answer is in the efficient cause of salvation and the choices made by God. We will discuss the latter later. As to the former, the one and only basis of salvation is the propitiating death of Christ, decreed in eternity past, effective from eternity past through eternity future, and accomplished in historical space-time. The efficient cause of salvation is the remission of sin's guilt and penalty by the application of Christ's limitless merit, by God's grace through the sinner's faith.

In those who are mentally competent to make a choice between faith and no-faith, Christ's merit is applied by their receiving God's gift of grace-faith-salvation (Ephesians 2:8), and through the means of personal faith in God and God's revealed way of salvation, they exercise saving faith.

However, the unborn, infants, small children, and adults who never became mentally or morally competent, as far as may be known, cannot grasp or express saving faith. Nor does Scripture deal with their need for salvation. Scripture makes plain those in that morally undeveloped group need salvation—the wages of sin is death—but

Scripture focuses on the responsibility of those who are able to make a decision for faith or no-faith. Scripture does not directly address the salvific needs of the unborn, infants, small children, and adults who never became mentally or morally competent.

The "saved until sinning" solution creates two ways of salvation, one where the sinner is not held accountable, and the scriptural view where every sinner is held accountable. Only one thing is certain. If one of those in the morally undeveloped group receives God's gift, Ephesians 2:8, he or she will respond with saving faith. There are not two ways of salvation, and that is another reason the "saved until sinning" solution does not agree with the Scripture.

Two Scriptures are often used to defend the salvation of infants and small children (neither of which addresses the unborn or the morally undeveloped adult.)

The first is 2 Samuel 12:15–23. The story is familiar to most Christians. David the king committed adultery with Bathsheba and she became pregnant. David recalled her husband from the battlefield so he could have sex with his wife and make it appear he was responsible for the pregnancy. He did not have sex with her, so David had him abandoned on the battlefield so he would die in conflict with the enemy; in God's eyes it was an act of murder. Then David married Bathsheba. The child was born. The child became ill and died.

During the illness, David prostrated himself in prayer and fasts. After the child died, David got up, washed and anointed himself, changed his clothes, went to the tabernacle, and worshiped YHWH. His servants were amazed he did not mourn. David replied,

> While the child yet lived, I fasted and wept; for I said, Who knows if the Lord will pity me, and the child live?

> But now it is dead, why should I fast thus? shall I be able to bring him back again? I shall go to him, but he shall not return to me. (LXX.)

Was David saying that when he died he would meet this infant in heaven, i.e., that this one infant had been saved prior to its physical death? (Salvation must occur prior to death, Hebrews 9:27.) To answer this question we must ask, who was speaking? Was it David the prophet or David the grieving father? We must ask, is what David said revelation from God? The words are inspired, which means that what David said was accurately recorded, but was what David said revelation from God the Holy Spirit regarding the spiritual state of all infants? Or even this one infant? David says his son cannot come back from death, but he, David, will go to him, the child, when he, David, dies.

If David was speaking as a prophet, and if David knew by divine revelation the eternal fate of this one infant, does that understanding apply to every other person dying in infancy from Adam forward to the end of the world? No. What David said was a singular statement, meaning that nothing like it, or corresponding to it, or parallel with it, or similar to it in thought or idea, appears anywhere else in Scripture.

One of the rules of theology is, do not build a doctrine from a single verse. I will respect that rule in regard to this singular verse. In my view, this one verse only answers the question concerning the salvation of either this one infant or all infants if you bring the answer with you. (And what about all the other morally undeveloped persons?)

The second verse used to justify all infants are saved, is the incident recorded in Matthew 19, Mark 10, and Luke 18, Jesus with little children. The passage says nothing conclusive about their salvation. Jesus was displeased that the disciples sought to prevent parents bringing their children to Jesus. However, it was culturally unusual, very unusual, that parents would bring their little children near to any "holy man," such as a rabbi, teacher, or prophet.

In the ancient world children were not prized as they are today. In modern times children are evaluated on their assumed adult potential. In the ancient world children were evaluated on what they might contribute to society or family as children. As a result, they were not valued at all (a high mortality rate for infants and children did not help the situation). Christianity is actually one of the impelling reasons the attitude toward children changed, because Christians know every human being is from the one, Adam, who was formed in God's image and likeness.

So it was unusual in those times for parents to bring their children to a teacher, a holy man, a prophet. But they did bring their children to Jesus and he did receive them. He used them as an illustration to teach that saving faith is trusting faith, on the order of the naïve kind of trust expressed by little children: faith without suspicion; faith without doubt. The passage does not say if little children will be saved, but it leaves no doubt they can be saved—if they can exercise saving faith.

Neither the 2 Samuel passage nor the gospel passages answer the question concerning the salvation of morally undeveloped unborn, infants, small children, and morally undeveloped adults. To answer the question we must return to the basis of salvation, Christ's propitiation and its efficient application, and add in the final point, the foreordaining choices made by God. What is required to save those who cannot express saving faith, who (as far as we can know) cannot make a choice between faith and no-faith, is the application of the merit of Christ to the sinful condition of their soul. What is required for that application is grace and faith.

That is, in fact, the need of everyone. No one seeks after God, no one understands, all have gone the way of sin. If no person seeks God, if the inclination of the sinful nature is to rebel against God, then how is anyone saved? The answer is God's foreordaining choices, Ephesians 1:4, "he chose us in him before the beginning of the universe." Not every human being is chosen, but no human being is beyond the reach of God's electing choice, from the moment of conception to physical death.

All those whom God has elected will certainly be saved. Those persons who are morally developed will be saved the same as every sinner may be saved: by responding to the Good News of salvation with faith. Scripture gives no other way to salvation. As to those God has not chosen to salvation, the election of some does not prevent the salvation of any; that is what the desire for sin does.

As to the unborn, infants, and others similarly so morally undeveloped that they are unable to make the moral choice between faith and no faith, if they are saved, "it cannot be on their own merits, or on the basis of their own righteousness or innocence, but must be entirely on the basis of Christ's redemptive work and regeneration by the work of the Holy Spirit within them" [Grudem, 500].

What I am saying is that if God has chosen any one of these morally undeveloped persons to salvation, then God will by grace give them the gift of grace-faith-salvation, and by grace they will positively respond to the gift by the exercise of saving faith, and by grace God will apply the merit of Christ to save their soul. The manner of their positive response—how they might express saving faith—cannot be known, because they cannot tell us by word or deed. But of course God is able to know.

Is the God who created human beings unable to effectively

communicate with the human soul that he designed and created *ex nihilo?* At any stage of human development, beginning at conception? The omnipotent God in whom my faith rests is able.

God's electing choice is the primary condition affecting the salvation of any human being from Adam forward to the end of this present universe: God acts to save all whom he has chosen; he takes no action to prevent any person from coming to him to be saved. The purpose of election is to guarantee salvation, nothing more, nothing less.

Beyond this no one can go with certainty. No one can say with scriptural certainty that all, some, or none of the unborn, infants, small children, or adults who never became morally developed are saved. Perhaps God has elected to salvation every single person who dies without having the moral development to decide for faith or no-faith. Perhaps some of these are saved and some not. Perhaps none are saved. Is God righteous, holy, and just only when I understand; or agree? Certainly not! For then how will God judge the world?

Whatever God has decided it is holy, it is righteous, it is just. As Abraham said, God does not execute the righteous with the wicked, Genesis 18:25. But none of the morally undeveloped are righteous until saved.

What are the options?

If all the unborn, infants, small children, and morally undeveloped adults are saved, God is just, God is holy.

If only some, or none, are saved God is just, God is holy.

Justice and holiness are essential characteristics of God. God has no sin and takes no action that would be unjust. There is an election according to grace—the blessing of God given to those with no merit. That is mercy. For those not elected that is deserved justice, because all human beings are sinners by nature from conception. The morally developed naturally choose sin. No one can say what the morally undeveloped choose, but they are sinners by nature, and therefore will chose to commit acts of sinning.

God does make a choice, "Jacob I have loved, but Esau have I hated," meaning God drew one into a covenant with himself but not the other, and "the children not yet being born, nor having done any good or evil, that the purpose of God according to election might stand, not of works, but of him who calls." God has chosen not to reveal the why or who of his electing choice. One must either accept that God is holy, righteous, and just in all his ways, or create a soteriology not based on Scripture, which is what many have done by making the morally undeveloped a special class of sinners.

What has been said about the unborn, infants, small children, and morally undeveloped adults cannot be applied to those who have developed the moral competence to make a decision for faith or no-faith. All morally developed persons of any physical age, in all the millennia of humankind on this earth, are morally required to believe in God and God's testimony as to the means of salvation. All Christians are required to go and "disciple all the peoples," Matthew 28:19. How God deals with that one class of sinners without moral development is one of the secret things that belong to YHWH our God (Deuteronomy 29:29). This also is part of the Ordo Salutis.

FREE WILL DOMINATED BY SIN

The will is the decision-making faculty of human nature. Free will may be defined as the moral authority God designed into his sentient creatures to make choices within the physical, moral, and spiritual boundaries of their nature, as further influenced by internal and external motivations and consequences.

The two important aspects of that definition are the "physical, moral, and spiritual boundaries," and "internal and external motivations and consequences."

Free will is not a license to think or do anything I want. Free will is limited by the attributes and characteristics of human nature. These form the boundaries in which free will may be exercised. If it helps, think of those attributes and characteristics of human nature as a fence beyond which one cannot go, whether physically, morally, or spiritually. Any decision may be made that the fence allows, including decisions to commit acts of sinning, and the decision to reject God and his salvation. The latter, in fact, that decision to reject God and his salvation, is the only decision regarding God and his salvation that the fence formed by the sinful unsaved human nature will allow.

The other important aspect to the exercise of free will is the influence of internal and external motivations and consequences. The internal motivations of the person, the external motivations applied to the person by influences outside the person, and the consequences arising from a person's freely made choices—all influence the exercise of free will, but do not change the fact the will freely makes decisions.

Right now, you are deciding to continue reading or stop. No one is making that decision for you. Your decision will be influenced by various internal motivations, such as your spiritual state (saved or unsaved), curiosity, the desire to learn, or perhaps the desire to respond to this "bloated windbag of a theologian" (as some have said). You are also experiencing various external motivations, including prior teaching you have received on the subject, and your own investigations of relevant scriptures. Whatever your decide, you exercised your free will.

As sinful human beings we try to hide, or even deny, our free will behind motivations and consequences. If the motivations and consequences are good we claim the choices we made. If the motivations and consequences are bad we say we were forced or coerced to make those choices. No, the choice is always yours, you alone are responsible for your choices.

Even the slave—even a slave to sin—makes a decision to obey or not to obey, as influenced by motivations and by the consequences of his choices. Even the slave is not prevented from exercising his free will because of the consequences of those choices.

So free will, like liberty or freedom, isn't a license to think or do anything I want. Just as a physical fence limits choices to "this far, no further," even so the fence formed by the physical, moral, and spiritual aspects of human nature say "this far, no further"; and these are fences one cannot climb over. One cannot freely choose to flap his arms and fly to the store because of the physical boundaries of human nature. Even so, the moral and spiritual boundaries limit the exercise of free will.

Free will is limited by the attributes and characteristics of human nature. Looking at the spiritual boundaries, the will is not neutrally suspended between good and evil, but is inclined toward one or the other by its spiritual attributes as created by God, corrupted by sin, and in the case of the saved, regenerated by salvation. The spiritual boundary does not allow the sinner to initiate salvation, nor believe and be saved unaided by the efficacious influence of God's gift of grace-faith-salvation (Ephesians 2:8).

In the case of unsaved human beings, the will is inclined toward sin because of the principle of rebellion (the sin attribute) that became part of human nature following Adam's sin and propagation. The inclination

68

of sin is to rebel against God and disobey his commandments, thereby effectively persuading human beings to choose their path in life apart from God. The sinner freely chooses to commit acts of sinning, including the sin to reject God and his salvation. The unsaved human being is unable to overcome the spiritual boundary of the sin attribute without God's gift of grace-faith-salvation.

The sinner freely chooses to sin, his choice conditioned by the moral and spiritual boundaries set by the sin attribute in his or her human nature. Without that freely made choice there is no responsibility, accountability, or liability. When we deny that free exercise of the will, we have denied God made humankind with the power to choose, the moral authority to exercise choice, the responsibility to choose rightly, and equally as important to God's justice, the accountability and liability for every freely made choice. When we deny the free exercise of will, we have proclaimed God made human beings programmed automatons who dance on the string of God's sovereignty.

God changes the spiritual boundary of the sinner through his gift, Ephesians 2:8, thereby changing the kind of choices that may be made. Staying with the same illustration, God moves the fence to a different spiritual boundary, so different choices may be made. God by his gift initiates salvation in the sinner by changing the spiritual boundary (1 Corinthians 2:14; Romans 6:14) in which free will operates. The gift enlivens the person's spiritual perception, whereby the sinner is able to understand the spiritual issues of his sin, Christ the only Savior, salvation by faith alone, and thereby the sinner willingly obeys God's command to believe and be saved, whereupon God completes that salvation through the regeneration of the human nature from unsaved to saved.

The saved, born-again believer freely chooses to deny temptation because those choices are within the spiritual boundary of the born-again human nature.

All decisions made by every human being are made within the limits imposed by the boundaries of the human nature of sinner or saint, as further influenced by internal and external motivations and consequences. That is free will.

Chapter Summary

In the previous chapter I disposed of the supralapsarian view that God elected some righteous persons to reprobation and then God decreed all human beings would be sinners. Election concerns only sinners, and only the salvation of sinners. This chapter explains what sin is and why all are sinners. The chapter then provides a biblical explanation of free will.

Sin is defined as an attribute of fallen human nature. The sin attribute makes the person a sinner who commits acts of sinning. The attributes of human nature are discussed, both their nature and their source. Man's moral, intellectual, and spiritual attributes were designed into human nature by God, patterned after God's communicable attributes. The attribute of rebellion and disobedience, which the Bible names "sin," came from Adam's rebellion and disobedience in response to God's command, Genesis 2:17; 3:6.

Sin is defined in both its moral and legal aspects. Morally sin is not being in the image and likeness of God in which humankind was created. Morally sin is violating God's moral values, whether by omission or commission. Legally sin is rebellion and disobedience to God's commandments and God's "Do this, Don't do that" rules for godly living.

The addition of sin into human nature through Adam's act of sinning is discussed. Then, the reason why all of Adam's descendants, the entire human race, have the sin attribute is explained as the consequence of God's Law of Biological Reproduction. That law is each kind of living being reproduces its own kind of living being and no other kind of living being.

The discussion explains the creation of the body and the soul, and the nature of each component of man's being. The explanation led into the reason why Adam and the Woman (Eve) could sin: their free will and their mutability. God gave humankind the moral authority to make decisions. God made humankind capable of change. Both of these aspects of human nature were designed with man's responsibility, his stewardship of the earth, in view. Both of those aspects allowed sinless Adam (and the Woman) to choose to sin, and both aspects made the effects of that choice permanent in their human nature.

Adam's misuse of the moral authority designed into his human nature by God, and the natural, God-designed mutability of his human nature, led not only to an act of sinning, but caused that act of sinning to permanently change Adam's human nature. God's Law of Biological Reproduction caused Adam's descendants to inherit that changed human nature, Genesis 5:3; Romans 5:12; 1 Corinthians 15:22.

The upside to moral authority (free will) and mutability is it allows the change in human nature that is the consequence of salvation: saved, born-again, a normal Christian life during this mortal life, and transformed to be sinless in the life yet to come.

The section on sin concludes with an in depth discussion of those who either have not developed, or never will develop, the moral capacity to decide for faith or no faith. All such are culpable for the sinful human nature they possess at conception. The Scripture does not directly address their salvation.

The conclusion of that discussion was any person lacking the moral development to decide for faith or no faith may be saved by grace through faith, because God is completely capable of communicating with the human nature he created, at any stage of human development, beginning at conception. However, no one can know if such are saved, because they don't have the capacity to demonstrate their salvation by testimony or works. Therefore one must have faith God will save, or not save, according to his purpose in creating humankind, and his foreordaining decrees effecting salvation.

The chapter concludes with an explanation of free will. Free will may be defined as the moral authority God designed into his sentient creatures to make choices within the physical, moral, and spiritual boundaries of their nature, as further influenced by internal and external motivations and consequences. That definition, and its consequences, are fully explained.

Free will always functions within the boundaries of human nature, physical, moral, and spiritual. God's gift of grace-faith-salvation (Ephesians 2:8) changes the spiritual boundary of sinful human nature, thereby changing the kind of choices that may be made. The sinner's choices are limited by the sin attribute to his freely made choices to sin. The choices of the person receiving God's gift are expanded to the exercise of saving faith.

Christ's Propitiation of God

Every Old Testament sacrifice for sin teaches this basic redemptive truth: propitiation and redemption are separate acts. Propitiation: the animal was sacrificed as a legal satisfaction for the sinner's judicial guilt for his crimes of sin. Redemption: the blood of the sacrifice, which represents the legal merit that cancels the judicial debt of sin, is by faith in its efficacy applied to the altar to effect forgiveness of sin. Even so, in agreement with the biblical principle, the limitless merit of Christ's propitiation of God for sin, in order to be salvific, must be applied to the sinner's spiritual need by the sinner's faith.

God made a legal satisfaction for his holiness, justice, and wrath against the crime of human sin through the propitiation of Jesus Christ on the cross. What is propitiation?

Statement Of The Doctrine.

> Propitiation. The satisfaction Christ made to God for sin by dying on the cross as the sin-bearer, 2 Corinthians 5:21; Romans 3:25; Hebrews 2:17; 1 John 2:2; 4:10, for the crime of sin committed by human beings, suffering in their place and on their behalf.

Christ alone propitiated God for the crime of sin. The purpose of Christ's propitiation was to fully satisfy (propitiate) God's holiness and justice for the crime of human sin. Christ's propitiation was of limitless merit, because his Person is of limitless worth.

The application of Christ's limitless merit to overcome the demerit of sin and save a soul, is through the election God decreed before he created the universe, and is personally applied by the sinner through the exercise of saving faith in response to God's gift of grace-faith-salvation (particular redemption), Ephesians 2:8. Christ's righteousness is imputed to the saved sinner so that he/she eternally stands uncondemned before a holy God, Romans 8:1, 31.

(The merit of Christ's propitiation is also applied in a manner consistent with God's mercy to give temporal benefits to all humankind. In the chapter on foreordination I defined mercy. God acts in mercy toward all human beings because of Christ's propitiation.)

Christ's propitiation was of infinite merit, because his Person is of infinite worth. The application of that merit is personally made by each sinner to his or her sin through faith in God and God's testimony as to the proper object and content of saving faith. The proper object of saving faith is God. The proper content of saving faith is God's historically current testimony as given in the progressive revelation of truth. Faith in God and God's testimony is how God's grace and Christ's merit in salvation is accessed.

Christ accomplished the propitiation of God for sin by enduring spiritual and physical death on the cross. Christ endured spiritual death when he was separated from fellowship with God ("My God, my God, why have you forsaken me?"), and physical death when he separated his soul from his body ("[B]owing his head, he gave up his spirit.")

Excursus: The God-man Suffered Death

Jesus suffered both penalties for sin: physical death and spiritual death. Remember, in Scripture, death is separation. Physical death is when the soul (the soul is the person) is separated from the physical body. Spiritual death is when the person is separated God, whether separated from a relationship (the unsaved) or separated in fellowship (the sinning believer). Therefore, during the crucifixion, Jesus suffered both kinds of separation, physical death and spiritual death, to pay the penalty for sin. Both were temporary, but both were genuine.

Jesus Christ endured spiritual death when he was separated from fellowship with God, and the Holy Spirit let us know that when he had Matthew and Mark record this word by Jesus on the cross: "My God, my God, why have you forsaken me?" That forsaking was a loss of fellowship. Not an interruption of his relationship with God, but an interruption of his fellowship with God.

Someone somewhere will say, "Jesus is God, so how can God be separated from fellowship with himself? The answer is Jesus the Christ is the God-man. Jesus of Nazareth is a human being, conceived in Mariam's womb, born into the world by Mariam's labor. God the Son is incarnate in Jesus of Nazareth, by that union forming one person, the God-man, Jesus the Christ, fully human and fully deity. The Scripture presents the God-man as one person, not two, not as though his deity did this or his humanity did that, but he is one person. The God-man slept, ate, perspired, eliminated bodily waste, and the God-man stilled the storm, created food in his hands, knew the future, healed the sick, demonized, and dead. One person, not a nature, did all, endured all, suffered all. The God-man is one person with one personality, that of God the Son, informed by his two natures, genuine deity and genuine human.

Therefore, in the crucifixion, the person suffered physical death although God the Son cannot die, and the person suffered a loss of fellowship, although God the Son cannot be separated from fellowship with the Father and Spirit. The God-man separated from his physical body: physical death; his human soul continued in active conscious existence, in the same union with the deity nature as before his physical death.

Even so, we know God did not lose fellowship with himself, but the person who was and is God-man did suffer a temporary loss of fellowship, a spiritual separation, as payment for the spiritual penalty of sin, and then continued in fellowship with God once the penalty was paid. We cannot fully explain it, but the testimony of the Scripture is this: "My God, my God, why have you forsaken me?"

Think on this, if the God-man Jesus Christ did not pay both the physical and spiritual penalties for the crime of sin, then God was not propitiated, and no one is saved. However your theology works that out, the God-man must suffer physical death and spiritual death on the cross, in order to propitiate God for your sin.

And after that loss of fellowship was endured and completed, he said, "Father," assuring us the fellowship had been restored, "into your hands I commit my spirit."

Returning to the discussion.

The merit of that propitiation is limitlessly sufficient to forgive all sin past, present, future. The reason the merit of Christ's propitiation is limitless is he was (and is) the God-man. His human nature was mortal, so he might suffer the penalty, but his deity nature is eternal and of limitless glory, therefore the efficacy of his propitiation has the value of his limitless merit. The humanity of the God-man is as important to propitiating God as the deity of the God-man. The God-man suffered the penalty due sin, and therefore the propitiatory merit of that suffering is limitless.

God's justice against sin having been fully satisfied by Christ's propitiation, God could act in temporal and eternal benefits toward humankind.

The eternal benefit is redemption to endless life. As I stated above, the limitless merit of Christ's propitiation of God for human sin must be applied by grace through faith to be salvific.

The work of salvation may be summarized in one sentence. "Place your trust at once and once for all in God and God's testimony concerning the Lord Jesus Christ, and you will be saved from the eternal penalty due your sins and given eternal life." Think not? That is what the Philippians jailor understood, Acts 16:31–32.

There are, however, a few details. An outline.

> God applies the limitless merit of the propitiation according to the decree of election (Ephesians 1:4),
>
> through the gift of grace-faith-salvation (Ephesians 2:8),
>
> which is efficacious to effect a change in the sinful human nature (giving life to the soul's faculty of spiritual perception, contra the natural state of 1 Corinthians 2:14),
>
> inevitably resulting in the freely made choice by the sinner to believe and be saved.

The biblical view is the unlimited propitiation made by Christ, and the particular redemption effected by God's foreordaining choice (election, Ephesians 1:4) to give his gift of grace-faith-salvation (Ephesians 2:8), results in the sinner's spiritual perception being enlivened to understand the spiritual issues of his or her sin, Jesus Christ the only Savior, and salvation not by works but by the limitless merit of Christ alone, inevitably bringing the sinner to have faith on God and God's testimony as to the way of salvation.

Or put another way, God's grace efficaciously works to change the unable and unwilling sinner to willing and able to believe and be saved, and by that faith the sinner is saved, not by works but by the limitless merit of Christ alone.

Therefore, salvation is not mere trust, nor is it only the sinner's choice, but is the consequence of a supra-natural work of God that results in the choice to commit one's eternal destiny to God and the Lord Jesus Christ.

The atonement-propitiation made by Christ is not redemption but is a legal satisfaction for sin. For the propitiation to be redemptive it must be applied by faith. There are three benefits to that legal satisfaction.

> One, the offer of the gospel to all persons is a legitimate offer. God does not prevent any sinner from coming and believing (their own desire for sin prevents them).

Two, salvation is not universal (not all human beings) but particular (some human beings as foreordained by God), by God's gift of grace (Ephesians 2:8) through the sinner's faith.

Three, God would act savingly toward any non-elect who would come, if they could overcome their desire for sin over God and God's salvation.

God chose to save some, but did not act to prevent any. God would have all persons to be saved (1 Timothy 2:4), but he wills for certain persons to believe (Ephesians 1:4; 2 Thessalonians 2:13)

The only limit to salvation is the sinner's desire for sin over God, because the grace that powers salvation and the propitiation that powers salvation is limitless to save when applied by the sinner's faith. No faith = no redemption. Because of the efficacy of God's grace (Ephesians 2:8), faith is the inevitable result of receiving God's gift.

Recognizing atonement-propitiation is not redemption but the judicial satisfaction of God's wrath and justice against sin, confirms Christ's propitiation of God had both temporal and eternal benefits to humankind.

The reason God may act in temporal benefits to all, e.g., allow his rain to fall on the unthankful evil as well as grateful good, is Christ's propitiation satisfied God's holiness and justice for sin: God is justly able to give temporal benefits to those who reject him and his salvation.

The reason God acts in eternal benefits to some is Christ's propitiation satisfied God's holiness and justice for sin: God justly saves those who believe in God and God's testimony as to the way of salvation. Election guarantees salvation; election does not prevent salvation.

Another reason to understand that propitiation is not redemption is the limitless merit of Christ propitiation of God for all human sin—sufficient for all—does not effect universal salvation, because the merit must be applied by grace through faith. That is the consistent testimony of the Scripture, Old and New Testament. That is the salvation principle: saved by God's grace alone, through the sinner's faith alone, by the limitless merit of Christ's propitiation alone.

The entire Scripture teaches this truth: without faith there is no salvation, Ephesians 2:8. That is the salvation principle, applicable and effective throughout the history of redemption, Old and New

Testaments. Even the elect must believe to be saved, which is why election is God giving the gift of grace-faith-salvation, so those receiving the gift will appropriate and apply the truth to their spiritual need, believe, and be saved.

The Purpose Of Christ's Propitiation

There is controversy within the Arminian, Reformed, and Dispensational camps over the extent of Christ's propitiation of God for human sin (aka: the "extent of the atonement"). This controversy is based on the question, "For whom did Christ die," a misstatement of the biblical doctrine, which is "What was the purpose of Christ's propitiation?" The purpose of Christ's propitiation was to fully satisfy God's justice for the crime of human sin, and out of that satisfaction comes temporal and eternal benefits. Let us look at the other views.

Arminian soteriology's foresight election has an easy answer: Christ died for everyone whom God omnipresently saw would believe. For Reformed and Dispensational believers there are three answers, depending on the person's lapsarian views.

Supra: Christ's Propitiation was limited to the elect only

Infra: Christ's Propitiation was sufficient for all efficient for the elect

Sub: Christ's Propitiation has eternal benefits to the elect, temporal benefits to all.

The limited position is held by supralapsarians. The unlimited sufficient-efficient position is held by infralapsarians and sublapsarians. The temporal-eternal benefits position is an historic Reformed and Dispensational view, often identified with Amyraldianism (but in truth simply one aspect of Moses Amyraut's [1596–1664] doctrine).

The True Nature Of Christ's Propitiation

My lapsarian order of God's pre-creation decrees is close to the sublapsarian order, but with a significant difference.

To create.

To permit the fall.

To satisfy God's justice and holiness through a propitiation for sin.

To elect some out of the fallen mass of humanity to be saved, and to take no action toward the others to affect or effect

78

their sinful state.

To send the Holy Spirit to apply the limitless merit of Christ's propitiation to the elect, thereby effecting their salvation.

What is the difference? The supra, infra, and sublapsarian orders teach propitiation = redemption. Those views make the purpose of Christ's propitiation man-centered. I believe the Scripture teaches the purpose of Christ's propitiation was God-centered (e.g., Romans 3:25). "To satisfy God's justice through a propitiation for sin." Salvation is an application of the propitiation, not the primary purpose. If no one was elected, if God had decided not to elect any but to leave all sinners to their own choices (as in Arminianism), and as a consequence none believed, God would still need to be propitiated, because his justice and holiness must act to satisfy itself.

Could God act to propitiate himself and save no one? He almost did in the Noahic Flood, when only eight were saved. How wonderful God's love and grace and mercy fully satisfied his justice and holiness so sinners could be saved, and that God chose to act directly to save some, and chose to not act directly to prevent any. Any individual could have entered the ark before God closed the door, Genesis 7:16. God chose to save some, but did not act to prevent any. God would have all persons to be saved (1 Timothy 2:4), but he wills for certain persons to believe (Ephesians 1:4; 2 Thessalonians 2:13), thereby guaranteeing the elect will believe, without any kind of decree preventing any from believing. Preach to all, proclaim to all, pray for all, and praise God for all those who are saved.

Christ's propitiation was the full satisfaction of God's justice for the crime of sin through a suitable vicarious sacrifice suffering the judicial penalty against sin. The primary purpose of the propitiation was to fully satisfy God's justice for the crime committed against his holiness.

Romans 3:25, Whom God set forth publicly as a propitiation, through faith in his blood, for declaring his [God's] righteousness.

Hebrews 2:17, in order to make propitiation for the sins of the people.

1 John 2:2, Now he is propitiation for our sins—but not for ours only but also for all the world [not only the elect].

1 John 5:10, In this is the love: not that we have loved God, but that he loved us, and sent his Son, a propitiation concerning

our sins.

In the interpretation of Scripture, every scripture relevant to a doctrine must be considered, and harmonized, which is to say, no contradictions allowed. The three lapsarian views discussed in the chapter on foreordination, the supra, infra, and sub views—and in fact almost every Reformed theology discussion on the subject—focuses on "a propitiation for redemption." But the simple scriptural fact is the purpose of Christ's propitiation was to satisfy God for the crime of sin, "for declaring God's righteousness," and salvation is one of the applications of that merit.

Therefore, the biblical doctrine is this: Christ propitiated God's holiness and justice for every human sin from Adam to the end of the world, and the limitless merit of that propitiation is applied according to God's decrees. The correct doctrine is not "limited atonement" as in supralapsarianism or the egregious TULIP, but unlimited propitiation of God and particular redemption of sinners.

What does the limitless merit of Christ's propitiation mean for all humankind? In the supra doctrine, nothing. In the infra doctrine, potentially something. In the sub doctrine most likely something. In the doctrine of others, including me, something for everyone: temporal and eternal blessings to each given according to God's mercy working through God's decrees.

My studies in the Scripture have led me to believe positively that the "something for everyone" is both temporal and eternal benefits to all humankind from Christ's propitiation of God for all human sin. I have already described the eternal benefits: conditioned upon saving faith. That condition is positively met for those saved by God's foreordaining choice, election, to give some sinners his gift of grace-faith-salvation, Ephesians 2:8. Therefore salvation is never a matter of personal merit, but of God's choice.

(Some may wonder why I refer to God's gift as grace-faith-salvation. The reasons are grammatical and doctrinal. Doctrinally, there is no salvation apart from God's grace and the believer's faith. Both are required for salvation, that is the salvation principle. Grammatically, the neuter pronoun "that," [and that not of yourselves] refers to both the masculine participle "you are saved" and the feminine noun "faith." See my commentary on Ephesians for more detail.)

The reason I believe in temporal benefits from Christ's propitiation is judicial: God's justice against the crime of sin has been satisfied. This is where the supralapsarian camp will shout out the accusation "universal salvation," but that is because their doctrine must make propitiation = redemption rather than propitiation = judicial satisfaction. The result of propitiation = judicial satisfaction is that there will be eternal benefits for some human beings and temporal benefits toward all humankind, each kind of benefit according to God's mercy and decrees.

Christ's propitiation of God for human sin fully satisfied God's justice for the crime against his holiness. Therefore, God can justly act in mercy toward the unforgiven sinner. God can justly delay judgment and justly relieve misery, which are the two aspects of God's mercy toward all humankind. (The delay in Satan's judgment to Revelation 20:10 is not due to Christ's act of propitiation, but God's purpose, plans, and processes. Christ propitiated God for human sin only.)

Above I criticized the supralapsarian doctrine for limiting God's mercy to the elect only, so that in the supralapsarian doctrine sunshine and rain on the non-elect is just an unhappy accident, not God's intent. The doctrine that propitiation = judicial satisfaction fully explains how God may be merciful to sinners. As one example,

> God's justice requires sin be immediately judged and the sinner immediately punished, no delay.

> Why is God able to delay judgment, and thereby give the sinner a lifetime to repent, belief, and be saved? Because propitiation = judicial satisfaction.

> How is God able to give blessings to the unforgiven sinner, when just wrath is required? Because propitiation = judicial satisfaction.

If Christ's propitiation = redemption, then God is justly unable to give mercy and blessing to any but the elect (the doctrine of many supralapsarian theologians). Because propitiation = judicial satisfaction, God is able (1) to give undeserved temporal benefits toward all human beings, saved or unsaved, elect or not elect and (2) gives eternal benefits to his elect.

The Application Of The Merit

How is God is able to be merciful when confronted by human sin? God's holy character has an automatic reaction to sin: immediate judgment. "God is light and darkness is not in him, none at all," 1 John

1:5. If, as is true, "in him we live and move and exist," Acts 17:28, then how does God tolerate our darkness within his light? The answer is Christ propitiated God for our darkness, i.e., our sin.

Jesus Christ "is propitiation for our sins—but not for ours only but also for all the world," 1 John 2:2. Was Christ's propitiation for all? Yes, and applied to each person according to God's foreordaining decrees in both temporal and eternal benefits, applied according to the rule governing God's grace: God blessing because he chooses to bless, even though blessing is always undeserved.

Today, Theodore Beza's supralapsarian order of God's pre-creation decrees is currently the most popular view of Christ's propitiation—the limited atonement view Christ died only for the elect, and therefore God's grace and love and mercy is allowed to affect only the elect. Supralapsarianism is the most popular, but not most biblical.

What did the person whom Beza claimed as his mentor, John Calvin, say? From *Calvin's Commentary* on the gospels (emphasis Calvin).

> On Matthew 22:22, The word *many* is not put definitively for a fixed number; for he contrasts himself with all others. And in this sense it is used in Romans 5:15, where Paul does not speak of any part of men, but embraces the whole human race. [*Commentary*, vol. 16, *On A Harmony of the Evangelists*, 2:427].

Calvin argues in Romans 5:15 the "many" are all those who are in Adam, which is the entire human race, as descended from Adam, the original human being.

> But observe, that a larger number (*plures*) are not here contrasted with many (*multis*) for he speaks not of the number of men: but as the sin of Adam has destroyed many, he draws this conclusion,—that the righteousness of Christ will be no less efficacious to save many. [*Commentary*, vol. 19, *Romans*, 207.]

Christ in some sense propitiated God for all human beings. In his comments on Romans 5:15, Calvin rightly contrasts the many who are sinners in Adam with the many who are in Christ. The "many" in Christ, Romans 5:15, are those who receive eternal life from Christ. But as Christ died for the many who are in Adam, in what sense do those not in Christ receive benefits from his death? Through temporal benefits.

In this way, God is able to justly have mercy toward all

humankind—delaying just judgment and relieving misery—because Christ propitiated God for all human sin, 1 John 2:2; Romans 3:23–25; Hebrews 2:17. The temporal benefits of that propitiation, God's mercy and goodness, apply to all human beings: the rain falls on all, good and evil. The eternal benefits of the propitiation are applied to some human beings according to God's decrees concerning salvation from the penalty of sin.

This is not only my doctrine, but a doctrine shared by many past and present.

> Martin Luther: "He bears all the sins of the world from its inception; this implies that He also bears yours, and offers you grace... Christ was given ... not for one or two sins, but for all sins ... Christ has taken away not only the sins of some men but your sins and those of the whole world. The offering was for the sins of the whole world, even though the whole world does not believe. So do not permit your sins to be merely sins; let them be your very own sins. That is, believe that Christ was given not only for the sins of others but also for yours." [Quoted by C. Daniel, "Hyper-Calvinism and John Gill," Ph.D. diss., University of Edinburgh, 1983), 512–513.]

The Synod of Dort taught Christ's propitiation of God was sufficient for all, efficient to salvation for the elect.

> Canons of Dort, Second Head of Doctrine, Article 3, "The death of the Son of God is the only and most perfect sacrifice and satisfaction for sin, and is of infinite worth and value, abundantly sufficient to expiate the sins of the whole world."

There is room in that statement for temporal benefits toward all humankind.

> C. Hodge: "It does not follow from the assertion of Christ's atonement having a special reference to the elect that it had no reference to the non-elect. Augustinians readily admit that the death of Christ had a relation to man, to the whole human family, which it had not to fallen angels. It is the ground on which salvation is offered to every creature under heaven who hears the gospel .... moreover, it secures to the whole race at large, and to all classes of men, innumerable blessings, both providential and religious. It was, of course, designed to produce these effects; and, therefore, he died to secure them...

. There is a sense, therefore, in which Christ died for all, and there is a sense in which he died for the elect alone." [Hodge, 2:545–546]

C.H. Spurgeon: "Our older Calvinistic friends deal with 1 Timothy 2:6 and 'all men' [and] they say, 'That is, some men'; as if the Holy Ghost could not have said 'some men' if he had meant some men. 'All men,' they say ... is 'some of all sorts of men'; as if the Lord could not have said 'all sorts of men' if he had meant that. The Holy Ghost by the apostle has written 'all men,' and unquestionably he means all men ... I was reading just now the exposition of a very able doctor who explains the text so as to explain it away: he applies grammatical gunpowder to it." [quoted in Ian Murray, *Spurgeon v. Hyper-Calvinism*, 150.]

Dr. John MacArthur is a recent voice noting God's love is both temporal and eternal. Dr. Keith Sherlin kindly provided these quotes from Dr. John MacArthur.

I am troubled by the tendency of some—often young people newly infatuated with Reformed doctrine—who insist that God cannot possibly love those who never repent and believe .... Those who hold this view often go to great lengths to argue that John 3:16 cannot really mean God loves the whole world. Perhaps the best-known argument for this view is found in A.W. Pink who wrote, "God loves whom he chooses. He does not love everybody" .... We must understand that it is God's very nature to love. The reason our Lord commanded us to love our enemies is 'in order that you may be sons of your Father ... for he causes his sun to rise on the evil and the good (Matt. 5:45) .... Reformed theologians have always affirmed the love of God for all sinners. John Calvin himself wrote regarding John 3:16 ... 'the Father loves the human race, and wishes that they should not perish' ... Calvin points out ... that [God's love is] by no means limited to the elect alone. [MacArthur, *The Love of God*, 12–18.]

Christ's atonement is unlimited as to its sufficiency, but limited as to its application. Real benefits accrue for all because of Christ's all sufficient atoning work. The gospel may be preached to all ... moreover, in a temporal sense the entire race was spared from immediate destruction ... and individual sinners experience a delay in God's judgment on their sins. [MacArthur, *First Timothy, New Testament Commentary*, 72]

The supralapsarian view, that God's love extends only toward those he elected to salvation, is simply not the testimony of the Scripture.

> Matthew 5:44–45, But I say to you, love your enemies, and pray for those persecuting you; bless those cursing you, do good to those misusing you and hating you, 45 so that you may be sons of your Father in the heavens. Because he makes his sun rise on evil and good, and sends rain on righteous and unrighteous.

> John 3:16, For God so loved the world that he gave the Son, the only begotten, that everyone believing in him should not perish but may have eternal life.

The "world" in the 3:16 context reasonably means the world of sinners.

The propitiation was and is sufficient for all, and therefore all are called upon to believe, because no act of God excludes any sinner from believing and being saved.

> John 12:32, And I, when I am lifted up from the earth, will draw all persons to myself.

> Revelation 22:17, And the Spirit and the bride say, 'Come.' And the one hearing let him say 'Come.' And the one thirsting—the one desiring—let him come, let him take freely the water of life.

The propitiation is sufficient for all, efficient to salvation for the elect, because the elect receive the gift of God that inevitably and infallibly results in the freely made choice to believe and be saved, by changing the unable and unwilling to willing and able.

> 1 John 5:15, Whoever confesses that Jesus Christ is the Son of God, God in him abides, and he in God.

If God's love and Christ's propitiation was restricted to a certain group (as per supralapsarianism), then the Holy Spirit lies in the many "whoever" texts proclaiming salvation to whoever believes. As I discussed earlier, the purpose of election is to guarantee salvation to the elect, not to prevent the salvation of the non-elect. That is what sin does, it prevents saving faith.

In relation to Dispensational, Reformed, and Arminian soteriology, all believe Christ's propitiation of God for human sin is efficient to completely save the believing sinner from the eternal penalty due sin. From the earliest days of church history the orthodox doctrine has been Christ's propitiation fully and completely saves the sinner. More plainly, there is no such thing as a partial salvation, and 2 Corinthians 5:8 applies to every saved person, Old Testament and New Testament.

I mention this because there is an unorthodox view the Old Testament saved went to a "good side" of Hades to wait for the historical event of Christ's propitiation so they could be fully saved and go to heaven. (See *Dispensational Soteriology*, chapter "Soteriology," for a discussion, or my work, *Did Jesus Go To Hell?*)

Popular Reformed preachers have turned this unorthodox view [a "good side of Hades," a sort of Protestant limbo] into a false doctrine. That doctrine first appeared in the "Apostle's Creed" in AD 390 and again in AD 650. There are fourteen versions of the Apostle's Creed, the first appearing in AD 107 (Ignatius) then AD 200, 220, 250, 260, 341, 390 (two versions), 400, 450, 650, 750, and the Nicaean-Constantinopolitan version. Only the AD 390, AD 650, and AD 750 have the "descended into hell" statement. Unfortunately, the AD 750 statement is the one adopted for popular use. You may investigate the development of the Apostle's Creed in Schaff, *Creeds*, 2:11–55. The Creed is part of the discussion in my book *Did Jesus Go To Hell?*

But that is a side issue. The consequence of Christ's propitiation of God for human sin is temporal benefits to all, eternal benefits to the elect. That is the teaching of the Scripture and has been the consistent historic teaching of the New Testament church.

Summary Of Propitiation

The New Testament concept of propitiation is exactly the same as the Old Testament concept of atonement: reconciliation with God through a full satisfaction for the crime of sin. Christians in times past thought the Old Testament atonement was a "covering for sin" because Hebrew language experts of the times defined the biblical atonement by a similar Arabic word that meant to cover. But time, better linguistic studies, and paying attention to the Scripture has revealed the Hebrew word atonement means the same thing as its Greek equivalent propitiation: a full satisfaction for the crime of sin.

There are two differences between the Old Testament atonement and the New Testament propitiation.

The Old Testament was through the believer offering an animal sacrifice, the New is through Jesus Christ's sacrifice of himself on the cross. Both satisfied God for the crime of sin.

The Old satisfied God for the past act or acts of sinning for which it was offered, the New Testament satisfied God for every act of sinning by every sinner in the past, present, and future of the whole world.

Both atonement and propitiation, Old and New Testament, mean God was fully satisfied and forgave the sinner on the basis of a sacrifice for sin. The difference is the extent of the satisfaction. The Old Testament atonement satisfied fully satisfied God's holiness and justice for the specific sin or sins for which it was offered. The propitiation of Christ fully satisfied God's holiness and justice for all sin.

How then was an Old Testament sinner saved if his atonement only satisfied for past sins? A comprehensive statement of salvation is required. A sinner is "saved by God's grace through the sinner's faith without personal merit from the sinner but by Christ's merit alone." Christ's merit for saving sinners was gained through his propitiation of God on the cross.

The salvation principle stated in Ephesians 2:8 has always been active in the world. An Old Testament sinner was saved by God's grace, through the sinner's faith, by Christ's merit. The sinner's faith was in God and God's testimony as to the way of salvation. That testimony of the way of salvation was given through the historic progressive revelation of truth.

Progressive Revelation: the doctrine of progressive revelation is the simple observation God does not reveal all things at the same time, but over time God's revelation is completed.

As God said through Isaiah 28:10 (ESV), "For it is precept upon precept, precept upon precept, line upon line, line upon line, here a little, there a little." Therefore, God's testimony as to the way of salvation at any one time in the history of redemption, was the historically current testimony that had been given up to any one particular time. Again, no one in Old Testament times could know what God had not yet revealed in his Word, but were responsible for what he had revealed in his Word current to their particular time in history.

The animal sacrifice the Old Testament believer offered as an atonement, agreed with God's historically current testimony of the times—what God required of the sinner to demonstrate faith. The sacrifice itself was not what saved, because the "blood of bulls and goats" cannot remit the judicial guilt of sin. That animal sacrifice saved because God by grace accepted the act of faith that offered the atoning sacrifice as the God-ordained means by which the limitless merit of Christ's propitiation was accessed, by grace through faith. The merit of Christ's propitiation, and the salvation principle (Ephesians 2:8–9) have always been in effect, from the beginning.

Therefore, in the Old Testament, before Moses and after Moses, the initial act of faith in YHWH as Savior saved the person completely (there is no such thing as a partial salvation). Repeated acts of faith, e.g., animal sacrifices, served the Old Testament saved the same way 1 John 1:9 serves the New Testament saved, by faith a confession of having sinned in response to conviction.

The propitiation of God made by Christ on the cross is the only limitless merit by which a sinner—any sinner living in Old or New Testament times—may be saved from the penalty due the crime of sin. That salvation always was, is, and always will be full and complete, never partial. All saved persons, Old and New Testaments, are affected by the principle expressed in 2 Corinthians 5:8.

Christ's propitiation is not synonymous with or equal to the redemption of sinners. Redemption is one of the applications God makes of the limitless merit of the propitiation. God applies that unlimited merit to redemption according to his foreordaining decree that accomplished the election of certain sinners, through choosing to give those sinners his gift of grace-faith-salvation.

God also makes use of and applies the limitless merit of the propitiation to justly act in mercy, goodness, and kindness toward all humankind, both delaying deserved justice for their unforgiven sin, and relieving the misery caused by sin.

Christ's propitiation was judicial in nature, legally satisfying God's justice for the crime of sin committed against his holiness. Because God's justice was satisfied (propitiated) God is justly able to act redemptively toward the elect, and with temporal benefits toward all human beings.

Chapter Summary

This chapter explained propitiation and corrected misunderstandings of the doctrine. Christ's propitiation of God on the cross was not the redemption of sinners, but was the legal satisfaction of God's holiness, justice, and wrath against the crime of human sin. That legal satisfaction powers redemption, in agreement with God's foreordaining decrees concerning redemption.

The discussion explained that every Old Testament sacrifice for sin, when offered by faith and accepted by grace, was a propitiation of God for the sin for which it was offered. Then, as explained, the merit of that propitiation must be applied to effect redemption: the blood of the sacrifice was applied to the altar, and the sacrifice was burned on the altar. In this way, by the many Old Testament examples, the Holy Spirit taught that no sacrifice is redemptive until applied. Christ's propitiation is not redemptive until applied to the sinner's spiritual need by God's gift of grace, Ephesians 2:8.

All redemption, Old Testament and New Testament, is the application of Christ's propitiation of God on the cross to the sinner's spiritual need, by God's grace through the sinner's faith. In the Old Testament that faith was shown according to God's testimony: an animal sacrifice. In the New Testament that faith is shown according to God's testimony: faith in Jesus Christ as Redeemer. There is only one way of salvation, Old Testament and New Testament: by God's grace, through the sinner's faith in God and God's testimony, without any merit from the sinner, but by the application of the limitless merit of Christ's propitiation of God for human sin.

Hearing the Good News

Introduction

That which God decreed in the Aeviternity before he created the universe, must be worked out in the time and space of the universe God created, from Genesis 1:1 to Revelation 20:15. (Revelation 21–22 are a new universe populated only by those saved during the times of this present universe).

Specifically, the way of salvation, the Ordo Salutis, must be worked out during the historical mortal lifespan of each human being. God's decree concerning the salvation of sinners is worked out in each human life sometime between the beginning of mortal human life, its conception, and the end of mortal human life, its physical death. There is no salvation from sinner to saved after physical death.

The working out of God's decrees in the time and space of the universe is the doctrine of providence. "That which God's foreordination effectuated in eternity-past, God's providence accomplishes in historical-present." Providence is a term used to describe "God's unceasing works by which he maintains and preserves the universe and all his creatures, and governs its operations and their actions, so as to accomplish his plans and eternal purpose."

In that part of the Ordo Salutis which we will examine in this chapter, God's providence effects the proclamation of the Good News of deliverance from the just and endless penalty due the unforgiven sinner. The proclamation of the Good News is part of the teaching of Scripture known as "soteriology," the theological term for the doctrine of salvation.

God has been proclaiming the Good News and thereby saving people since the first human being who was saved, Abel. That may sound strange to some who have been conditioned to think of the Good News as faith in Jesus Christ. However, the Good News is not a specific content of faith, but the fact that sinners may be forgiven and thereby delivered from the just and endless penalty due the unforgiven sinner. A little ways below, I will discuss the object and content of saving faith that effects that deliverance from the penalty due sin. (Why does the Good News begin with Cain and Abel? Adam and the Woman were created in a relationship with God, so they were never lost, and were restored to fellowship after their sin. Cain and Abel were conceived as sinners.)

The reason it is important to begin with Abel, is because modern soteriology tends to focus on salvation in the New Testament, and express Old Testament salvation in New Testament terms. The principle of salvation is not "by grace alone, by faith alone, in Christ alone." Why? Two reasons. One, the Old Testament sinner could not have saving faith in someone they did not know as the Savior. Two, YHWH is the ever-present Savior in the Old Testament. The principle of salvation that applies to both testaments is "by grace alone, by faith alone, by Christ's merit alone."

Two simple principles: no one can know what has not yet been revealed; the Old Testament had meaning for the Old Testament peoples without the revelation in the New Testament. Adam and all his Old Testament descendants did not see Jesus Christ in Genesis 3:15. Noah did not see Jesus Christ in the Ark. Abraham and all his Old Testament descendants did not see Jesus Christ in Genesis 15. David the King did not see Jesus Christ in 2 Samuel 7 or Psalm 2. Isaiah did not see Jesus Christ in chapter 53 (look at Acts 8:34). Daniel did not see Jesus Christ in the prophecy in chapter 9.

Why did they did not see Jesus Christ in the Scripture revealed to them? No one in Old Testament times could know what God had not yet revealed in his Word. When was Jesus Christ revealed? Luke 1:31-32.

But all those Old Testament peoples were responsible for what God had revealed in his Word current to their particular time in history. What was that word? YHWH is the ever present Savior, and this is how you will demonstrate your faith in me: obedience to my commandments, sacrifices for your sins. It is any different today? No, e.g., John 14:15; 1 John 2:2.

A principle is an unchanging fundamental truth that is always applicable. The principle of salvation was, is, and always will be "by grace alone, by faith alone, by Christ's limitless merit alone." Faith in the person Jesus the Christ cannot be the salvation principle, because he was not revealed in the Old Testament scriptures. The Hebrew word *māshîah*, anointed, is used of the coming anointed one only twice in the Old Testament: Psalm 2:2, which speaks of the Messiah-King; Daniel 9:25–26, which speaks of the Messiah-Redeemer. The king the Old Testament peoples understood. The redeemer they did not understand. Want proof? Matthew 16:21–22; Acts 8:34.

God's grace, the sinner's faith in God and God's historically current testimony, and Christ's limitless merit are the elements of salvation, the unchanging principle of salvation, in every age of humankind. It is not faith in Christ that saved the Old Testament sinner, nor saves the New Testament sinner, it is God's grace, plus the sinner's faith in God and God's testimony of salvation, plus the limitless merit of Christ's propitiation of God on the cross. In this age of the New Testament church God's testimony of salvation is Jesus the Christ is the Savior.

What saves the soul from the penalty due sin is the application of Christ's limitless merit, effected by God's grace through the sinner's faith in God and God's historically current testimony of the way of salvation. By "historically current testimony" I mean the scripture as possessed by Adam, or Noah, or Abraham, or Moses, or Isaiah, or Daniel, or Peter on the day of Pentecost, or Paul on the road to Damascus. The content of faith, which is to say the Good News, changed as scripture accumulated through the centuries, from Genesis through the Revelation.

The content of God's testimony of the way of salvation is God's historically current testimony in the progressive revelation of truth. The "progressive revelation of truth" is the observable fact that God gave his revelation, the Scripture, a little bit here and a little bit there.

All the Scripture Israel had for more than forty years was Genesis through Deuteronomy, written by Moses. Then the Book of Joshua was written. Then, after about 375 years, the Book of Judges was published, probably by Samuel the judge and prophet. Isaiah had more books of the Bible than King David. Malachi had access to the entire Old Testament canon, after he had written his book.

YHWH was saving people during that entire Genesis to Malachi period of time. Therefore, the content of their faith in YHWH was the accumulated scripture extant during their times. The means of salvation was always the same: God's grace, the sinner's faith in God and God's testimony, Christ's limitless merit.

But the content of saving faith changed from Cain to Christ because that content, God's testimony, was informed by the scripture available to sinners during their particular times: God's testimony as delivered in the progressive revelation of truth. YHWH was the Savior, even as he is today. The content of faith in these New Testament times, as revealed by God's testimony, the New Testament Scripture, is Jesus Christ the Redeemer.

In Scripture, YHWH (the Old Testament name for the Triune God) is the Savior, during both Old Testament and New Testament times. Therefore, the principle of salvation, Ephesians 2:8, must be explained in a way that applies to both the Old Testament and New Testament sinner.

> Saved by God's grace through the sinner's faith in God and God's testimony, as given in the historical progressive revelation of truth, without personal merit from the sinner, but by Christ's limitless merit alone.

That is the one and only way of salvation from the beginning of this universe, Genesis 1:1, to its end, 2 Peter 3:10; Revelation 20:11.

The Object And Content Of Saving Faith

The proclamation of the Good News I am speaking of relates to the object of saving faith and the content of saving faith. Another has stated it well [Ryrie, *Dispensational*, 115.].

> The basis of salvation in every age is the death [i.e., propitiation] of Christ; the requirement of salvation in every age is faith; the object of faith in every age is God; the content of faith changes in the various dispensations.

Contrary to this principle, that the object of faith in every age is God, Reformed soteriology proclaims Christ as the content of the Good News in both Old and New Testaments. Below is a comparison between Dispensational soteriology and Reformed soteriology in the proclamation of the Good News. [Quiggle, *Understanding*, 107.]

> Dispensational soteriology: the object of faith in every age is God.

> Reformed soteriology: the object of faith in every age is Christ.

> Dispensational soteriology: the content of faith changes in the various dispensations.

> Reformed soteriology: the content of faith is always Christ, either coming (OT), or arrived (NT).

I agree with the doctrinal statement of Dallas Theological Seminary, Article V. [Quoted in Ryrie, *Dispensationalism*, 116.]

> We believe ... that the principle of faith was prevalent in the lives of all the Old Testament saints. However, it was impossible

that they should have had as the conscious object of their faith the incarnate, crucified Son, the Lamb of God (John 1:29), and it is evident that they did not comprehend as we do that the sacrifices depicted the person and work of Christ.

Some will claim all the Old Testament peoples, at least those who were saved, knew of Christ from Genesis 3:15, where Christ is never mentioned. They are suggesting extra-biblical revelation: a New Testament understanding of an Old Testament scripture using New Testament revelation not yet written.

I have a lengthy discussion of that claim in my book *Dispensational Soteriology*, with an exegesis of Genesis 3:15, so will not pursue the issue here. Suffice it to say here, that finding Christ in Genesis 3:15 is wholly contrary to the grammatical-historical (literal) hermeneutic, which seeks the plain and normal meaning of the words of Scripture within their historical-cultural setting.

What, then, is the principle that should guide the proclamation of the Good News of salvation in every age in the history of redemption, Old and New Testament? "Saved by God's grace through the sinner's faith in God, through God's historically current testimony as given in the historical progressive revelation of truth." This is the "content of faith" concept in Ryrie's definition. To repeat.

> The basis of salvation in every age is the death [i.e., propitiation] of Christ; the requirement of salvation in every age is faith; the object of faith in every age is God; *the content of faith changes in the various dispensations.*

The content of faith in every age during the history of redemption is God's historical testimony, as it was given in the progressive revelation of truth.

As God the Holy Spirit gave new revelation in succeeding generations of humankind, that new revelation joined with prior revelation in the accumulation of revelation, until the revelation was completed, Genesis 1:1 through Revelation 22:21. Until the revelation the Holy Spirit was giving throughout history was accumulated to completion, no one could know what was not yet revealed, a simple and obvious principle often ignored.

To say the Old Testament peoples knew what was not yet revealed in the written Scripture is saying what the cults say, possession of extra-biblical (not in the Bible, or not yet revealed in the Bible) revelation from God. To say the Old Testament sinner knew what was not yet written in the New Testament revelation is the same as saying they were given extra-biblical revelation, because it was not yet written.

A few examples of the content of faith in Old Testament history. Enoch's content of faith was to live the manner of life prescribed by God: he believed and walked with God. The content of Noah's faith was judgment is coming, get into the ark to be saved (the Good News Noah proclaimed to all who would listen). The content of Abraham's faith was the promise of the land to him and his descendants through an heir from his own body. The content of faith under the Mosaic Law was faith in God and God's testimony that repentance of sin with confession of sin and a proper sacrifice for sin would result in forgiveness of sin. In these New Testament times, the content of faith is God's testimony that salvation is through faith in God and God's testimony concerning Jesus Christ, Acts 2:38; 3:19–20; 11:18; Romans 3:22–26; 10:9–10, 13; Galatians 3:22; 1 Corinthians 15:3–4; 1 Peter 1:21; 1 John 3:23.

But let us make sure we understand that there is one and only one way of salvation in every age of humankind. The one and only way to be saved in any age of humankind from the age of Adam forward is this.

> By God's grace, through the sinner's faith in God and God's historical testimony as to the way of salvation, apart from any merit of the sinner, but by Christ's limitless merit alone that propitiated God for sin.

Does a sinner need to know all those parts? No, that is doctrine learned by discipleship after salvation. We as believers err when we add to the simplicity of the gospel message of sin, the Savior, and salvation any theological understanding that may only be gained by discipleship after salvation.

No one could believe what the written Scripture present in their times did not tell them. As the revelation of truth was slowly given, a little here, a little there, with more being revealed as the revelation accumulated throughout the history of humankind, saving faith was a positive response to the existing accumulated revelation at any one time in the history of redemption. (To view the content of faith in every age of humankind from the beginning to the end, see my book, *Covenants and Dispensations in the Scripture.*)

Responsibility To Proclaim The Good News

We will now turn to the age we live in, the age of the New Testament church. The New Testament church age stretches from the AD 33 Pentecost proclamation of the Good News of salvation in the risen Jesus Christ, to Christ taking his New Testament church into heaven, the event known in Scripture as the "catching away," but more commonly known as the Rapture (from a Latin translation of the Greek *hárpazō*, "to snatch away"), 1 Thessalonians 4:17; 1 Corinthians 15:51–52).

If your eschatology is Reformed, you do not believe in a Rapture or a Tribulation. If your ecclesiology is Reformed, you believe the church began with Adam. But you do believe in the times of the New Testament church from Christ's ascension to his return, and the proclamation of the Good News of the risen Jesus Christ for this time in the history of redemption.

The proclamation of the Good News, in every generation of humankind, always proclaims faith in God and God's testimony as to the way of salvation. The Good News is the means of learning the way of salvation for every sinner who was saved or will be saved. God has ordained that faith is from hearing and hearing through the Word of God.

Was not the Good News in Noah's time—the Word given by God—get in the ark, YHWH is bringing judgment upon the whole earth? Yes. Could any person have entered the ark before God shut the door (Genesis 7:16)? Yes. The Good News of salvation in the ark was proclaimed to all, requiring only the positive response of faith to enter in. God did not prevent people from believing and entering the ark; that is what sin does.

God has ordained in these times of the New Testament church age that "faith [is] from hearing and hearing through a word about Christ," Romans 10:17. With that faith, "all that may call upon the Lord's name will be saved," Romans 10:13.

But, "How then may they call on whom they have not believed? Now how may they believe of whom they have not heard? Now how may they hear without proclaiming? Now how may they proclaim if they might not be sent?" Romans 10:14–15. God is pleased through the absurdity of the proclamation of the Good News that those who believe (cf. 1 Corinthians 1:21) may be saved. You have been sent; use every opportunity the Holy Spirit provides to you to proclaim the Good News.

Your duty in these times of the New Testament church is to proclaim the Good News given to the New Testament church in the completed revelation of the Word of God. The duties of the New Testament church may be summed in this manner: evangelize the lost, disciple the saved. The proclamation of the Good News, then, is the first step on the road to salvation. But let us remember God alone is the Savior. We proclaim, God saves when and whom he wills.

Content Of The Good News

What are the elements of the Good News? Sin, the Savior, and salvation, which is to say, personal sin, the risen Savior, and salvation from the penalty due sin. The genuine Good News leading to salvation requires the accusation of sin and the proclamation of the risen Savior. These things may be communicated in many ways.

> The Good News is, "I am a sinner and the risen Christ is the only Savior for me."

> The Good News is, "I am a sinner, the risen Jesus Christ is the Savior who died to pay for my sins, through faith in the risen Jesus Christ my sins are forgiven without my works."

> The Good News is, "I am a sinner; my sins have completely separated me from God, so that I am without hope in the world; Jesus Christ satisfied God for my sins; through faith in the risen Jesus Christ, God will forgive my sins and bring me into a relationship with himself in Christ."

> The Good News is, "Christ was crucified for your sins, he died and was buried, and he resurrected the third day having satisfied God for your crime of sin. At once submit yourself to God by placing your trust in the only person whom God has appointed to be Savior, the Lord Jesus Christ. Agree with God, from within your innermost being, that God sent Jesus to die for your sin, and that God raised him from the dead because the judicial debt for your sin had been paid. Through your repentance and faith God will apply Christ's payment for sin to your spiritual need."

The Good News may be expressed in many ways, as long as it has the elements of personal sin, Christ the risen Savior, and salvation for the penalty due sin.

However, there are modern proclamations that are not the Good News.

The Good News is not, "God has a wonderful plan for your life." That only applies for those who believe. For those who do not believe God has a not so wonderful plan. God has a wonderful plan for the sinner whose sin is forgiven because he/she believed on Christ the risen Savior. None else are included in that "wonderful plan."

The Good News is not, "The coming of the kingdom of Christ." There is a kingdom coming, the Davidic-Messianic Kingdom of 2 Samuel 7:13, 16; Psalm 2, but only those sinners whose sins have been forgiven because of faith in Christ as risen Savior will enter that kingdom when it arrives.

The Good News is not, "God's kingdom has broken into human affairs. The kingdom of God is not about going to heaven when we die. The kingdom of God is God's reign working in the here and now." No. There is work for the believer to do in this life, and heaven is the assured destination of every believer, 2 Corinthians 5:8. Heaven is not the kingdom.

The Good News is not, "The time is fulfilled, and the kingdom of God is near." That was the message of Messiah the King (Psalm 2) to the nation Israel, Mark 1:15, concerning the Davidic-Messianic Kingdom. The message required of the New Testament church concerns Messiah the Redeemer (Isaiah 53; Daniel 9:26a; Romans 10:9; 1 Corinthians 15:3–4).

The Good News is not, "Jesus Christ gave his life as the price for this fallen and broken world. He is the good news we need to help us restore our lives. Jesus, more than anything, wants to be a part of our lives and build a relationship with us." No, God is willing to forgive the penalty due sin, through faith in the death and resurrection of Jesus Christ, and that is the Good News. What comes after is working out (daily living in) your salvation, Philippians 2:12.

The Good News is not, "Jesus will transform your life." Actually, "transforming your life," is the work of the Holy Spirit, occurring only in those who have believed on Christ as Savior. Your life will be transformed only if you come to Jesus as a hopeless and helpless sinner, seeking pardon from God through the work of Christ the Redeemer on the cross and resurrected, so that your rebellion against God may be ended and you are given peace with God through Christ.

The Good News is not some media sound bite that fits onto a bumper sticker, is given a line or two in a sermon, a page or two in a tract, that fits into a FB meme, or is accompanied by a pleasing melody in a video. The Good News is not a solution to your worldly problems, not a message of prosperity in worldly terms, not a mantra to chant until you feel comforted by a warm spiritual presence, not feeding the poor, and not in seeking social justice for all.

What are the parts of the Good News in these New Testament times?

The Good News always has the accusation of personal sin against God and therefore sin's judicial guilt as a crime against a just and holy God.

The Good News always has the explanation of the Savior, suffering the just wrath of God against the sinner's sin, suffering and dying in the sinner's place as just punishment for the sinner's sin.

The Good News always has the announcement of the Savior's resurrection out of the dead to be the sinner's savior. He rose from the dead because he paid in full the penalty for the sinner's sin.

The Good News always has the duty to act with faith in God and God's testimony about Jesus Christ the Savior.

The Good News is the requirement to believe and be forgiven of the penalty due sin, and delivered from the dominating influence of sin, and live in a relationship with God because by his grace through your faith in the risen Savior your sins have been forgiven and you will be born-again.

All those things are parts of the Good News in these New Testament times, because Christ the Redeemer has come, suffered for the sins of others (2 Corinthians 5:21), died, and resurrected.

The Good News may be expressed in many ways, as long as it has the facts of sin, the risen Savior, and salvation. Those facts are personal sin, the eternal punishment due to the sinner for sin, that Jesus suffered the penalty for the sinner's sin by dying in the place of the sinner before a just and holy God, and that personal faith in the risen Jesus Christ will save the sinner from the penalty due their sin, which is separation from God in this mortal life and in the endless life to come after physical death.

Don't pity the unsaved person who has died. That person has received what he or she wanted: a life without God. Pity the living unsaved by telling them about sin, the risen Savior, and salvation. Don't warn the unsaved about an eternity without Christ, it is no warning because that is what they want. Tell them about their sin and its consequences, the Savior and what he did for them, and salvation that will change their life in the here and now and the hereafter. Then, having done your best, pray for them, commit them to God, who alone is the Savior of sinners.

Hearing the Good News

The Good News is not found in nature. There is a universal proclamation of the existence of God through his creation of the universe, Psalm 19:1–4; Romans 1:19–20. This natural proclamation is not salvific but the Holy Spirit may use it as an introduction to the Good News.

How does a sinner hear the Good News? The Scripture says there are two ways.

1. Reading the Good News in the Word of God. This means of receiving the Good News is able to be salvific.

2. Hearing the Good News. This means of receiving the Good News is able to be salvific.

The universal proclamation of the existence of God through his creation of the universe is not salvific, but does leave the sinner without excuse to seek God and God's salvation. With those who deny the existence of God, here is a place to begin. If the Holy Spirit gives understanding, the way is opened for the proclamation of the Good News.

Reading the Good News in the Word of God. This means of receiving the Good News is able to be salvific. The Word of God is itself, by itself, salvific. If, as is the case, God is the Savior, then God is able to effect salvation by a person reading the written Word of God. The New Testament Scripture does not focus on this means of proclamation, because in New Testament times the New Testament scriptures were being written, they were not yet copied and distributed, and therefore the Good News was delivered orally. As the Holy Spirit guided individual believers to copy the Word of God and distribute those copies, then reading the Good News in the Word of God became a means to effect salvation. The Holy Spirit has given us an instance of both reading the Good News and oral proclamation of the good news, Acts 8:29–35

Hearing the Good News. This means of receiving the Good News is able to be salvific. This is the norm for proclaiming the Good News. Although 1 Corinthians 1:18, says, "to those who are perishing the word of the cross is absurd," God's choice was "through the absurdity of the preaching to save those believing," 1 Corinthians 1:21. Why? That it will be obvious God alone is the Savior. Human beings are made perverse by sin, and that same perversity makes some believers believe their proclamation of the Good News is what saves the sinner. May it never be! God is the Savior, we are the proclaimers of the message of reconciliation, 2 Corinthians 5:18–20.

A story is told of the 19th century evangelist D. L. Moody. One morning, Moody and a friend were walking along in the city after a night of one of Moody's evangelistic campaigns. The friend saw a drunken man in the gutter and said to Moody, "There is one of your converts from last night." Moody replied, "He must be one of mine, because if he was one the Lord's coverts he would not be there." Moody understood that God only is the Savior.

Therefore, "proclaim the word, be prepared for any opportunity convenient or inconvenient" (2 Timothy 4:2). How shall they hear the good news if the one's sent do not go. The Holy Spirit does not expect every believer to evangelize non-stop 24/7. There are some the Spirit gifts with the spiritual gift of evangelism, that is their calling.

For the rest of us, the Holy Spirit will from time to time provide an opportunity to give the Good news, and our duty is to be aware of those opportunities, and use them, 1 Peter 2:15; 2 Timothy 4:2. This book, in this chapter, was one of my opportunities. As a writer my fingers are my breath, and with that breath I will praise the Lord.

Chapter Summary

This chapter, "Hearing the Good News," begins with a lengthy introduction of how God's decrees work out in historical time. The Good News begins in the Old Testament with Abel, the first person the Scripture says was saved from the penalty due sin. God has been saving people since Abel, but Jesus Christ was not the specific content of the Good News of salvation in Old Testament times. In Old Testament times the ever present YHWH is the Savior in which faith resides.

The introduction explains how and why the specific content of the Good News of salvation changes throughout the history of redemption. The reason is God's progressive revelation of truth. God did not say everything he had to say at the same time, but a little here and a little there throughout the history of humankind. Therefore, the revelation of God accumulated over time, and humankind was responsible for the revelation that had been given up to their time. Two common sense principles apply to the Old Testament Good News: no one can know what has not yet been revealed; the Old Testament had meaning for the Old Testament peoples without the revelation in the New Testament.

Therefore, the Old Testament peoples were responsible for what God had revealed in his Word current to their particular time in history. That Old Testament revelation was YHWH is the ever present Savior; you will demonstrate your faith in me through obedience to my commandments, and by sacrifices for your sins. In that respect the New Testament proclamation is the same, John 14:15; 1 John 2:2.

The specific content of the Good News, then, has changed throughout the history of humankind, from Adam to Jesus Christ, according to what God has revealed as his revelation accumulated, a little here, a little there. But salvation is always the same from Adam to Jesus Christ: God's grace, the sinner's faith in God and God's historically current testimony, and Christ's limitless merit are the elements of salvation. Only the details in the proclamation change to reflect the accumulation of God's testimony as his revelation of truth progressed.

Those details are explained in this way, using a comparison of two theologies, Dispensational theology and Reformed theology.

> Dispensational soteriology: the object of faith in every age is God.
>
> Reformed soteriology: the object of faith in every age is Christ.
>
> Dispensational soteriology: the content of faith changes in the various dispensations.
>
> Reformed soteriology: the content of faith is always Christ, either coming (OT), or arrived (NT).

Looking back to the principles, no one can know what has not yet been revealed. In Old Testament times, a coming redeemer from the penalty due sin had not yet been clearly revealed, YHWH is the

Redeemer in the Old Testament Good News. (This is not the place for an extended discussion, but Matthew 16:21–23; Acts 8:31–35 reveal the coming Christ was not understood as Redeemer of individuals from the penalty due sin. That is why the New Testament revelation was given. He was understood as the King, 2 Samuel 7:13, 16; Psalm 2, who would rescue Israel from gentile oppression.)

As God the Holy Spirit gave new revelation in succeeding generations of humankind, that new revelation joined with prior revelation in the accumulation of revelation, until the revelation was completed, Genesis 1:1 through Revelation 22:21. Until the revelation the Holy Spirit was giving throughout history was accumulated to completion, no one could know what was not yet revealed, a simple and obvious principle.

The believer has a responsibility to proclaim the Good News. Romans 10:14–15 states the believer's responsibility: we are sent to proclaim. This obligation fits into the duties of the New Testament church: evangelize the lost, disciple the saved.

The next section of the chapter focuses on the content of the Good News in this New Testament age—what the sinner is supposed to hear from the believer. The essential elements of the Good News are personal sin, the risen Savior, and salvation from the penalty due sin. The genuine Good News leading to salvation requires the accusation of sin and the proclamation of the risen Savior.

The three essential elements of the Good News may be communicated in many ways. A detailed discussion is given contrasting what is and it not the proclamation of the Good News.

The final section of the chapter focuses on how one may hear the Good News. In this time of the completed Old Testament and New Testament revelation, the Good News may be received by reading the Word of God, or by hearing God's Word in the proclamation of the message of salvation.

Responding to the Good News

Sometimes a sinner hears the Good News for the first time and then and there believes and is saved. Other sinners must hear the Good News over and over at various times in their life before they believe and become saved. Some hear and never believe, whether hearing one time or multiple times. I didn't hear the Good News—I knew nothing about Christianity—until about two months before my twenty-second birthday, and then by God's grace I heard the Good News twice on Sunday and once on Wednesday, in a little church in a little village, and believed on May 19, 1974, four days before my twenty-second birthday. The Holy Spirit works with us as the individuals we are.

How does a sinner respond to the Good News of salvation? He or she rejects the good news. Rejecting the Good News is automatic and natural in the sinner, the reflex action of a sinful human nature under the influence of the sin attribute in human nature. First Corinthians 2:14, "But a natural person [the unsaved person] does not accept the things of the Spirit of God, for they are absurd to him, and he is not able to know them, because they are discerned spiritually."

The natural person, the unsaved person, lacks the spiritual perception to understand spiritual things. When the Scripture speaks of the unsaved person as "spiritually dead," what the human writer and the Holy Spirit mean is the soul's, i.e., the person's, faculty of spiritual perception is so grossly dulled by the sin attribute that he or she is unable to comprehend spiritual things, and reacts to spiritual things by rejecting them.

The evil attribute sin influences every other attribute in human nature with the inclination to sin, and in that sense sin can be said to dominate the will. The sinner freely chooses sinning because his will is of itself always inclined to choose sinning, and as being rebellious and disobedient toward God never desires to change its inclination to choose sinning to rebel against God, disobey his commandments, and seek a path in life apart from God.

Thus, the unsaved sinner, lacking a working faculty of spiritual perception to understand spiritual things, and possessing the disposition, inclination, and tendency to reject spiritual things, naturally acts in rebellion against God and his salvation. Spiritually dead does not mean inactive, as though a corpse, but actively responding in rebellion to reject God and God's salvation.

How, then, does a sinner respond in positive manner (saving faith) to the Good News of salvation? God must give prevenient grace. Prevenient Grace is the theological and biblical concept that God gives grace to enable the sinner's faith. Ephesians 2:8 describes prevenient grace as the gift of God.

> For by grace you are having been saved, through faith, and that not of yourselves. Of God the gift, not from works, so that no one should boast.

(The unfamiliar "having been saved," translates the combination of the Greek present and perfect tenses, indicating the present continuing result of a past completed action. Salvation having once occurred continues.)

What is grace? Grace is God choosing to bless because he wants to, although blessing is undeserved. The Scripture teaches God's grace does many different things: salvation, thanksgiving, knowledge, wisdom, ministry, hope, strength, justification, and sanctification: Titus 2:11; 2 Corinthians 4:15; 1 Corinthians 1:3; 2 Corinthians 1:12; Ephesians 4:7; 2 Thessalonians 2:16; 2 Corinthians 12:9; Romans 5:17; Ephesians 1:6.

Excursus: Prevenient Grace for Salvation

God's prevenient grace is required to overcome the dominion of sin in human nature. Below (following this Excursus) I will explain the way prevenient grace works to effect salvation. However, different theologies have differing views as to how God applies his prevenient grace. This excurses will focus on the two major views, Arminian and Calvinistic soteriology.

Calvinistic soteriology views prevenient grace as given by God to specific individuals through his foreordaining choice to give the gift of grace-faith-salvation to certain persons, Ephesians 1:4; 2:8; 2 Thessalonians 2:13. God's gift of grace-faith-salvation always results in the salvation of the individual receiving God's gift. God's gift of grace-faith-salvation is given only to those whom he chose to give his gift (election) before the creation of the universe, Ephesians 1:4.

Modern Arminian (Wesleyan) soteriology views prevenient grace as given by God indiscriminately to every sinner, with the result every sinner is freed from the dominion of sin. Therefore, every sinner is made able to freely decide for him or herself whether or not to believe the Good News and be saved. In Arminian soteriology God gives this prevenient grace because of Christ's work on the cross, so that all people are capable of hearing and responding to the gospel as they may choose, with faith or no faith.

The Arminian view of prevenient grace is universal in its scope (every human being) and effect (completely freed from the effects of sin), but ineffectual to save, because in Arminian soteriology salvation depends wholly on the sinner's choice, not God's foreordaining choices.

In regard to the Calvinistic view, neither election nor prevenient grace prevents salvation. That is what sin does. Thus, in Calvinistic soteriology, prevenient grace is particular in its scope (Ephesians 1:4) and effect (spiritual perception is enlivened in the individual receiving grace), and always effectual to save the individual receiving prevenient grace In Calvinistic soteriology the purpose of election and the prevenient grace given to individuals is to guarantee salvation. Nothing more, nothing less.

Returning to the main discussion.

How Does God Save A Sinner?

My views on soteriology conform to the sublapsarian order of God's pre-creation decrees (see chapter, "Foreordination"). I have a Calvinistic view of how God gives his prevenient grace.

God gives all human beings what is known as "common grace," which is the call of the gospel of salvation to establish the moral responsibility of all men to believe and be saved. Common grace is not prevenient grace. Common grace does not save, only prevenient grace is effective to save. Prevenient grace is given to particular individuals according to God's foreordaining choices. Only the prevenient grace of the gift of God works efficaciously to save sinners.

> Efficacious means God's prevenient grace working effectively in the sinner's human nature to enliven the soul's faculty of spiritual perception, thereby freeing the will from the spiritual ignorance caused by the dominion of sin.

> The sinner having received God's gift, and now having the spiritual perception to understand spiritual things, believes the gospel message of his or her judicial guilt for the crime of sin, and understands from the Good News his or her spiritual need to be rescued from the penalty for sin.

Therefore, it is by God's gift of prevenient, efficacious grace that the unable and unwilling sinner is made able and willing to choose to act in agreement with the command to believe and be saved.

Choosing to act in agreement with the command to believe and be saved is saving faith. What is faith?

Faith is belief, trust, confidence. All human beings have faith as an attribute of their human nature. However, natural faith is not the same as the living, saving, empowering faith the Scripture requires of sinner and believer. Biblical living, saving, empowering faith is belief, trust, confidence plus a commitment to God as the Savior from the penalty due sin, through the infallible conviction given by the Holy Spirit.

The kind of faith that saves and empowers the Christian's life is inwardly believing the testimony of God through the infallible conviction given by the Holy Spirit, and faith is outwardly acting through the power given by the Holy Spirit to conform one's thoughts and actions to that conviction. A person is not "enabled" to believe by the Spirit's convicting power, but rather as being convicted of the truth, and on the basis of that conviction, each person appropriates and applies the truth to his or her specific circumstance, whether the spiritual issue is salvation or discipleship. That phrase, "appropriates and applies the truth," is what the Bible names living, saving, empowering faith.

God's gift of prevenient grace is efficacious because it is the work of the Holy Spirit (2 Thessalonians 2:13; 1 Peter 1:2) applying God's gift of grace-faith-salvation to effect salvation. Efficacious grace enlivens the sinner's faculty of spiritual perception, infallibly leading to the exercise of saving faith.

In More Detail

Some repetition of what was said above is unavoidable.

Prevenient grace is God's gift of grace-faith-salvation. The term "grace-faith-salvation" is derived from Ephesians 2:8 indicating the complete salvation principle: saved by grace through faith. The Greek grammatical construction of the sentence reveals God's gift is not only grace, or not only faith, or not only salvation, but grace and faith and salvation are God's gift. The gift of God (prevenient grace) in the salvation of sinners is grace-faith-salvation.

How then does God's gift of grace-faith-salvation work in the sinner? In 1 Corinthians 2:14, Paul and the Holy Spirit tell us the unsaved person does not accept the things of the Spirit of God, because such things are absurd to the sinner. Spiritual discernment and spiritual understanding depend on the human soul's faculty of spiritual perception.

Human beings are a union of material body and immaterial soul. The immaterial soul contains the human essence, the immaterial essence life, and the human nature with all its attributes. The human nature as designed by God possesses a faculty to perceive spiritual things, through which human beings perceive, understand, and communicate with God (e.g., prayer, worship). In the unsaved person the sin attribute (added to human nature by Adam's sin) has rendered spiritual perception so grossly dulled that the unsaved person does not have the spiritual discernment to receive or understand the things of the Spirit of God, 1 Corinthians 2:14. I say "grossly dulled" because the sinner can respond to spiritual issues, but that response is always rebellion and rejection against God and God's salvation.

What must happen to save the sinner is the person's faculty of spiritual perception must be enlivened so the sinner may receive and understand spiritual things. The gift of God is the means whereby the faculty of spiritual perception becomes perceptive: able to receive, understand, and appropriately apply the biblical knowledge relevant to his spiritual state of unsaved. (That knowledge is communicated by the Good News: personal sin, the risen Savior, and salvation.)

Put another way, the sinner's will is freed from the dominion of sin that motivates human beings to rebel against God, disobey his commandments, and seek a path in life apart from God.

What is the dominion of sin? Sin is an attribute of fallen human nature, a principle or attribute of evil that motivates human beings to rebel against God, disobey his commandments, and seek a path in life apart from God. Sin has authority (dominion, rule) over the sinner, not as some invincible overlord, but as an innate part of human nature constructively working with all the other attributes of human nature to persuasively incline the will to choose an act of sinning. The evil attribute sin influences every other attribute with the inclination to sin, and in that sense sin can be said to dominate the will. The sinner freely chooses sinning because his will is of itself always inclined to choose sinning, and as being rebellious and disobedient toward God never desires to change its inclination to choose sinning to rebel against God, disobey his commandments, and seek a path in life apart from God.

God's prevenient grace in his gift of grace-faith-salvation enlivens spiritual perception and sets the sinner's will free from sin's dominion. (See chapter "Why All Are Sinners" for a discussion of free will.)

God's Gift And Free Will

If, as is the case, the unsaved sinner is irrevocably opposed to God and God's salvation, does God's grace overcome or force the sinner to believe? No.

In a few words, God's efficacious grace changes the unable and unwilling sinner to able and willing. God's efficacious grace (I described it above) works effectively in the sinner's human nature to free the will from the dominion of sin, and inform the sinner of his or her spiritual guilt and spiritual need, so that the unwilling sinner is made willing to choose to act in agreement with the command to believe and be saved.

To believe and be saved is not a mechanical exercise, but the consequence of God's supra-natural grace. In terms of free will, the sinner's spiritual boundaries are changed by God's gift of grace-faith-salvation from unable and unwilling to able and willing. The sinner receiving God's gift of grace does not struggle against God's grace, his sinful nature is so changed by God's grace that he or she willingly cooperates. As I said, not a mechanical exercise, but the consequence of God's supra-natural grace.

Thus the exercise of saving faith is a freely made decision, but also an inevitable decision, because God's grace cannot fail to accomplish its objective, which is the salvation of the sinner receiving God's gift of grace-faith-salvation. The enlivened spiritual perception understands and responds in faith.

What we are speaking of is otherwise known as conviction, which is the work of the Holy Spirit in the individual to infallibly reveal right and wrong according to the testimony of Scripture.

Conviction leads to faith. What is faith? I will discuss faith in the next chapter, but here a brief definition. Faith is inwardly believing the testimony of God through the infallible conviction given by the Holy Spirit, and faith is outwardly acting through the power given by the Holy Spirit to conform one's thoughts and actions to that conviction. Genuine biblical saving faith is supra-natural, the gift of God.

Is Grace Efficacious Or Irresistible

Some Calvinists view God's gift of grace-faith-salvation as irresistible: too powerful or convincing to be resisted. However, an irresistible grace contradicts the moral authority (free will) God designed into his sentient creatures. God has respect for what he created. His grace in salvation is efficacious not irresistible.

The term "irresistible grace" is more accurately "efficacious grace." The grace God gives for salvation is efficacious in that it always accomplishes the purposes for which God bestowed that grace, through that synergy of God's sovereignty and human choice that characterizes all of God's interactions with all human beings.

That word "synergy" may confuse some readers. Salvation is monergistic in that God alone is the origin and source of salvation. God alone initiates salvation through his gift of grace-faith-salvation, Ephesians 2:8. Salvation is synergistic in that it is both the gift of God, Ephesians 2:8, and the duty of the sinner to believe, Acts 16:31; Romans 10:9–13.

God the Holy Spirit applies the gift of grace-faith-salvation (Ephesians 2:8) to the elect sinner (Ephesians 1:4), which works efficaciously to enliven the soul's faculty of spiritual perception (2 Thessalonians 2:13; 1 Peter 1:2), such that the sinner to whom the Spirit has given the gift is able to perceive and understand and apply the truth of sin, the Savior, and salvation to his/her personal spiritual condition, and thereby exercise saving faith.

More simply, saving faith is what the elect sinner is elected to, so that he/she freely and infallibly chooses to believe, because freed from the deception of sin by God's gift. I agree with Spurgeon, "I do not find it difficult to believe faith to be at the same time the duty of man and the gift of God" (Metropolitan Tabernacle, Vol. 17, Sermon No. 979).

The grace of God in salvation is efficacious because the inclination of the will, once freed from the dominion of sin, is to freely believe and be saved, which is the happy synergy of God's sovereignty working through man's responsibility.

Thus, efficacious grace (the work of the Holy Spirit in applying God's gift to effect salvation) is not irresistible in the sense that it is resisted and all such resistance is overcome, but it is efficacious in that it is never resisted. Its nature forbids it. It is only "irresistible" in the sense that it is always effectual.

Chapter Summary

In this chapter I answer the question, how can the spiritually dead believe when they hear the Good News, because to the sinner the Good News is absurd, 1 Corinthians 2:14. The answer is salvation is a supra-natural act of God from beginning to end. I discuss the details. I explain what spiritually dead means and how being spiritually dead affects the hearers response to the Good News. I explain God's prevenient grace (Ephesians 2:8), and briefly explore the difference between Calvinistic and Arminian views of prevenient grace: to whom it is given and what it does according to each of those theologies, and according to Scripture.

I also define and explain efficacious grace, spiritual perception, and the exercise of faith in perspective with the dominion of sin. God's gift of grace-faith-salvation enlivens the soul's faculty of spiritual perception, so that the sinner is freed from sin's dominion, understands the essentials of the Good News, and that efficacious grace inevitably leads to the personal exercise of saving faith.

The interaction between God's gift and free will is briefly explored. To believe and be saved is not a mechanical exercise, but the consequence of God's supra-natural grace. The sinner's spiritual boundaries are changed by God's gift of grace-faith-salvation. God's efficacious grace changes the unable and unwilling sinner to able and willing.

The chapter ends with a discussion of God's grace as efficacious or irresistible. God's grace is not irresistible in the sense that it is resisted and all such resistance is overcome, but it is efficacious in that it is never resisted.

Saving faith, Forgiveness, Eternal life, Regeneration

Salvation is the remission of sin's penalty by the application of the merit of Christ's propitiation of God on the cross to the sinner's spiritual need. The limitless merit of the propitiation is applied to the sinner's spiritual need by God's grace through the means of the sinner's personal faith in God and God's testimony as to the way of salvation.

In salvation, God rescues a sinner out of the state of spiritual death and delivers him/her into a permanent state of spiritual life. In finer detail, God forgives the sin that caused the spiritual separation, and gives the saved person spiritual life, and that eternal life which regenerates human nature, and declares the person justified from all crimes against God, and declares the person sanctified, which is to be separated from sin and dedicated to God.

What is spiritual life? It is participation in God's spiritual life. Spiritual life has two components. One, the soul's faculty of spiritual perception is relieved from the gross dullness caused by sin and is enlivened for conscious communion with God. Two, spiritual life is participation in the life of God in all the fullness possible for a finite being: God communicates the communicable attributes of his eternal life to the saved person.

In this New Testament age, salvation occurs when a sinner repents of his or her sins and believes on Christ as their Savior, according to God's testimony, Acts 2:38; 3:19–20; 11:18; Romans 3:22–26; 10:9–10, 13; Galatians 3:22; 1 Peter 1:21; 1 John 3:23, and other relevant scriptures.

Salvation is obtained by God's grace, through the sinner's faith not works, and the limitless merit of Christ's propitiation of God. Salvation is maintained by God's grace and the limitless merit of Christ's propitiation.

Salvation is an instantaneous event as the result of the exercise of saving faith. However, there is a process leading to that moment of the exercise of saving faith. Although the process is applied by the Holy Spirit to each sinner in individual ways consistent with each sinner's internal and external circumstances, it may be summarized as knowledge of the applicable scriptures, conviction, repentance, and the exercise of faith. Repentance is not a separate action, but is in integral part of faith. Repentance is that decision of faith to turn to God from sin.

Because the Holy Spirit works with each sinner as the individual he or she is, that process leading to the exercise of saving faith has no specific or average duration.

Salvation is the inevitable consequence of the exercise of saving faith, resulting in forgiveness, eternal life, and regeneration. Salvation is in fact comprised of those four elements: faith, forgiveness, eternal life, and regeneration. This chapter will examine each of those elements of salvation.

SAVING FAITH

Again, in looking at the details, some repetition is unavoidable. Saving faith receives forgiveness and the eternal life that regenerates human nature. What is saving faith? In the previous chapter I gave a brief definition of faith.

> Faith is inwardly believing the testimony of God through the infallible conviction given by the Holy Spirit, and faith is outwardly acting through the power given by the Holy Spirit to conform one's thoughts and actions to that conviction.

Here is a more complete definition.

> The conformity of thought and action to the infallible conviction of the Holy Spirit through volitional simple trust or confidence in the testimony of God that the risen Jesus Christ is the only Person who is able to save the sinner from the penalty due sin.

> A sinner is not enabled to believe, he or she is convicted through the work of God the Holy Spirit of the truth of personal sin, the judicial guilt and punishment of sin, the need for salvation by faith not works, and the all-sufficiency of the propitiation made by Jesus Christ the Savior required to save his or her soul. On the basis of that conviction the sinner personally appropriates these truths to satisfy his or her spiritual need for salvation. That personal appropriation of truth to satisfy the spiritual need for salvation is the exercise of saving faith.

The sinner who exercises saving faith has been convicted: the infallible spiritual understanding given by the Holy Spirit that a belief or action is right or wrong according to the Scripture, resulting in a spiritual change. The Holy Spirit gives conviction consistent with the individuality of each sinner. For some it may be a process of persuasion, long or short, leading to the conclusion, "I am a sinner in need of the

Savior." For others it may be a "light bulb" moment. By whatever means the Holy Spirit uses, the moment of conviction comes to each sinner who is being saved.

Having been convicted of sin, the Savior, and salvation by God's efficacious grace given in God's gift of grace-faith-salvation, the sinner receiving God's gift is convicted of his or her need for salvation, and inevitably chooses to believe and be saved.

The most important thing to understand about saving faith is it is supra-natural in origin.

Without question an unsaved person has faith as an attribute of their human nature, in the sense of belief, trust, and confidence. That is not saving faith

Saving faith is the result of a supra-natural conviction from the Holy Spirit. The sinner decides to exercise saving faith in response to the work of the Holy Spirit, in obedience to the conviction received from the Holy Spirit: I am a sinner, the risen Jesus Christ is the only Savior.

However, a decision alone does not save. The exercise of saving faith must be the end result of God's gift of grace-faith-salvation, of conviction by the Holy Spirit, of personally appropriating the truth to satisfy the spiritual need for salvation. All those things have their origin and source in God initiating his processes of salvation.

Do not misunderstand. Salvation is an instantaneous event, the inevitable consequence of the exercise of saving faith. That choice to exercise saving faith is the inevitable consequence of the Holy Spirit working through his gift of grace-faith-salvation. However, there is a process leading to the exercise of saving faith that begins with God the Holy Spirit applying God's gift of grace-faith-salvation.

The most important thing to understand about salvation is the message of reconciliation (the Good News), 2 Corinthians 5:18, may be delivered to the sinner in many ways, but God alone gives conviction and God alone is the Savior. Many hear the Good News. God will have mercy on whom he will have mercy. Either God is sovereign in all things, or he is sovereign in none. Therefore, God alone, not man, is the Savior.

An In Depth Look At Saving Faith

Saving faith is initiated by prevenient grace, which is given by God in his gift of grace-faith-salvation, Ephesians 2:8–9. The meaning of Ephesians 2:8–9 is clear: the source of salvation is God not the sinner.

115

The grammar of 2:8 indicates God's gift is not only grace, not only faith, not only salvation but is grace and faith and salvation.

The grammatical question to be answered in Ephesians 2:8 is, what does the Greek pronoun, *toúto*, "that," refer to in the phrase, "and that (*toúto*) not of yourselves"? In biblical Greek, grammatical associations are indicated by the gender of a word. This book is written in American English. In English grammatical associations are indicated by word order. Did the cat eat the rat, or did the rat eat the cat. Word order makes clear the meaning of each sentence: "cat eat rat" or rat eat cat."

In biblical Greek (the Koine dialect of the ancient Greek language), the grammatical structure of the words would associate "eat" with cat or rat. If the cat ate the rat, then the gender of the words would tell the reader who did the eating and who was eaten (there are also other grammatical associations).

Greek had three genders, neuter, masculine, feminine, used for grammatical purposes. Grammatical gender is not sexual gender. For example, the Greek word for "moon" is always feminine. The Greek word for "spirit" is often neuter, even when referring to the Holy Spirit. Context, not grammar, decides when sexual gender is in view.

In Ephesians 2:8, the grammar is more complicated than the usual Greek sentence. The word *toúto*, "that," is a neuter demonstrative pronoun. "You are saved" is a masculine participle, (formed from the masculine *esté*, "you are," and *sesosménoi*, the perfect passive participle of *sózō*, "saved"). The word "grace" is feminine as is the word "faith." The neuter pronoun *toúto* could refer to the feminine noun "grace," the feminine noun "faith," or the masculine participle "you are saved." However, neither the feminine or the masculine matches the neuter pronoun in gender.

The best view [Hoehner, *Ephesians*, 343; Robertson, *Word Pictures*, 4:525] is that the neuter *toúto* refers to the complete salvation principle: saved by grace through faith. The gift of God is grace-faith-salvation: "and that [gift of grace-faith-salvation] is not of yourselves." God is the Savior from beginning to end.

Some saved persons struggle with faith being part of God's gift of grace-faith-salvation. The function of the sin attribute is to rebel against God, to refuse to submit to God, and to rob God of his glory by ascribing to ourselves the works of God. Some want themselves, not God, to be the source of their faith. But, "Of God is the gift."

The interpretive problem is failure to distinguish between things that differ. There is a difference between the origin of faith and the exercise of faith. God is the origin of faith. The one receiving the gift of grace-faith-salvation is to exercise the faith he/she has been given through the gift of God.

How is that faith given? God's gift enlivens the sinner's faculty of spiritual perception, leading to understanding and conviction of the spiritual issues necessary to salvation. Not a natural understanding, i.e., not by unaided reasoning alone. In the processes leading to the exercise of saving faith, the sinner's natural faculty of reasoning (designed into human nature by God when he created Adam) is engaged to reason with and about the scriptures (cf. Isaiah 1:18), and is able to come to the right conclusions, as a consequence of God's gift enlivening the sinner's faculty of spiritual perception. Without God's gift of efficacious grace the sinner is unable to understand spiritual things by his natural power of reasoning, 1 Corinthians 2:14.

The unsaved sinner who has been given God's gift will exercise faith, because the conviction of the Holy Spirit and the enlivening of the soul's faculty of spiritual perception by God's gift is efficacious to give the sinner spiritual understanding of sin, the Savior, and salvation, thereby changing the sinner from unwilling and unable to willing and able to exercise the faith he/she has been given, and thereby be saved.

Saving faith, therefore, is both rational and supra-natural: there is a supra-natural God-ward perspective and there is a rational man-ward perspective. First, in the supra-natural God-ward perspective, faith is God-given conviction of truth in the inner experience of the soul. God-given conviction is the absolute, undeniable, unquestioned, certain, and sure receipt of truth as originating in and communicated from God.

No person—saved or unsaved—can obtain this certainty through his or her unaided rational faculties. Only God, by his Holy Spirit, can give absolute certainty, unwavering conviction. Conviction is part of the faith that is God's gift in salvation. In the God-ward perspective, God-given conviction of truth infallibly results in the sinner's positive response of faith toward God and God's testimony given in Scripture.

(As in all things spiritual, Satan has his counterfeit, a fanatical zeal. Satan's counterfeit is always in some manner destructive; God's conviction is a life-changing, positive, constructive force for the good of the soul.)

Second, from the rational man-ward perspective, the unsaved sinner as prompted, informed, and given the ability to understand by God's gift, considers the facts of salvation as to their authenticity, credibility, and accuracy. Did these facts originate in God? Can they be believed? Is the information true as opposed to false?

The sinner may come to a rational conclusion that the facts are authentic, credible, and accurate. The rational conclusion may be persuasive, perhaps even life-changing, but it cannot effect change in the soul's state of sin. A rational conclusion cannot change the sinful state of the soul because such a conclusion is part of the sinner's rational faculties, which are corrupted and dominated by sin. A rational conclusion may be accepted, modified, or rejected, according to the disposition of a person's nature. There may be reformation, but not the transformation from sinner to saved accomplished only by God's efficacious grace, saving faith, and the limitless merit of Christ's propitiation.

Only a supra-natural intervention—God's gift of conviction, given by his grace, and thus infallibly leading to the exercise of faith—can turn a rational conclusion into saving faith and change the state of the soul from sinner to saved. A rational assessment and conclusion are not faith, they are only a part of faith. Without a supra-natural God-given conviction, rationally accepted facts cannot effect a spiritual change. From the sinner's perspective, faith is the necessary positive response to God's convicting testimony given in the Scripture.

God's part in saving faith is to give a sinner personal understanding and infallible conviction that the facts concerning his/her spiritual state are true. Those facts are personal sin, the eternal punishment due to the sinner for sin, that Jesus suffered the penalty for the sinner's sin, resurrected, and faith in Jesus will save him/her from the penalty due their sin.

The sinner's part is to exercise his rational faculties in the certainty of spiritual truth and respond with saving faith to the conviction given by the Holy Spirit. The sinner who receives God's gift will respond to the inner experience of God-given conviction of truth (God's gift of faith) with an outward response (the exercise of faith) that conforms his/her thoughts and actions to the truth conveyed in that inner conviction of truth.

Thereby, the conviction-faith that I am a sinner and Jesus is the only Savior, has its origin and source in God alone. The sinner's response to God given conviction-faith is the personal exercise of faith, that "Jesus is the only Savior for me!"

Saving faith always consists of God's gift and the sinner's response. The sinner is not "enabled" to believe, he/she is convicted of the truth, and on the basis of that conviction personally appropriates the truth to his or her specific circumstances, which is the exercise of saving faith. The unsaved sinner responds to God's gift of grace-faith-salvation by means of faith: he/she believes-accepts-receives-responds to Jesus as "My Savior." This is God's sovereignty, working through the sinner's responsibility, to infallibly accomplish God's purposes and plans in his election of sinners in Christ to salvation, in love by grace through faith.

The Result Of Salvation

Salvation is an instantaneous act with several results. The initial result of saving faith is the forgiveness of sin. The now-saved sinner is free from the judicial guilt and penalty of sin because Christ has satisfied God's law on behalf of the sinner, Romans 6:23. The now-saved sinner has been reconciled to God, 2 Corinthians 2:18–19. This brings peace with God, Romans 5:1, for with sin forgiven (Ephesians 1:7), and the penalty satisfied (1 John 2:2), there is no more enmity between God and the believer. With his faculty of spiritual perception enlivened the now saved sinner is capable of intimate communion with God and understanding God's word.

The Holy Spirit accomplishes the sanctification of the believer, which is to set the believer apart from the defilement caused by sin and dedicate him to God, Ephesians 1:4; 1 Corinthians 1:30; 1 Peter 1:2. God imparts to the believer eternal life, John 17:2–3; Romans 6:23b; 1 John 2:25, which is God communicating the communicable aspects of his eternal life. God's eternal life is the "seed" (1 John 3:9) that regenerates the human nature (born-again) of the believer.

In the act of sanctification, sin loses its dominating power, Romans 6:14-23, and a new principle of life, holiness, is added to the believer, Ephesians 4:24, becoming the dominating principle in his human nature, 1 Thessalonians 4:7; 1 Corinthians 17b; Colossians 3:12; 1 Peter 1:15.

In addition to these, the righteousness of Christ is imputed to the believer, and he is justified, meaning all the (judicial) guilt of sin is removed. In what might be called both the initiating and culminating event (for the New Testament believer), the Holy Spirit takes up permanent residence in the believer's soul, John 14:17; Acts 10:44-48; 1 Corinthians 6:19.

The believer now stands before God in Christ as forgiven, sanctified, justified, regenerated, filled with eternal life, indwelt by the Holy Spirit, and in intimate communion with God in Christ. He/she is freed from the penalty, power, and pleasure of sin, with absolute assurance of the future transformation and glorification of his human nature and body, so that he/she will be freed eternally from the presence of sin. The believer is empowered to resist sin's temptations, live a holy life, understand the Scripture, worship, obey, and serve God, and fellowship with God, and know God hears and answers his prayers, all the while persevering in the faith by means of faith to lead a holy life, looking toward resurrection and an eternal life in God's presence.

THE FORGIVENESS OF SAVING FAITH

The exercise of saving faith results in forgiveness. It is often said the sinner is saved from hell. No, the sinner is saved from the endless punishment due sin in hell (the lake of fire), having been delivered [*sózó*, Zodhiates, s. v. 4982, to save, deliver, preserve from danger] from God's wrath against sin.

It is true that salvation from God's just wrath against sin means all the believer's sins (past present, future) have been forgiven so that there is no longer the condemnation (Romans 8:1) of endless punishment after physical death, first in Hades, then in the lake of fire (the true hell) which is the consequence of dying with unforgiven sin. The forgiveness that is part of salvation has several consequences.

In discussing forgiveness, I am going to make use of a simple alliterative mnemonic: penalty, power, pleasure, presence. Salvation is deliverance from: the Penalty due sin; the dominating Power of sin; the Pleasure of sin; the Presence of sin.

Delivered From The Penalty Due Sin

To be delivered from God's just wrath against the crime of sin is salvation from the penalty due sin. One is delivered from the penalty due sin by forgiveness of the crime of sin.

> Luke 23:46-47, Thus it has been written: the Christ was to suffer, and rise out from the dead the third day, and to be proclaimed in his name repentance and forgiveness of sins.

> Acts 10:43, To him [Jesus Christ] all the prophets bear witness, that everyone believing on him receives forgiveness of sins through his name.

> Romans 8:1, Therefore now there is not even one condemnatory judgment to those in Christ Jesus.

"The wages of sin is death," Romans 6:23, both physical death and spiritual death. Christ suffered both kinds of death on the cross, thereby paying the legal debt for the crime of sin, as a substitutionary, vicarious propitiating sacrifice for the crime of sin: in the place of the sinner (substitutionary) and on behalf of the sinner (vicarious), thereby completely satisfying (propitiating) God's holiness and justice against the sinner for the crime of sin, because the limitless merit of his person as the God-man gave the limitless merit of his deity to his human death for the crime of sin, 2 Corinthians 5:21.

Christ's suffering and death on the cross was a legal transaction between Jesus Christ and God in judicial payment for the crime of human sin against God.

Christ's limitless merit, that made in full the payment for the judicial debt of the crime of sin, is applied to the believing sinner's sin, by God's grace, through the sinner's faith in God and God's testimony, and the sinner's sins are forgiven, and the penalty is canceled. All sins past, present, and future are forgiven, because the merit of Jesus Christ's propitiating payment for the crime of sin was and is without limit, an overwhelming judicial payment for the crime. The full demerit of human sin compared to the limitless merit of Jesus Christ's propitiation is like a tear drop in an ocean.

Therefore, there is no condemnatory judgment against the sinner, Romans 8:1, which is to say, the penalty having been paid in full, the forgiven sinner no longer owes the judicial debt for the crime. He or she is no longer subject to the penalty due sin, which is spiritual separation from God during this mortal life, and endless separation and punishment in the life to come. The sins are forgiven, the penalty is canceled, forever.

Someone will surely ask, if there is now no more condemnation for every past, present, and future sin, why do believer's confess their acts of sinning, 1 John 1:9? The difference is between condemnatory judgment preventing a relationship with God in Christ, and acts of sinning injuring a believer's fellowship with God in Christ. God must always act against sin. Therefore any act of sinning requires a just action by God. Because of salvation that just action against sin is not eternal judgment, but a temporary separation from fellowship.

Delivered From The Dominating Power Of Sin

In the unsaved person, sin is an attribute of fallen human nature, a principle or attribute of evil, that motivates human beings to rebel against God, disobey his commandments, and seek a path in life apart from God.

Sin has authority (dominion, rule) over the sinner, not as some invincible overlord, but as an innate part of human nature constructively working with all the other attributes of human nature to persuasively incline the will to choose an act of sinning.

The evil attribute sin influences every other attribute with the inclination to sin, and in that sense sin can be said to dominate the will. The sinner freely chooses sinning because his will is of itself always inclined to choose sinning, and as being rebellious and disobedient toward God never desires to change its inclination to choose sinning to rebel against God, disobey his commandments, and seek a path in life apart from God.

Salvation from the penalty due the crime of sin releases the believer from the dominion of sin (through positional sanctification). Romans 6:14 states sin no longer has dominion over the believer. The saved person freely chooses righteousness because the saved person's will is of itself always inclined to choose righteousness, and as being in salvific relationship with God, doesn't desire to change its inclination to choose righteousness. The choice to live righteously is freely made, because the person's disposition is inclined to holiness and righteousness toward God.

(Sometimes the saved act on temptation, because the sin attribute remains as part of human nature, always tempting; but the saved will habitually act righteously, sinning only occasionally and always confessing their acts of sinning when committed, out of love for Christ and a desire to please him.)

In the saved, sinning is not a natural reflex of the regenerated human nature, because salvation has delivered the believer from the dominating power of sin. Whereas before the choice to deny temptation was limited to things such as self-interest, now the believer has the spiritual power to say "No" to temptation and enforce the decision.

Delivered From The Pleasure Of Sin

It is a simple fact of salvation that sin and acts of sinning become repugnant to the believer. Relief from the pleasure of sin is replaced by the pleasure of intimate fellowship with God. The believer wants to please God, and experiences satisfaction when he or she has pleased God. Any pleasure that might be derived from an act of sinning is fleeting.

Sin and sinning really bother the Christian. The believer hates sin because God hates sin. The believer defines sin just like God defines sin. Sin is doing what I want to do, just because I don't want to do what God says. Sin is doing what I think is right not what God says is right. Sin is pleasing myself, not pleasing God. The Christian's whole-hearted desire is to want the things God wants and to do the things that please God.

Sometimes believers are so tempted by sin that they do the sin. Temptation is not sin, sinning is sin. Sometimes believers follow temptation into sin. When a believer does sin he or she knows they have done wrong. When a believer sins he or she feels as though they have disappointed God. There are feelings of "I am guilty," and feelings of shame (or embarrassment).

The sinning believer doesn't like what he has done, and may wonder if God can still like him. That is because an act of sinning forms a spiritual barrier between the believer and God. The sinning believer is still God's saved child—a parent does not disown their child just because he has done something wrong. But friendly relations between the believer and God are strained by sin. God must, because he is God the Savior, convict the believer of his wrong-doing and bring the believer back to fellowship.

When a believer sins God convicts him that he (or she) has sinned. This leads to the desire to leave that sin behind and return to fellowship with God. The believer can recover from sin and be restored to fellowship with God because Jesus has already paid for that sin on the cross.

What God requires from the sinning believer is confession and repentance. Confession is agreeing with God that I have sinned. Repentance is turning my back on the sin by turning myself to face God. God teaches the path to recovery in a simple verse, 1 John 1:9, if the believer confesses his or her sin (confession includes repentance),

God himself is faithful and just to cleanse the believer from the sin, and restore him or her to fellowship. Why? Because Christ is the believer's legal advocate in the matter of sin, and he presents his propitiation as the cause to forgive sin, 1 John 2:1–2.

The genuine Christian thinks about obeying God. His or her desire is to obey God by not sinning. The pleasure of sin is diminished. The believer is strongly bothered by sin and sinning. The believer actively resists the temptation to commit an act of sinning. He doesn't want to sin. He doesn't want to sin because he doesn't want to disappoint God and he doesn't like how he feels when he sins. Sometimes the believer does sin. When a believer sins he (or she) is bothered by the sin. The believer knows sin injures his fellowship with God. The believer looks to God's way of recovery (1 John 1:9) so he can get rid of the "guilty" of the sin and return to fellowship with God.

Delivered From The Presence Of Sin

At physical death or rapture the believer is freed from the presence of sin. The sin attribute is removed from the believer's human nature, and the believer is given the grace of indefectability. This is the same grace that was given the angels who did not sin, and by that grace have never sinned.

Let us reason together from the scriptures. When Lucifer sinned and became Satan, he was cast out of the third heaven, Ezekiel 28:16; Revelation 12:4. All angels live in the second heaven of the spirit domain (the first heaven is the material atmosphere and starry sky). Just as the material domain was created for material things and beings, such as human beings, even so a spirit domain was created for immaterial beings.

The third heaven (2 Corinthians 12:2) is a place in the spirit domain where only holy angels and redeemed human beings live. When Lucifer sinned and became Satan he was cast out of the third heaven, and never allowed to return there again. Why? God maintains a manifestation of himself in the third heaven (cf. Revelation 4:2–3). No sin is allowed in God's presence in the third heaven. (Satan talks to God just as you do, by speaking or thinking.)

In every presentation of the third heaven in the Scripture, there is no sin and there are no sinners in the third heaven.

Therefore, before the believer may live in heaven, the sin attribute must be removed from his or her human nature. In 1 Corinthians 15:52

Paul says the dead in Christ will be resurrected, and then "we" the living "will be transformed," because, 15:53, "it is necessary that this the corruptible to put on incorruption." That is the removal of the sin attribute in human nature.

Scripture gives another indication that believers are sinless in the life after this life. At the end of the ages, all sin will be confined in the lake of fire.

> Revelation 20:15, And if anyone was not found having been written in the book of life, he was thrown into the lake of fire.

> Revelation 21:8, But to fearful, and to unbelieving, and to having become abhorrent, and to murderers, and to sexually immoral, and to sorcerers, and to idolators, and to all liars, their portion is in the lake burning with fire and sulfur, which is the second death."

> Revelation 21:27, And never no never may enter into it anything defiling, and those practicing anything detestable to God, and a lie; only those being written in the book of life of the Lamb.

> Revelation 22:3, And there will not be any curse anymore. And the throne of God and of the Lamb will be in it, and his servants will serve him.

When a saved person leaves this mortal life, whether by death or rapture, the sin attribute is permanently removed from his or her human nature, delivering the believer from the presence of sin forever. The believer's human nature becomes incorruptible, and is preserved incorruptible by the grace of indefectability. The believer's body is resurrected immortal and incorruptible. Then the believer's immaterial immortal incorruptible soul (the soul is the person) is reunited with the resurrected body made immortal and incorruptible, thereby animating the body, and the believer lives endlessly in incorruptible and immortal body and soul in the presence of God.

I will discuss the grace of indefectability in chapter "Physical Death, Soul Transformed, Intermediate State."

ETERNAL LIFE

The quality of endless physical life is not eternal life but immortal life. The human soul was created naturally immortal, being given as one of its components the animating principle we know as "life.' The aminating principle life comes from God, who alone has life-in-himself, John 5:26, Exodus 3:14, "I am he who exists." Unlike the physical body, the human soul has no know means of dissolution (death). The body is mortal until the resurrection.

The eternal life of the believer is the duration and quality of life experienced by the believer. The duration is everlasting. The quality of eternal life is God sharing his communicable attributes in the fullest measure possible for a saved finite soul to receive, thus effecting intimate fellowship and communion between God and the believer in this mortal life and in the life hereafter.

The believer has eternal life as a present possession, and experiences it in part during his or her mortal life (as he or she is being made conformed by the Holy Spirit to the likeness of Christ), but the fullness of eternal life begins following physical death, when the immortal soul is washed clean of the sin attribute, and continues when reunited with the incorruptible immortal resurrected body.

Eternal life is that "seed," 1 John 3:9, that makes the believer born-again. The Greek word translated seed is *spérma*, meaning what is sown, the germ of new fruit, or what is growing out of what was sown, i.e., the product of the seed [Zodhiates, s. v. 4690]. The use at 3:9 is obviously figurative. The reference to "born from God" indicates the regeneration of the soul (born-again) through being given eternal life. Eternal life is the seed that prevents habitual sinning during this mortal life.

Eternal life is a quality of life. Godly life principles, such as holiness, righteousness, and love, are given at salvation to regenerate human nature from sinner to saved. Eternal life gives spiritual life to the soul. Spiritual life overcomes the power, pleasure, and temptations of sin, enabling the believer to habitually say "No" to temptation and habitually practice righteousness.

Eternal life is God sharing his communicable attributes with the believer. Human kind was created in God's image and likeness. Human nature was fashioned with godly attributes in the likeness of God's communicable attributes, in finite measure, in a greater or lesser degree, depending on the attribute in question.

Stated a little differently, the pattern God used to create human nature in Adam's soul was God's communicable attributes. Sin did not destroy the attributes of human nature, it reprioritized them to serve self not God. "Man fallen is but the anagram of man in innocency" [Manton, *James*, 73]. Every aspect of the created nature remains, but has been repurposed by sin.

The communicable attributes of God are holiness, love, faithfulness, intellect, wisdom, righteousness, mercy, goodness, kindness, personality, will, volition, and veracity. These can be arranged into moral, intellectual, and spiritual qualities that define human nature [Quiggle, *Adam*, 64]. (Mercy is listed in both the moral and spiritual areas because mercy may delay justice, a moral quality, or relieve suffering, a spiritual quality.)

> Moral: holiness, sanctification, righteousness, justice, mercy, faithfulness

> Intellectual: personality, will, volition, veracity, knowledge, wisdom

> Spiritual: love, compassion, goodness, kindness, longsuffering, mercy

Human kind created in God's image is human nature fashioned according to God's communicable moral, intellectual, and spiritual attributes. The eternal life the saved receive is a quality of spiritual life given by God to regenerate human nature to its original design.

The process of regeneration begins with salvation from the penalty, power, and pleasure of sin and becomes complete with deliverance from the presence of sin, e.g., John 10:28; Romans 6:14, 23; 8:1; 1 Corinthians 15:22; 53; Ephesians 1:14; Revelation 21:4. At physical death or (for a few) at the rapture, "this corruptible [human nature] will put on incorruption." Then at resurrection "this mortal [physical body] will put on immortality." (The human soul is immortal from the moment it comes into existence.)

For the saved, eternal life is being fit for immortal, incorruptible life body and soul in God's presence. The eternal life Christ gives the believer consists of four characteristics: knowing God; sharing in God's communicable attributes; denying temptation; living forever in God's presence.

REGENERATION

There is a question some pose: which is first, saving faith or regeneration? Does saving faith lead to regeneration, or is saving faith the consequence of regeneration? If the regeneration (born-again) of the sinner's human nature precedes saving faith, then what is the purpose of faith in salvation? If one must be regenerated in order to be saved, then where is the exercise of faith that saves? Is not the scriptural order believe and be saved, Acts 16:31? To be regenerated is to have been saved. Salvation precedes regeneration. Even as the earth must turn toward the sun receive sunlight, the sinner must turn toward the Son to be saved in order to be regenerated.

The true question is not, "Does regeneration precede faith or follow faith?" The true question is "How does someone unable and unwilling to understand spiritual things, become able and willing and believing?" If, as the Scripture teaches, the unsaved person does not have the spiritual perception to understand spiritual things, 1 Corinthians 2:14, then how does the unsaved person understand those spiritual things necessary to salvation?

The answer, as I described above under "Saving Faith," is the Holy Spirit applies God's gift of grace-faith-salvation (Ephesians 2:8) to enliven spiritual perception, thereby changing the spiritual boundaries of the sinner's human nature, so the sinner is able to understand the spiritual things of salvation: his or her sin, Christ the only Savior, and salvation by faith not works.

Then, by God's gift, and by the Holy Spirit's convicting work, the sinner understands the spiritual things necessary to salvation, and he or she inevitably and freely chooses to believe on God and God's testimony as to the way of salvation.

Then having believed, his or her human nature is fully regenerated. The order is God's gift, spiritual perception, conviction, faith, regeneration.

There are two things one looks for in sinners when giving testimony of sin, the Savior, and salvation (the Good News). The first is the ability to understand those spiritual things necessary to salvation—that is the consequence of receiving God's gift of grace-faith-salvation. The second is conviction of sin and conviction the risen Jesus Christ is the only Savior. When those two things are present, one knows the Holy Spirit is at work.

(There is an intellectual ability that mimics spiritual perception but cannot mimic Holy Spirit given conviction, which always results in the genuine expression of saving faith. "Easy Believism" is the mimicry of spiritual perception that agrees with Good News, but is not convicted by the Good News.)

Whatever you believe about faith and regeneration, give the gospel and look for spiritual understanding and conviction. If God is at work, his presence will be known.

BORN AGAIN

I briefly touched on regeneration above, under the heading "The Result Of Salvation." Here I will explain regeneration in depth.

Salvation is an instantaneous act with several results, which may be separated for the purpose of discussion. The unbeliever is unable to understand the things of the Spirit of God (1 Corinthians 2:14), because his/her faculty of spiritual perception is "dead," unable to perceive spiritual things (Ephesians 2:1, 5). The first part of "born-again" is the believer's faculty of spiritual perception is brought to life, thus enabling the spiritual understanding required to be convicted of sin, the Savior, and salvation. This is accomplished through God's gift of grace-faith-salvation (Ephesians 2:8) by the work of the Holy Spirit to accomplish the salvation decreed by God (Ephesians 1:4; 2 Thessalonians 2:13; 1 Peter 1:2). The exercise of saving faith is the sure and certain outcome of God's gift of grace-faith-salvation.

Upon the exercise of saving faith by the sinner, God imparts to him/her eternal life, John 10:27–29; 17:2–3; Romans 6:23b; 1 John 2:25, which is God sharing (in a participatory way) the communicable aspects of his eternal life, creating communion with God and spiritual understanding. To be born-again, or regeneration, is the result of God sharing the communicable aspects of his eternal life. The attributes of human nature, which were jumbled and wrongly prioritized by the sin attribute, are normalized, which is to say, godliness is restored to human nature through the godly attributes of holiness, righteousness, love, mercy, etc. The believer is given new wants and new desires. His/her human nature is re-prioritized toward God.

Upon the exercise of saving faith, God imputes the righteousness of Christ to the now-believing sinner, freeing him or her from the judicial guilt and penalty of sin (justification) because Christ has satisfied God's law on behalf of the sinner, Romans 6:23. The now-saved sinner has been reconciled to God, 2 Corinthians 5:18–19. This brings peace with God, Romans 5:1, because with sin forgiven (Ephesians 1:7), and the judicial penalty satisfied through Christ's propitiation (1 John 2:2), there is no more enmity between God and the believer.

Upon the exercise of saving faith, the Holy Spirit accomplishes the sanctification of the believer, which is to set the believer apart from the defilement caused by sin and dedicate him to God, Ephesians 1:4; 1 Corinthians 1:30; 1 Peter 1:2. In the act of sanctification sin loses its dominating power, Romans 6:14–23, and a new principle of life, holiness, is added to the believer, Ephesians 4:24, becoming the dominating principle in his human nature, 1 Thessalonians 4:7; 1 Corinthians 3:17b; Colossians 3:12; 1 Peter 1:15.

The believer now stands before God in Christ as forgiven, justified, sanctified, regenerated, and filled with eternal life. He is freed from the penalty, power, and pleasure of sin, with absolute assurance of the future transformation and glorification of human nature and body that frees the believer eternally from the presence of sin. The believer is empowered to resist sin's temptations, live a holy life, understand the Scripture, worship, obey, fellowship with, and serve God. God hears and answers his prayers, and he (or she) perseveres in the faith to lead a holy life, looking toward resurrection and an eternal life in God's presence.

The Holy Spirit is always present with his saved people in any age of humankind, but the Old Testament believer was not indwelt by the Holy Spirit. The New Testament believer is indwelt by the Holy Spirit. In this age of the NT church, when the human nature has been regenerated by the work of the Holy Spirit, the Holy Spirit then takes up permanent residence in the believer's soul, John 14:17; Acts 10:44–48; 1 Corinthians 6:19.

Five Characteristics Of The Saved Person

1. Sin and sinning bother the believer: Christ has delivered the Christian from the pleasure of sin. Before salvation sin was a pleasure taken without guilt or shame. The saved person struggles against and overcomes sin.

2. The Word of God is precious and pleasurable. The believer delights in God's Word: to read it, study it, apply it, live it, and share it. Before salvation the Word was incomprehensible and impractical.

3. Believers enjoy the company of those with like precious faith. Believers share Christ, the Bible, worship, service, and a future in common, bringing them together in fellowship. Before salvation the company of Christians was tiresome, or threatening, or boring, and unlikely.

4. Believer's pray and worship. This is performed as a group publicly and as an individual devotionally. We worship because we

know God and have a deeply seated desire to ascribe to him praise and glory and thanksgiving. We pray because we have a deep seated trust in God and desire to submit ourselves to his will in all things. Before salvation God was an afterthought, if he was thought of at all. Now his will, his Word, and his glory are all important.

5. The believer develops a character, expressed in attitudes and actions, which is informed and guided by Scripture. The believer becomes like Christ, which is to say he becomes godly and does godly works. This is Peter's emphasis: God's character manifested in the believer's character. Before salvation Christ was a curse word, not a person, and godly character was unknown. Now Christ is worshiped.

The unsaved person finds it easy to turn away from Christ. The saved person perseveres in his faith to the very end of life. He may stumble, he may falter, he may stand still for a little while, but he always gets up and presses on to the goal. That is salvation.

Chapter Summary

In this chapter salvation is closely defined as "the remission of sin's penalty by the application of the merit of Christ's propitiation of God on the cross to the sinner's spiritual need." This chapter explains the consequences of salvation under four headings: the kind of faith that saves the person from the penalty due sin, what is the forgiveness experienced in saving faith, what is that eternal life one receives in response to saving faith, and the regeneration of human nature as a consequence of saving faith.

Saving faith is examined in great detail, forming the bulk of the chapter. I present a complete definition of faith as acting on the conviction given by the Holy Spirit, and then discuss faith in detail. The grammatical aspects of Ephesians 2:8 are explored, resulting in the understanding the salvation principle is not grace alone or faith alone, or salvation alone, but all three as one principle: God's gift is grace-faith-salvation.

How God's gift is given (to foreordained individuals), and how the sinner receiving the gift responds (the exercise of saving faith), is explained as both rational and supra-natural. Both aspects are explored in detail, with the conclusion a rational faith only is not saving, the supra-natural aspect is also required. A rational faith alone may reform but cannot transform—cannot be salvific. The consequences of saving faith—in a word, regeneration—are explained.

The exercise of saving faith results in forgiveness, of which being saved from hell is the end result, but not the only result; there are consequences for this mortal life. All the believer's sins (past present, future) are forgiven so that there is no longer the condemnation of endless punishment after physical death, first in Hades, then in the lake of fire (the true hell) which is the consequence of dying with unforgiven sin. The consequences of saving faith during this mortal life are explored under an alliterative outline, delivered from the penalty, power, pleasure, and presence of sin.

In the next section, eternal life is defined as both a quality and duration of life. The duration is everlasting. The quality of eternal life is God sharing his communicable attributes in the fullest measure possible for a saved finite soul to receive, thus effecting intimate fellowship and communion between God and the believer in this mortal life and in the life hereafter. Eternal life is that "seed," 1 John 3:9, that makes the believer born-again. Eternal life is the godly life principles, such as holiness, righteousness, and love, given at salvation to regenerate human nature from sinner to saved.

In the section, "Regeneration," I discuss the conundrum, "which is first, saving faith or regeneration," concluding that salvation precedes regeneration. Even as the earth must turn toward the sun receive sunlight, the sinner must turn toward the Son to be saved in order to be regenerated.

Following this section the processes and consequences of regeneration are listed in a logical order. The chapter concludes with six characteristics of salvation, which the reader may use to evaluate his or her own state of salvation.

Positional Justification and Sanctification in Christ

The believer's standing before God and his or her state in the world are two aspects of salvation. This chapter discusses the believer's standing before God in Christ. See chapter "Perseverance and Experiential Sanctification" for a discussion of the believer's state in the world.

The word "positional" is used in theology to describe the believer's "standing" before God the Judge. The believer stands before God the Judge in Jesus Christ forgiven, justified, sanctified.

POSITIONAL JUSTIFICATION

The word "justification" has several meanings.

In printing text, the spacing between words in a line of type so that left and right margins are even (Dictionary.com).

Showing something to be right or reasonable (Oxford Languages Dictionary).

An acceptable reason for doing something or behaving in a certain way (Miriam Webster).

In law a type of defense that exempts the defendant from liability because the defendant's actions were justified, or not wrong.

How does the Scripture define justification? Not as it is defined in law.

The Scripture recognizes the sinner's actions were wrong and deserving of punishment. Scripture's definition of justification is the consequence of the wrongful actions of the guilty sinner punished by executing the punishment due the sinner on a legal and innocent substitute, Jesus Christ, who imputed the sinner's sins to himself, 2 Corinthians 5:21, and bore the just punishment due those sins on behalf of the guilty sinner. Because the penalty was paid on behalf of the sinner, the sinner may be justified.

Justification. A believer is permanently positionally justified in Christ: in his court of justice God declares those whom he has saved "not judicially guilty," of the crimes of their sins, Romans 8:1. [Quiggle, *Dictionary.*]

When one is in Christ by grace through faith by Christ's limitless merit, then he or she is acquitted of the moral and legal crimes of sin, because Christ paid in full the penalty due those sins, on the guilty sinner's behalf, in the place of the guilty sinner.

The word "positional" means God views the believer as though standing in Christ before God. God always sees the believer as vitally united in Christ by the salvific relationship. This was the goal of election, "he chose us in him," Ephesians 1:4. As the believer stands before God for judgment of his or her sins, God sees the believer in a salvific relationship with himself in Jesus Christ, imputes Christ's righteousness to the believer, and there is no judgment because Jesus paid it all in his propitiation. A believer's standing is as permanent as the salvific relationship (see chapter "Security and Assurance of Salvation").

Positional justification is purely a legal matter. Possessing the sin attribute in human nature, and committing acts of sinning, are crimes against the laws of God. The sinner is guilty of the crime of sin. Justification declares the sinner Not Guilty of the crimes of sin. The legal basis for justification is the legal satisfaction Christ made to God's justice and holiness on the cross: Jesus Christ's propitiation of God for human sin (see chapter "Christ's Propitiation of God")

The reason a sinner may be declared "Not Guilty" for the crime of sin is someone else paid the penalty for the crime. That someone else was Jesus the Christ. The limitless merit of Christ's propitiation is applied by God to remit the judicial guilt of the person God is saving. Christ's righteousness as the Redeemer is permanently imputed to the believer. The believer stands before God the Judge in the permanent state of not guilty, no condemnation.

The permanent "Not Guilty" of positional justification immediately brings to mind the fact that believer's do occasionally commit acts of sinning, 1 John 1:8, 10—though habitually living righteously, 1 John 3:9—and are required to "confess our sins," 1 John 1:9, to be cleansed from the unrighteousness caused by that act of sinning. What is the relationship between positional justification and confession of acts of sinning? One's standing before God and one's state in the world. Standing is permanent but state fluctuates because every believer occasionally commits an act of sinning. A believer's standing in Christ means no condemnation for occasional acts of sinning.

The purpose of positional justification is the believer can never no never be condemned to the endless judgment due the unforgiven sinner. The believer's state in the world may and will change as he or she lives righteously, or occasionally succumbs to temptation and commits an act of sinning. The believer's standing before God as righteous in Christ cannot change. Standing is permanent because created by the limitless merit of Christ's propitiation, that was applied by God's grace and the believer's faith, to permanently save the believer through the forgiveness of sin and imputation of Christ's righteousness. Because positional justification is grounded in Christ's limitless merit which never changes, the believer's standing of positionally justified never changes.

Salvation is a permanent relationship with God in Christ. Salvation is God by his grace rescuing a believing sinner out of the state of spiritual death and placing the believing sinner into a permanent state of spiritual life. Because the merit that overcame the demerit of sin is the limitless merit of Christ's propitiation of God for sin, no act of sinning can overcome that limitless merit and change the believer's salvific relationship with God. "Therefore now there is not even one condemnatory judgment to those in Christ Jesus," Romans 8:1.

What an act of sinning does is injure the believer's fellowship with God. God cannot ignore sin. Every act of sinning deserves a just punishment. For the believer, Christ vicariously experienced that punishment on the cross as the believer's legal substitute, 1 John 2:1–2. For the believer the spiritual separation because of an act of sinning is not the salvific relationship but separation in fellowship.

For the unsaved the just punishment is separation from a relationship with God—spiritually separated during this mortal life, and if sin remains unforgiven by salvation then permanently separated both spiritually and physically after this mortal life. The power of physical death confirms the unsaved sinner in his or her separation from God, there is no salvation after physical death, only judgment, Hebrews 9:27, "And inasmuch as it awaits for men to die once, then after that judgment."

For the saved, an act of sinning cannot undo salvation. When a believer commits an act of sinning God responds by limiting his fellowship with the believer, convicting the believer of his sin to prompt repentance and confession (1 John 1:9), or sending chastisement to prompt repentance and confession.

I have answered the question of the relationship between the permanent standing of positional justification and the commission of acts of sinning. The legal satisfaction of the propitiation, which has been permanently applied to the believer by salvation, is the basis for the believer's positional justification (his or her permanent standing of not guilty before God the Judge) that prevents the condemnation of endless punishment for an act of sinning, and maintains the believer's salvific relationship.

However, acts of sinning injure the believer's fellowship with God, because God's holiness, and righteousness, and justice require God act against every sin. God takes action against a believer's occasional acts of sinning by conviction or chastisement to lead the sinning believer to repentance and confession, so that he may "forgive us the sins, and to cleanse us from every unrighteousness," 1 John 1:9, and restore the believer to intimate fellowship.

How then does God forgive acts of sinning? Through the same limitless merit of Jesus Christ that forgives all sins.

> 1 John 2:1–2, My little children, I am writing these things to you that you may not commit acts of sinning. Now if anyone should commit an act of sinning, we have one who represents us with the Father, Jesus Christ the righteous. 2 Now he is propitiation for our sins—but not for ours only but also for all the world.

Because of the salvific relationship, Christ represents the believer before the Father in all matters. In the matter of an act of sinning, the believer has a representative, Jesus Christ the righteous, standing before the Father on his behalf. Christ is the *paráklētos*, the Helper, the believer's legal representative, who pleads the believer's cause with the Father when the believer has committed an act of sinning; the condemnation of endless punishment has been satisfied by Christ's propitiation applied by God's grace through the believer's saving faith.

In what way does Christ plead the believer's cause with the Father when an act of sinning has been committed? He does so by confessing to the Father that one of his believers has committed an act of sinning. Then he applies the merit of his propitiation to the act of sinning as the ground for forgiveness and cleansing. The believer confesses his/her sin, 1 John 1:9, in faith depending on Christ's propitiation. The penalty for any sin is death—spiritual and physical. Christ's propitiation paid the penalty for every sin past, present, and future. The believer's present act of sinning is forgiven on the basis of Christ's eternally efficient propitiation and the believer's prior historical act of saving faith.

John presents the effect of Christ's propitiation on a believer's act of sinning as a legal transaction between Father and Son. He presents this transaction as though when a believer sins, Christ appears before the Father in the court of divine justice to plead why the believer should be forgiven; as though Christ's legal pleading reminds the Father that the eternal penalty which might affect the relationship has already been resolved, and the temporary penalty, the loss of fellowship, is then and there resolved. Of course, the Father does not need reminding, and the Son need not plead, but here is an imaginative illustration of the spiritual transaction:

> "Yes Father," says Christ, "that person has sinned and deserves death. Remember that I paid for that sin. When I was on the cross I suffered your wrath and my physical death for this person's sin. The debt has been paid, and this saved person, who is Your child (Romans 8:16) and my brethren (Hebrews 2:11), must be forgiven. He/she has confessed and repented their sin and must be restored to our fellowship and our service."

Every issue related to sin and sinning has been, and will continue to be, resolved by the Son's propitiation and the believer's faith in Christ.

Because Jesus Christ is righteous, a sinner can be saved from the penalty of sin, and a believer will be forgiven for committing acts of sinning. That is positional justification. In regard to salvation, Christ's righteousness gave unlimited merit to his propitiation of God, thereby satisfying the demands of God's holiness and justice. In regard to the believer who has committed an act of sinning, when the believer confesses sinning, Christ's righteousness, the same righteousness possessed by the Father, represents the sinning believer before the Father. That also is positional justification.

In positional justification, Christ's righteousness is imputed to the believing sinner, giving him or her permanent righteous standing before God the Judge.

POSITIONAL SANCTIFICATION

The word "positional" means the believer's standing before God in Christ. What is sanctification? The word is sometimes used in a secular sense of declaring something to be moral or ethical. What we want is the biblical meaning of sanctification.

The word "sanctification" comes from a group of Greek words

meaning "holy." The basic meaning of "holy" and "holiness" is separation and dedication (in the sense of consecration). Sanctification is the act of declaring something is holy. A discussion of holiness is necessary.

God is essentially holy, meaning the essence of his being, his essential nature as God, is holy. God's holiness means God is separate from all that is unlike himself.

1 John 1:5, God is light and darkness is not in him, none at all.

All that is in God is God, with no admixture of anything that is not God. All that is unlike God is not essentially holy. God is separate from all unlike himself and dedicated to being himself. In more familiar terms, God is pure, meaning he is sinless in every thought and action. But more than that, God himself is the standard for holiness. He alone is essentially holy as a necessary characteristic of his being.

Job 25:1–6 (LXX, Brenton) For how shall a mortal be just before the Lord? or who that is born of a woman shall purify himself? If he gives an order to the moon, then it shines not; and the stars are not pure before him. But alas! man is corruption, and the son of man a worm.

Romans 3:10–18, As it was written, none is righteous, not one. 11 None is understanding. None is seeking God. 12 They all turned away. Together they became vile. None is practicing good: there is not so much as one. 13 Their voice box: a grave opening; with their tongues always deceiving. Under their lips: venom of vipers; 14 of whom the mouth is full of bitterness and imprecation. 15 Their feet: swift to shed blood. 16 Their paths: ruin and misery; 17 and the way leading to peace they have not known. 18 There is not fear of God before their eyes.

Even a believer standing in God's light would be a spot of darkness, his presence rejected. But his presence is allowed because he stands in Christ (positional justification), with Christ's imputed righteousness, and the positional sanctification (separated from sin and dedicated to God) caused by his relationship with God in Christ.

In relation to the things and living beings God has created, a mundane illustration captures the essential meaning of sanctification. My toothbrush is holy: it is set aside from all tasks but one, and it is dedicated to that one task only. The pans and shovels and censers in the tabernacle/temple were holy: dedicated to service in the tabernacle/temple to do nothing else nowhere else. The believer is made holy when saved: set apart from sin and dedicated to God. Regardless of a believer's experiential state of sanctification in the world, his standing of positional sanctification in Christ before God is permanently holy.

All holy creatures are holy because God has 1) added holiness to their character and 2) set them apart from sin and dedicated them to himself. To be holy is to be like God. Jesus Christ is perfectly holy because his character is perfectly exactly like God (an aspect of his deity nature and the consequence of his sinless human nature).

The believer is made positionally holy by being brought into a relationship with God in Christ. The believer during this mortal life is to live like Christ, separating him or herself from all that is unlike Christ, striving by the power and guidance of the Holy Spirit to lead a Christ-like life: experiential sanctification. After this mortal life, God will transform the believer to be sinless and give the believer the grace of indefectibility so he/she will for eternity be holy: final (permanent, eternal) sanctification.

Positional sanctification, then, is the standing of holy before God in Christ resulting from the salvation experience. Sanctification has three aspects: positional, experiential, and eternal.

Positional Sanctification: A result of salvation that occurs at the moment of salvation. The judicial guilt of personal sin is forgiven. The soul is regenerated to spiritual life. God shares the communicable aspects of his eternal life. The righteousness of Christ is imputed to the believer. Positional sanctification defines the believer as he or she stands before God in Christ: forgiven, regenerated, possessing eternal life, judged as holy and righteous, placed into an eternal relationship with God. This status never changes, because secured for the believer by Christ.

Experiential Sanctification: The sanctified believer uses the means of grace to conform his manner of living (thoughts and actions) to be more like Christ. God has given the believer new and eternal life, but has left the old nature (the sin nature) resident in the flesh. The new life a believer has is a product of grace and is maintained by grace, but requires personal effort to apply that grace so as to overcome the temptation of sin.

Experiential sanctification is the believer's state before God in the world. One lives his or her life in such a manner so as to conform one's lifestyle to be godly and Christ-like. The believer makes a conscious effort to bring his state in the world to the same level of godliness, holiness, and righteousness as his standing in Christ. This is a life-long process in which the believer should steadily progress.

A stairway illustrates the believers' progress in experiential sanctification. We learn, we practice what we learned (standing on a step), we progress (going up a step), sometimes we go down a step, we learn, we practice, we progress, etc. throughout life.

Eternal sanctification is that transformation of soul and body that occurs in the soul at physical death and in the body at the resurrection. Eternal sanctification eliminates the sin attribute in body and soul. In eternal sanctification the believer's state is the same as his standing. In every aspect of his or her life, for all eternity, the believer possesses godliness, holiness, and righteousness in every desire, every thought, and every action, sustained by God's grace.

Chapter Summary

Positional justification is a believer's permanent standing before God as not guilty of his or her crimes of sin, because God has imputed the righteousness of Jesus Christ to the believer.

Positional sanctification is a believer's permanent standing before God as separated from sin and dedicated to God. This is also because God has imputed the righteousness of Jesus Christ to the believer.

Both justification and sanctification have experiential aspects in the believer's life. The experiential state of the believer in the world does not affect the believer's permanent standing before God in Christ.

Experientially, the believer is sanctified by denying temptation and living righteously. The sin attribute in believer's human nature no longer has dominion, but it never stops tempting the believer to commit an act of sinning. Saying "No," to temptation and enforcing that decision is the act of experiential sanctification: continuously separating one's self from acts of sinning by continuously dedicating one's self to maintaining fellowship with God.

But occasionally a believer will say "Yes" to a temptation and commit an act of sinning.

Experientially, the believer is justified from his or her occasional acts of sinning through repentance, confession, and Christ's representation of the sinning believer before God on the basis of the limitless merit of his propitiation of God for the believer's every past, present, and future acts of sinning. "If we continue to confess our sins, he is faithful and righteous to forgive us the sins, and to cleanse us from every unrighteousness" because "if anyone should commit an act of sinning, we have one who represents us with the Father, Jesus Christ the righteous" (1 John 1:9, 2:2).

The tension between the believer's positional standing and experiential state of justification and sanctification will be resolved at physical death or rapture, when the sin attribute is removed from the believer's human nature. The transformed and glorified believer will be given the grace of indefectability so that the incorruptible state of his transformed human nature is maintained endlessly forever.

Adoption as a Consequence of Predestination

To understand adoption, we must first understand predestination. Centuries ago, the Reformers confused predestination by using the word as a synonym for election. In Reformed theology, the term "predestination" smashes together four distinct biblical doctrines: foreordination + election + predestination + providence. I mentioned this before in the chapter on Foreordination.

Election is a decree affecting the spiritual state of the sinner, effecting a permanent change in the sinner from unsaved to saved. Predestination is a decree affecting the spiritual state of the saved, effecting a change in the believer's human nature to be like Christ.

> Predestination. God's decree to conform the believer to be like Christ according to certain aspects of Christ's spiritual character and physical form (Romans 8:29–30; 1 John 3:2), and to place the believer in the legal position of God's son and heir (adoption) (Ephesians 1:5, 11), so that the believer has an inheritance from God and is God's heritage.

God's decree of predestination, not his decree of election, is why a believer is adopted by God to place the believer in the legal position of God's son and heir and joint-heir with Jesus Christ, Romans 8:17.

Adoption is that spiritual state in which God places the believer as an adult son and heir of God, making them "sons of God." God has one natural child, Jesus Christ the Son of God, the "only begotten," who is heir of all things. God takes those who are not his natural children, sinners, saves them by his grace through their faith, and adopts them into the position of a natural born child (Ephesians 1:5). Adoption and son-ship are not gender-specific terms but a position of relationship and inheritance applicable to every believer.

> Galatians 4:4–7, But when the fullness of the time had come, God sent forth his Son, having been born of a woman, having been born under the Law, 5 that he may redeem those under the Law, so that we may receive the adoption as sons. 6 Now because you are sons, God sent forth the Spirit of his Son into our hearts, crying out, "Abba, Father." 7 So you are no longer a servant, but a son; if now a son, also an heir through God.
>
> Ephesians 1:5–6, In love 5 he predestined us for sonship to himself through Jesus Christ, according to the good pleasure of

his will, 6 to praise and glory of his grace.

The apostle Paul's use of the term "adoption" comes from a Roman legal custom. A Roman citizen (only certain people in the Roman Republic, and later the Roman Empire, were citizens), could adopt any person—free, freed, or slave—to legally make that person his son and legal heir.

From being slaves to sin to being made sons of God, all believers are sons of God by adoption. The word "sons" in reference to believers reflects the salvific relationship a believer has with God and incorporates the idea of being adopted by God as an adult son and heir.

A discussion of the biblical term "sons of" is necessary. The biblical term "sons of" is description of character. The biblical terms "seed of," "offspring of" "sons of," or "daughters of," are, when speaking metaphorically, those persons whose characteristics are like the person of whom they are a "seed of," "offspring of," "son of," or "daughter of."

When used symbolically neither "sons of" nor "daughters of" is a gender specific term. The terms "seed of," "offspring of," daughter of," or "sons of," means a person possesses the characteristics of the person or thing he or she is a "seed/offspring/daughter/sons of." The "sons of rebellion," at 2 Samuel 23:6 were the rebellious. The "sons of the prophets," 2 Kings 2:3, were those men who were faithful to God and preached his Word. The sons of fools, and the sons of vile men, Job 30:8, were fools and vile.

The terms "sons of God" means any person, human or angel, who is in a faith-based relationship with God.

The term "sons of God" (Hebrew: *benê 'ĕlōhîm;* Greek: *huiós theós*) is used in Genesis 6:2, 4; Job 1:6; 2:1; 38:7; Matthew 5:9; Luke 20:36; Romans 8:14, 19; Galatians 3:26. In every use it refers to persons who are like God because they are in a faith-based relationship with God. No fallen angel and no unsaved human being are ever characterized as sons of God.

The human sons of God are God's legal heirs because by their adoption they have become joint-heirs, Romans 8:17, with God's heir, Jesus Christ the Son of God. (Below in chronological order of writing.)

> Galatians 4:7, So you are no longer a servant, but a son; if now a son, also an heir through God.
>
> Romans 8:16–17, The Spirit himself bears witness with our spirit that we are children of God. 17 Now if children, also heirs, truly

heirs of God, now joint-heirs of Christ, seeing that we suffer together so that also we may be glorified together.

Colossians 1:12, With joy 12 giving thanks to the Father, the one having qualified us for the share of the inheritance of the saints in the light.

1 Peter 1:3–5, Blessed be the God and Father of our Lord Jesus Christ, who according to his great mercy regenerated us to a living hope through resurrection of Jesus Christ out from the dead ones, 4 to an inheritance not-corruptible and not-defiled and not-fading, reserved in heaven for you, 5 the ones by the power of God being guarded through faith unto a salvation ready to be revealed in a last season.

The full receipt of the inheritance waits for the redemption of the body, Ephesians 1:14. What is the inheritance of the sons of God? The inheritance of the saved consists of several things.

Matthew 5:5, Blessed the meek, because they will inherit the earth.

Matthew 19:29, And everyone who has left houses, or brothers, or sisters, or father, or mother, or wife, or children, or lands for my name's sake, a hundredfold will receive, and will inherit eternal life.

Matthew 25:34, Then the King will say to those on his right hand, 'Come, those blessed of my Father, inherit the kingdom prepared for you from the foundation of the world.

The inheritance is also expressed by defining who will not inherit.

1 Corinthians 6:9–10, Or know you not unrighteous ones will not inherit God's Kingdom? Be not led astray. Not sexually immoral, nor idolators, nor adulterers, nor effeminate with other males, nor homosexuals, 10 nor thieves, nor those greedy for what others have, nor drunkards, nor verbal abusers, nor extortioners, will inherit God's Kingdom.

Galatians 5:19–21, Now, the works of the flesh are plain, which are sexual immorality, moral impurity, a shameless love of sin, 20 idolatry, sorcery, enmities, strife, envies, outbursts of anger, personal ambition and partisan rivalry, division, factions, 21 embittered resentment, drunkenness, debauchery, and things like these, of which I forewarn you, even as I warned before, that those habitually doing such things will not inherit God's kingdom.

The inheritance, then, is eternal life and the kingdom. I have before defined eternal life as both the duration of life and the quality of life, which is God sharing his communicable attributes in a measure suitable to finite creatures.

What is the kingdom the saved shall inherit? A kingdom consists of ruler(s), ruled, and realm. Scripture teaches several aspects of the kingdom. The "kingdom" has several meaning in Scripture.

The Universal Kingdom: God's universal rule over his creation. This kingdom is present for all time and eternity.

Kingdom of God/Kingdom of Heaven. The reign of God through Jesus Christ (1 Corinthians 15:24–28).

The Spiritual Kingdom: the kingdom during the New Testament church age between the two advents, composed only of believers saved during the New Testament church age, entered by the new birth. This is the New Testament church that is the body of Christ.

The Mystery Kingdom: the kingdom during the New Testament church age between the two advents, composed of believers saved during the New Testament church age, and of people professing (not possessing) faith, rejecters of faith, and opponents of faith, who are visibly in the New Testament church, but are not spiritually part of the New Testament church through the new birth. This is the New Testament church the world sees.

The Davidic-Messianic Kingdom: based on the Davidic covenant (2 Samuel 7:11b-17; 1 Chronicles 17:10b-15) promised to national ethnic Israel through King David's heir, who is Christ. The ruler is Christ through national ethnic Israel. The ruled will be all the inhabitants of the earth. The resurrected church will reign with Christ in this kingdom (2 Timothy 2:12; Revelation 5:10; 20:6).

The Eternal state of the new heavens and earth, Revelation 21:1–22:5. Though not named a "kingdom," it is the eternal dominion of God when all other dominion, authority, and power, and death itself (1 Corinthians 15:24–25), are eliminated and Good's rule is unopposed, forever, Revelation 21:822:3.

There are two kingdoms in view as the inheritance of the saints.

The first is the Davidic-Messianic Kingdom. This is the Christ's inheritance as the heir of King David, 2 Samiel 7:13, 16; Psalm 2. Because believer's are joint-heirs with Christ, their inheritance incudes that kingdom. It is the kingdom mentioned in Matthew 25:34.

That inheritance is not yet, as the Christ currently sits on God's throne in heaven. Hebrews 10:12–13, "But this one, having offered one sacrifice for sins in perpetuity, sat down at the right hand of God, 13 hence forward expecting until his enemies may be placed as a footstool for his feet." Compare Psalm 110:1. When he returns, at his second advent, Jesus Christ will inaugurate that kingdom and rule for a thousand years, Revelation 20:4–6, and the New Testament church will be part of his rule, Revelation 1:6; 5:10.

The second kingdom that is the inheritance of the saints is the Eternal kingdom, Revelation 21:1–22:5.

Revelation 21:7, The one prevailing will inherit all things, and I will be his God, and he will be my son.

Revelation 21:22–27, And I did not see a temple in it, for the Lord God Almighty is its temple, and the Lamb. 23 And the city has no need of the sun nor of the moon, so that they should give light in it. For the glory of God gives it light, and its lamp is the Lamb. 24 And the nations will walk by its light, and the kings of the earth bring their glory into it. 25 And its gates may never no never be closed by day, for there will not be night. 26 And they will bring the glory and the honor of the nations into it. 27 And never no never may enter into it anything defiling, and those practicing anything detestable to God, and a lie; only those being written in the book of life of the Lamb.

Revelation 22:1–5, And he showed me a river of water of life radiant as crystal, going out of the throne of God and of the Lamb. 2 The river was in the middle of the broad street. On this side and on that side a tree of life producing twelve fruits according to month, each giving its fruit. And the leaves of the tree for healing the nations. 3 And there will not be any curse anymore. And the throne of God and of the Lamb will be in it, and his servants will serve him. 4 And they will see his face, and his name is on their foreheads. 5 And there will not be night there, and they do not have need of a lamp, and of light of the sun, because the Lord God will shine upon them; and they will rule to the ages of the ages.

All that by adoption.

Chapter Summary

A consequence of salvation is the believer's adoption as "sons of God." "Sons of God" is not gender-based, every believer, male or female, is one of the sons of God. To be one of the sons of God is to be a joint-heir with Christ, with the eternal life to enjoy the inheritance. All the saved inherit the Kingdom, but only the New Testament church is identified in Scripture as adopted and as joint-heirs with Christ.

Security and Assurance of Salvation

The permanence of the state of salvation (security) and the believer's confidence (assurance) that their personal state of salvation is permanent, are distinct doctrines. However, the state of one's assurance of a permanent salvation is deeply affected by one's confidence that salvation once gained is permanent and secure. This chapter will examine the security of salvation from seven perspectives. Then, I will examine the believer's assurance of salvation.

SEVEN PERSPECTIVES OF SALVATION'S SECURITY

1. Christ's Propitiation Of God For Sin

If one understands Christ's propitiation of God for sin, then one has a firm foundation for understanding the permanence of salvation, that is, its security. Jesus Christ on the cross made a complete and completed legal satisfaction to God for every past, present, and future crime of every sin every human being ever has or ever will commit. Jesus Christ made a legal satisfaction to God for the moral crime of not being in the image and likeness of God in which human beings were created—which is to say, possessing a sin attribute in his or her human nature. Jesus Christ made a legal satisfaction to God for the legal crime of committing acts of sinning.

Although I said this in the chapter "Christ's Propitiation of God," it bears repeating. Propitiation is not redemption. Christ's propitiation, his legal satisfaction of God's justice and holiness for sin, it is not in itself salvation. To be salvation, Christ's legal satisfaction for sin must be applied by God's grace through the sinner's faith in God and God's testimony as to the way of salvation. God's grace + the sinner's faith + the limitless merit of Christ's propitiation = salvation.

2. The Scripture Testimony For Security

Therefore, because Christ's propitiation was and is the only complete legal satisfaction of God for sin, the propitiation is the one and only foundation for the security of salvation. First John 2:2 teaches the eternal security of the believer's salvation. "Now he is propitiation for our sins." The "our" is not only John's audience, and John himself, but includes all believers out of every age of humankind during the entire history of salvation: from the first saved person forward to the last person saved before the end of this present universe.

John states "all our sins." The are no exceptions or exclusions stated. Every sin past, present, and future. If, as is the case, "he is propitiation for our sins," then there is no sin the believer has done, is doing, or will do that will take them out of their salvific relationship with God, because Christ made propitiation for that sin. That is the endless security of salvation.

In 1 John 2:1, John states, "if anyone should commit an act of sinning, we have one who represents us with the Father, Jesus Christ the righteous." Whatever act of sinning a believer might commit, Christ represents that sinner before God the Father as the one who propitiated God for that sin. As the believer's legal representative, Jesus Christ acknowledges to the Father that one of his saved people has sinned, and presents the limitless merit of his propitiation as judicial payment for that crime.

3. Jesus is the Believer's High Priest

Jesus functions as the believer's high priest and makes an acceptable intercession on behalf of the believer for that sin. Jesus as high priest and intercessor is also taught by the Hebrews Writer.

> Hebrews 5:3, So also Christ did not glorify himself to become a high priest, but the One having said to him, "You are my son, today I have begotten you." 6 Just as also in another place he says, "You: a priest for the age according to the order of Melchizedek."

> Hebrews 7:23–25, And truly, those many [sons of Aaron] being made priests, through death are prevented from continuing. 24 But through his [Christ's] abiding to the age, he holds an unchangeable priesthood. 25 Wherefore also, he is able to forever save all those drawing near to God through him, always living to intercede for them.

The illustration the Hebrews Writer gives, in Hebrews 9, are the Day of Atonement sacrifices by Israel's high priest.

> Hebrews 9:7 But into the second [the Holy of Holies] the high priest, only once in the year, not without blood, which he offers for himself and the errors of the people

> Hebrews 9:11–12, But when Christ appeared as high priest of the good things having now come, through the greater and more perfect tabernacle not made by hands, that is, not of this creation, 12 nor by the blood of goats and young bullocks, but through his own blood entered once for all into the holies,

having obtained eternal redemption.

Hebrews 10:12, But this one [Christ], having offered one sacrifice for sins in perpetuity, sat down at the right hand of God, 13 hence forward expecting until his enemies may be placed as a footstool for his feet. 14 For by one offering he has completed continually those being sanctified.

One of the rituals during the Day of Atonement is one animal was sacrificed as judicial payment for sins, and the other animal was taken outside the camp and set free. The illustration is sin is forgiven and forgotten. That is the endless security of salvation.

We see then, that Jesus Christ is the believer's ever living high priest, who continuously intercedes for his sinning people, and effects forgiveness for their sinning, based on the limitless merit of his propitiation. That is the endless security of salvation.

4. Jesus Keeps His Saved People Saved

Jesus Christ made an unmistakably clear statement that he acts to maintain the salvation of his saved people. John 10:26–29.

... my sheep hear my voice, and I know them, and they follow me, 28 and I give them life eternal; and never no never will they perish for the age; and never will anyone take them out of my hand. 29 My Father who has given them to me is greater than all; and no one is able to take them out of the Father's hand. 30 I and the Father are one."

Christ says he knows his sheep; his sheep follow him; he gives his sheep eternal life; because he has given his sheep eternal life they will never no never perish.

In English two negatives imply a positive. In the Koine Greek dialect in which the New Testament was written two negatives emphasize the negative. That phrase "never no never" is the translation of two negatives, *ou mē*. Never (*ou*) no never (*mē*), literally "never not." The first negative states the event absolutely cannot happen, the second negative implies such a thing could not exist. Though some might think there is a possibility (*mē*) of a believer losing his or her salvation, the loss of salvation is absolutely impossible (*ou*).

Christ also says never (*ou*, the absolute negative) will anyone take any one of his saved people out of his hand. Christ says God the Father, who gave Christ his saved people, also keeps the saved in the state of salvation because *oudeís*, not even one (not another person, not the believer), is "is able to take them out of the Father's hand." Then Christ states his oneness with God the Father—his own deity nature and the fact he and the Father are one God—as the guarantee of eternal security of salvation. Salvation once gained cannot be lost; that is the endless security of salvation.

5. A Believer Is Habitually Abiding In Christ

The Christian's path in the world is difficult. As someone has said, the Christian life is uphill all the way. Occasionally a believer steps off the path—he or she commits an act of sinning. Has that act of sinning caused the believer to lose salvation? Some think it does.

The believer knows from scripture that acts of sinning will occur, 1 John 1:8—2:2.

> If we should say that we have no sin, we deceive ourselves and the truth is not in us. 9 If we continue to confess our sins, he is faithful and righteous to forgive us the sins, and to cleanse us from every unrighteousness. 10 If we should say that we have not sinned, and as a result are not now sinning, we make him a liar, and his word is not in us.

> 2:1 My little children, I am writing these things to you that you may not commit acts of sinning. Now if anyone should commit an act of sinning, we have one who represents us with the Father, Jesus Christ the righteous. 2 Now he is propitiation for our sins—but not for ours only but also for all the world.

What is it John says about acts of sinning?

In 1:8 John states every believer has the sin attribute resident in their born-again human nature.

In 1:10 John says every believer does in fact commit acts of sinning.

In 1:9 John tells us how to react to an act of sinning: confession of the act and faith God forgives.

In 2:1 John says when there is an act of sinning, Jesus Christ the righteous represents the believer before God the Father.

In 2:2 John tells us the basis for Christ's representation, and why acts of sinning can be forgiven, by the complete satisfaction (propitiation) for sin Jesus made on the cross: the propitiation of God's holiness and justice against sin.

The limitless merit that saved the sinner is the same merit that forgives the sinning believer, thereby maintaining the believer's salvation.

But, says someone, 1 John 3:9 says believers do not sin, therefore when we commit an act of sinning we are no longer believers, until we confess our sin and God restores our salvation.

Which translation of 1 John 3:9 one reads makes a difference.

> KJV, Whosoever is born of God doth not commit sin; for his seed remaineth in him: and he cannot sin, because he is born of God.

> NKJV, Whoever has been born of God does not sin, for His seed remains in him; and he cannot sin, because he has been born of God.

> NIV, No one who is born of God will continue to sin, because God's seed remains in him; he cannot go on sinning, because he has been born of God.

> ESV, No one born of God makes a practice of sinning, for God's seed abides in him, and he cannot keep on sinning because he has been born of God.

> JQTNT, Every person who has been born from God does not habitually practice sin, because his seed abides in him, and he is not able to habitually sin, because from God he is born.

If the translation is "does not commit sin ... cannot sin," then the conclusion must be that if an act of sinning is committed then the person is no longer born of God: he has lost his salvation. The only security is to never commit an act of sinning.

Of course, translations such as the KJV/NKJV contradict 1 John 1:10, "If we say should that we have not sinned, and as a result are not now sinning, we make him [God] a liar, and the truth is not in us." No Christian is sinless during this mortal life.

The correct translation is "does not habitually practice sin ... he is not able to habitually sin." Acknowledging believers commit acts of sinning leads to the conclusion an act of sinning does not cause loss of salvation. (Loss of fellowship, yes, until 1 John 1:9; 2:1. Loss of relationship, aka: salvation, no.)

Thus, the translation issue is an interpretation issue. The translation issue is this, how should the present tense of the Greek verbs in 1 John 3:9 be expressed in translation. All the verbs in 3:9 are in the present tense. What does the Greek present tense express? The

Greek present tense gives an action a linear/progressive/in process/ongoing aspect. I study the Bible: I am continually (not continuously) studying the Bible; studying the Bible is an ongoing event in my life; I habitually study the Bible.

(The word "continuous" refers to something that happens without interruption or ceasing. "Continual" refers to something that recurs frequently or regularly.)

There is a debate amongst the Language Experts, which is reflected in the translations listed above. You may read about this issue in my commentary on John's Epistles, Appendix one.

Most readers do not have an understanding of the Koine Greek language. So let us interact with this issue using the context, without the necessity of knowing the grammatical and syntactical technicalities of the Greek text. The interaction between three indisputable facts indicates the believer habitually lives In righteousness but occasionally sins:

> First, there is the context of 1:5–10. Fellowship with Christ requires no sinning (walking in the light as he is in the light), 1:7, but believers have sin and may commit acts of sinning, 1:8, 10. Fellowship is restored by 1:9. The tension between 1:8, 9, and 10 reveals the believer may occasionally sin but habitually remains in fellowship.

> Second, there are the many exhortations in the Scripture to live righteously, indicating there are times when a believer does not live righteously, the opposite being that believers usually do live righteously. Therefore righteous living is the normal, i.e., habitual state of the Christian.

> Third, there is the immediate context of 3:6. The person who is abiding is the one who does not sin. If one is not abiding then he/she will be sinning. Thus, a believer may sin, but will not sin when abiding. Abiding is to be the habitual state of believers.

Setting aside, for a moment, the ongoing meaning of the present tense, John says, "Whoever abides in Christ does not sin." The opposite must be true: whoever is not abiding in him does sin. Therefore an occasion of sinning is inversely related to the habit of abiding. Sinning is habitual when not abiding; not sinning is habitual when abiding. All this from the context, without resort to technical questions of grammar and syntax.

This was the conclusion Augustine came to. Augustine lived AD 354–430 and, although his native language was Latin, he also spoke the Greek of the day, and was probably more familiar with the Koine Greek of the Bible than the moderns of today. He wrote, "In so far as he [the believer] abideth in Him [Christ], in so far he sinneth not" [Schaff, *NPNF, First Series,* 7:485, *Ten Homilies on the First Epistle of John,* homily IV].

I understand Augustine's comment to mean when the believer is abiding in Christ he/she is not committing acts of sinning. During those times when a believer is not abiding, he/she is committing acts of sinning. The conclusion is that not sinning is as habitual as abiding, acts of sinning are as occasional as not abiding. An interpretation from the context supports a view of the present tense at 1 John 3:6 as having an ongoing kind of action, i.e., habitual.

Therefore I agree those persons recognized in their day as Language Authorities. Westcott wrote [104], "it [*ouch hamartanei*] describes a character, 'a prevailing habit,' and not primarily an act." Wuest wrote, "The tense of the verb is present, the kind of action, continuous, habitual" [Wuest, *Word Studies,* 2:147]. Robertson wrote [6:222], "Sinneth not (*ouch hamartanei*). Linear present active indicative of *hamartánō,* 'does not keep on sinning.' Whosoever sinneth (*ho hamartanōn*) [is] 'the one who keeps on sinning' (lives a life of sin, not mere occasional acts of sin) ... The habit of sin is proof that one has not the vision or knowledge of Christ." The opposite must be true: the habit of not sinning is proof that one has the knowledge of Christ.

Another question arises from the above discussion. If a believer is not abiding, does that indicate a loss of salvation? The Greek word translated abide or abiding is *ménō* [Zodhiates, s. v. 3306], "to remain, abide, dwell, live." Like many words it is used in several contexts with some variation of meaning, the concept of semantic range. Semantic range is illustrated in these examples: I ran a mile, I ran a business, I ran him down with a car, I ran her down with gossip.

When looking at *ménō,* sometimes it means to remain forever, sometimes it means to be in or out of fellowship. Examples.

> Forever. 1 Peter 1:23, having been born-again not from corruptible seed but by the not-corruptible word of God which lives and abides forever.
>
> Fellowship. 1 John 2:28, And now, little children, abide in him,

that when he appears we may have confidence, and not be put to shame before him at his coming.

In 1 John 3:9, the thing that is abiding permanently is "God's seed." The Greek word translated seed is *spérma*, meaning what is sown, the germ of new fruit, or what is growing out of what was sown, i.e., the product of the seed [Zodhiates, s. v. 4690]. The use at 3:9 is obviously figurative. The reference to "born from God" indicates the regeneration of the soul through being given eternal life. Eternal life is the seed that prevents habitual sinning. Eternal life regenerates the believer's human nature to be like Christ. This seed constantly remains, dwells, continues, and lives in the believer. That eternal life Christ gives his saved people cannot lead a believer to sin but does lead a believer to choose righteousness.

Eternal life is also the power to deny temptation. The godly attributes of eternal life never influence the will to choose sin. Their action in human nature is to strongly influence the will to deny sin and decide for God. When the believer abides in fellowship with Christ he/she does not sin, because God's seed—the eternal life, the born-again nature—cannot sin. When the believer is out of fellowship, i.e., not abiding, acts of sinning will occur, because the sin attribute, still present in the believer's human nature, is always trying to influence the will to choose sinning. Paul names this decision to sin the old man or the flesh, which may be defined as sin acting out through mind and body. The sin attribute influences the will to decide against the influence of the godly life attributes God has regenerated in human nature through salvation.

Therefore, because that eternal life God gives the believer abides, remains, dwells forever, having regenerated the believer's human nature, an occasional act of sinning cannot cause that eternal life to leave the believer, the born-again soul cannot become un-born-again.

6. Continual Cleansing From Sin

There is another scripture that is seldom brought into the discussion of the endless security of salvation, but should be. That Scripture is 1 John 1:7, "... the blood of Jesus Christ his Son is continually cleansing us from every sin." My translation gives the sense, "continually cleansing," because the verb here is in the present indicative, indicating an action continually taking place. The meaning is cleansing from sin takes place when an act of sinning has occurred. Looking at all of 1:7, cleansing from sin takes place whenever a believer is not ordering his or her behavior in the light that is God (1:5), so that the believer may continue to order his or her behavior in the light.

The tension between committing acts of sinning and not committing acts of sinning, is resolved by three facts.

> One. The present tense of the verbs in 1 John 3:9 tell us a believer habitually lives a righteous life but occasionally commits an act of sinning.

> Two. God's seed, that eternal life Christ gives his saved people, John 10:28, and thereby regenerates the saved human nature, remains, continues, lives, abides in the believer without cessation or interruption.

> Three. The limitless merit of Jesus Christ, 1 John 2:1–2, forgives acts of sinning, and thereby maintains the believer's salvation.

A believer in Christ cannot lose his or her salvation by committing an act of sinning.

7. Salvation is an Unconditional Covenant

In all things relating to the genuine Christian faith there is God's responsibility and our responsibility. God's responsibility is to maintain our salvation, that he has promised, John 8:27–30. Our responsibility is to believe and live like Christ. Sometimes believers fail in their responsibility. But salvation is an unconditional covenant between Christ and God, Hebrews 2:13, "Look, I and the children whom God has given me"; 5:5; 7:21–22, 25; 10:12. The definition of an unconditional covenant, which may be verified by examining all the covenants in Scripture (only the Mosaic covenant is conditional) is that God will unfailingly fulfill his responsibilities, even if the believer experiences failure in his responsibilities.

Summary

There is a principle of interpretation that applies to the endless security of salvation: never reinterpret a clear scripture with one that is not as clear. There are several scriptures one might interpret as saying salvation may be lost. However, the clear scriptures, some of which I examined in this chapter, teach salvation cannot be lost.

An excellent work on this subject is A.W. Pink, *Eternal Security*. Next, I will examine assurance of salvation.

THE ASSURANCE OF SALVATION.

In his first letter, John the apostle confidently states a believer can know he or she is saved. First John 5:13, "These things I have written to you, in order for you to have assurance that you do possess eternal life, to you who believe on the name of the Son of God." What things did John write that give assurance?

1:7, if we habitually order our behavior in the light, as he is in the light, we have fellowship with one another, and the blood of Jesus Christ his Son is continually cleansing us from every sin.

1:9, If we continue to confess our sins, he is faithful and righteous to forgive us the sins, and to cleanse us from every unrighteousness.

2:3, Now in this we know that we have come to know him: if his commandments we are continually keeping.

2:6, the person claiming to abide in him is obligated, even as he lived his life, also himself to behave in the same manner.

2:10, The person habitually loving his brother abides in the light, and there is no cause for stumbling in him.

2:17, the person habitually doing God's will abides for the age.

2:23, Every person who is denying the Son, neither has he the Father. The person who is confessing the Son has the Father also.

2:24–27, That which each one of you have heard from the beginning, let it constantly abide in you. If that which you have heard from the beginning should abide in you, you will also abide in the Son and in the Father. 25 Now this is the promise that he promised us: the eternal life. 26 These things I have written to you concerning those leading you astray. 27 And you, the anointing that you received from him abides in you, and you have no constant need that anyone should continuously teach you, but as the same anointing teaches you about all things, and is true and is not a lie, and just as it has taught you, you will be constantly abiding in him.

2:29, If you understand that he is righteous, you also know that every person habitually practicing righteousness is born from him.

3:6, Every person habitually abiding in him is not habitually sinning. Every person habitually sinning has not discerned him, nor does he know him.

3:9, Every person who has been born from God does not habitually practice sin, because his seed abides in him, and he is not able to habitually sin, because from God he is born.

3:14, We know with certainty we have permanently passed out of death to life, because we are habitually loving the brethren.

3:18, Little children we should not love in word or in speech, but in action and truth. 19 In this we will know that we are of the truth, and will quiet our heart in his presence.

3:24, the person habitually keeping his commandments, abides in him, and he in him; and by this we know that he abides in us, from the Spirit whom he gave to us.

4:7, Beloved ones, let us be habitually loving one another, because love is from God; and every person who is habitually loving has been born from God and knows God.

4:15, Whoever confesses that Jesus Christ is the Son of God, God in him abides, and he in God.

5:2, In this we know that we are habitually loving the children of God: when we habitually love God, and his commandments we are habitually doing.

5:3–4, For this is the love for God, that his commandments we are habitually obeying; and his commandments are not heavy burdens. 4 Because every person born from God constantly overcomes the world; and this is the victory that is constantly overcoming the world: our faith.

5:10–12, The person believing on the Son of God has the testimony in himself; the person not believing God has made him a liar and presently considers him a liar, because he has not believed in the testimony that God has testified concerning his Son. 11 Now this is the testimony: that God gave us eternal life, and this life is in his Son. 12 The person who has the Son has life. The person not having the Son of God does not have life.

5:18, We know that everyone having been born from God does not keep on habitually sinning. But rather, the One having been born from God guards him, and the evildoer does not influence him.

John has a "yes or no" view of the Christian life. One believes the right doctrine, or is not saved. One habitually does God's will, or is not saved. One practices his life according to God's moral values, principles, and applicable precepts, or is not saved. However, John also recognizes acts of sinning will occur, 1 John 1:8–2:2, and so his "yes or no" view of salvation is saying the normal, habitual manner of the Christian's life gives assurance of salvation.

If your Christian life is not the normal, habitual practice of righteousness, then you should "examine yourselves if you are in the faith; put yourselves to the proof. Or do you not yourselves really know that Jesus Christ is in you, unless you are without proof?" 2 Corinthians 13:5. The following discusses five ways to examine yourself.

In conclusion to this section, salvation is not gained by works and salvation cannot be lost by works. The grace of God and the limitless merit of Christ that saves the sinner is greater than good or evil works.

How Can I Know I Am A Christian?

In the chapter "Saving Faith, Forgiveness, Eternal Life, Regeneration," I briefly gave "Five Characteristics Of The Saved Person." Here are those same characteristics, but in greater detail in relation to assurance of salvation.

1. What is my relationship with Jesus?

There should be a definite time or moment in every Christian's life when he or she was able to say with conviction, Jesus is "My Savior." For some it may have been an intensely personal moment when they understood they were a desperate sinner facing punishment from God, and only faith in Jesus Christ could save their soul. For others it may have been a very emotional moment when God flooded their soul with the magnificence of his presence and the joy of their salvation through faith in Jesus. For some it may have been a quiet moment when God spoke to their soul and said, "I am your God and Savior." Whether the moment was dramatic or quiet, a Christian should be able to remember a definite moment when he or she believed on Jesus and received him as "My Savior." The memory need not include all the details, but a Christian should remember the experience of salvation.

The believer delights to worship the One God who is Father-Son-Holy Spirit. Worship is more than singing songs and listening to sermons. Worship happens inside our heart and mind. Singing a song or listening to a sermon is just a way for the believer to pour out his love, worship, and praise of God. Worship is focusing the heart and mind on God, in order to applaud him for who he is and thank him for what he has done. Worship is praising God as worthy of honor, and glory, and blessing, because he is God, because he made me, because he saved me. Worship is recognizing that God has power, and riches, and wisdom, and strength. Worship is saying that God is in charge and I am his servant. Believers sincerely want to take time in their life to stop everything they are doing and focus everything on God.

The believer actively seeks to have fellowship with God, and keeps on seeking even when he feels he is failing. Fellowship means you share your life and feelings with God. Fellowship means you ask him for guidance in everyday matters, and thank him for all the things that happen. Fellowship means taking time to speak to God in prayer, listen to him from the Bible, and worship him under all circumstances. Fellowship with God—having God as a friend—means sharing things in common with God: love for Christ, a righteous life, good works, a moral character, kindness toward others, sharing the gospel. Christians think about God a lot, and want him to be a part of everything they do. Believers want God to be a part of their life, and believers ask God to be a part of their life.

When you are a believer you want to serve God. How do you serve God? Some people stand up in front of others and speak about Jesus and the Bible. But most serve in ways that don't get much attention. They are part of a ministry, such as to children, seniors, or other adults. They might change diapers in the nursery, or clean the church building after services. Some spend a lot of time praying for others. Some teach a Bible study. Some play piano, some lead singing, some sing, some devote themselves to worship and praise. There are many ways to serve. How a person serves is much less important than wanting to serve and finding some way to serve. The Christian believes God is in charge, that he wants the believer to serve him, and therefore he will show believers how and where and when to serve him. The believer has a very strong desire to serve God.

The Christian knows that loving God and living for God requires supra-natural power from God. That power is present when a person has a relationship with the Father and Holy Spirit through the Son. Simple faith in the death and resurrection of the Son saves the person from the penalty, power, and pleasure of sin. The Holy Spirit enables the Christian to understand God's word and do the works of God. The believer seeks that power, depends on it, and uses it to live for God.

The unsaved person tries to build a relationship with God by trying to be the best person he or she can be. But good works don't create salvation; faith in Jesus as "My Savior" is what saves. Works come after salvation because they are the product of salvation. A person's good works don't maintain their salvation; the work of the Son and the Spirit keep the saved person saved. The saved person continues to worship, fellowship with, obey, and serve God because of their relationship with God through faith in Jesus Christ as Savior.

2. How important is the Bible?

In the Bible God says: this is who I am; this is who you are; this is what I want you to believe; this is how I want you to live. The Bible is important to the Christian. In the Bible the believer discovers more about God and more about him or herself. In the Bible the believer learns how to live for God by following God's rules and living by God's values. In the Bible the Christian sees how others lived and learns from their (good or bad) example. The Bible has God's instructions for living the Christian life.

The Bible is important to the Christian because the Christian has a strong desire to learn about God: who he is, what he has done, how to live for him. God's existence can be seen in the world he has created, but knowledge about God is found only in the Bible, because in the Bible God has revealed himself.

The Christian knows the Bible is food for the soul that keeps him or her spiritually healthy and leads to spiritual maturity. To the Christian it is important to spend time reading, studying, and learning from the Bible. The Bible calls this "growing in knowledge." However, the Christian knows that knowledge is not enough. The Christian wants to be like Jesus. He knows the Holy Spirit works through the Bible to tell him how to live like Jesus lived: to be completely dependent on God for worship, fellowship, obedience, and service to God. Only the Bible can tell him these things, only the Holy Spirit can help him understand these things, and only the Spirit can give the spiritual power the believer needs to live for God. The Bible is very important to the Christian. The Christian reads his Bible often. When he reads it, he wants to learn what it says so he can do what it says.

The Bible is important for personal, private worship. Through the Bible the believer focuses his heart and mind on God. He praises and worships God for who God is and what he has done. Reading and studying, learning and understanding the Bible will always lead the believer to worship and praise God. The Christian understands the Bible is a very important part of his or her life.

3. Do I like being with fellow believers?

The Christian enjoys and seeks out the company of other believers. He or she wants to be with others who believe in and serve the same God and Christ. When the believer has God for his friend, then he wants to know and be with others who also have God for their friend. The believer values the company, friendship, and advice of his saved friends above that of his unsaved friends.

The Christian wants to participate in public worship with others who believe as he believes and worship as he worships. Their common faith in the same God and Christ draw believers together, so they can together worship and praise God. The Christian strongly desires to be with other believers and join his or her worship to theirs.

The Christian enjoys being part of a group of believers who serve God. They know that their unity in faith, fellowship, and service bring honor to God. Together they supply a joint witness that God is worthy of faith and worship, and worthy of fellowship, obedience, and service. The Christian really wants to be with others of like precious faith, and really enjoys their company.

4. Do I live according to God's Rules?

A relationship with God changes a person. The saved person values the things of God more than the things they have in the world. A Christian wants to know God's values and follow God's rules for living. The world has a set of philosophies about how to live one's life: a world view. The Christian believes in and strives to follow God's view. The Christian genuinely wants to do what God says is right. In the Bible God defines "do right" for the Christian life.

The Christian reads these rules and understands that they apply to his or her life. Most of God's rules are plain and simple. For example, do not steal or lie, run away from sexual immorality, honor your parents, don't be intoxicated with alcohol or drugs, value God above everyone and everything else. These and the other "do this" and "don't do that" rules of the biblical, godly way of living are easy to understand.

Above I spoke of the biblical, godly way of living. What is godliness? God living and active in humanity, humanity acting and living according to God's values. Godliness may be described as thought, will, and action that conforms the believer's manner of life to the moral, holy, and righteous standard set by God's own character. In simpler terms, to be Christ-like. God takes delight in those whose character and actions reflect his character and actions. God's character defines the worth of the actions performed by all beings: they are godly or ungodly.

Godliness is not naturally generated by the believing soul, but depends on the work of the Holy Spirit through the grace he gives to all believers to live a godly life pleasing to God. While it is true a life of faith is the product of God's grace, it is also true that a lot of personal effort must be expended in order to live a godly and righteous life. There is a cost to living a life of faith: denying the temptations of sin in the mind and flesh; alienation from the world and worldly practices; separation from sinning and sinners engaged in sin; caution in one's relationships with sinners.

The Bible requires moral, ethical, and sexual purity in the way that God, not the world, defines these things. God's values are not hard to find in the Bible. The Christian seeks out God's rules for living in the Bible and depends on God the Holy Spirit for the moral and spiritual power to live as God wants him or her to live. The genuine Christian earnestly desires to live according to God's rules for living, and makes every effort to make those rules active in his or her life.

5. Does Sin and Sinning bother me?

Sin and sinning really bother the Christian. The believer hates sin because God hates sin. The believer defines sin just like God defines sin. Sin is doing what I want to do, just because I don't want to do what God says. Sin is doing what I think is right not what God says is right. Sin is pleasing myself, not pleasing God. The Christian's whole-hearted desire is to want the things God wants and to do the things that please God.

Sometimes believers are so tempted by sin that they do the sin. Temptation is not sin, sinning is sin. Sometimes believers follow temptation into sin. When a believer does sin he or she knows they have done wrong. When a believer sins he or she feels as though they have disappointed God. There are feelings of "I am guilty," and feelings of shame (or embarrassment). The sinning believer doesn't like what he has done, and may wonder if God can still like him. That is because a sin forms a spiritual barrier between the believer and God. The sinning believer is still God's saved child—a parent does not disown their child just because he has done something wrong. But friendly relations between the believer and God are strained by sin. God must, because he is God, convict the believer of his wrong-doing and lead the believer back to fellowship.

When a believer sins God convicts him that he (or she) has sinned. This leads to the desire to leave that sin behind and return to fellowship with God. The believer can recover from sin and be restored to fellowship with God because Jesus has already paid for that sin on the cross. What God requires from the sinning believer is confession and repentance. Confession is agreeing with God that I have sinned. Repentance is turning my back on the sin by turning myself to face God. God teaches the path to recovery in a simple verse, 1 John 1:9: if the believer confesses his or her sin (confession includes repentance), God himself is faithful and just to cleanse the believer from the sin, and restore him or her to fellowship.

The genuine Christian thinks about obeying God. His or her desire is to obey God by not sinning. The believer is strongly bothered by sin and sinning. The believer actively resists the temptation to commit an act of sin. He doesn't want to sin. He doesn't want to sin because he doesn't want to disappoint God and he doesn't like how he feels when he sins. Sometimes the believer does sin. When a believer sins he (or she) is bothered by the sin. The believer knows sin injures his fellowship with God. The believer looks to God's way of recovery (1 John 1:9) so he can get rid of the "guilty" of the sin and return to fellowship with God.

How can I know I am a Christian?

How have you answered the five questions? Is God—Father, Son, Spirit—significant to your daily life? Is reading and doing what the Bible says important in how you live your life? Do you really desire the company of other Christians? Do you think about how God wants you to live? Do sin and sinning always bother you? If the answer is "No," then you are probably not a Christian. To be a Christian begins with a relationship with God through faith in Jesus as Savior. Ask God for his gift of grace-faith-salvation, accept the gift from him, and receive Jesus Christ as "My Savior."

Chapter Summary

The security and assurance of salvation troubles some believers. This chapter addresses the issues in depth.

Security of salvation. Seven perspectives on security are given and explained by which the believer may know salvation is endless. Those reasons are:

1. Christ's Propitiation Of God For Sin
2. The Scripture Testimony For Security
3. Jesus is the Believer's High Priest
4. Jesus Keeps His Saved People Saved
5. A Believer Is Habitually Abiding In Christ
6. Continual Cleansing From Sin
7. Salvation is an Unconditional Covenant

The testimony of the Scripture is clear, salvation once gained cannot be lost.

Assurance of salvation. The apostle John stated, 1 John 5:13, "These things I have written to you, in order for you to have assurance that you do possess eternal life, to you who believe on the name of the Son of God." Twenty passages from John's letter are given demonstrating how the believer may be assured of his salvation. John recognizes acts of sinning will occur, 1 John 1:8–2:2, and so is saying the normal, habitual manner of the Christian's life gives assurance of salvation.

The section on assurance concludes with five characteristics of the saved person, by which a believer may evaluate and confirm his assurance and security.

Perseverance and Experiential Sanctification

Introduction

The grace to persevere in the faith by means of faith, and the choice to deny sin and choose righteousness—experiential sanctification—are closely related in the Christian life.

Defining Perseverance

In the chapter on positional justification and sanctification, I wrote in detail about experiential sanctification. Here, a brief definition.

> Experiential sanctification. That on-going process whereby the believer strives to become in daily living that which he or she is by salvation in Christ: holy and righteous.

Experiential sanctification, then, is the work of the Holy Spirit and the believer to conform the believer to be like Christ during this mortal life.

What is the definition of perseverance? There are two aspects to perseverance: persevering grace and persevering faith.

> Perseverance is a grace God gives the believer to overcome all spiritual and physical obstacles to faith and persevering faith is the believer using the means of grace God has provided for him or her to continue in the faith by faith.

The relationship between perseverance and experiential sanctification is this:

> The grace of perseverance is the cause of experiential sanctification, and experiential sanctification is the means by which one exercises persevering faith.

God tells his saved people to persevere, and he gives his saved people every grace and spiritual power necessary to be able to persevere. By means of the grace of perseverance, every believer will persevere in the faith by means of faith all the way throughout life and through physical death into the endless life yet to come. Perseverance in the faith is guaranteed by God's gift of persevering grace. Perseverance in the faith by faith is accomplished by means of experiential sanctification.

Experiential Sanctification

What is experiential sanctification? The positionally sanctified believer uses the means of grace to conform his manner of living (thoughts and actions) to be more like Christ. (The "means of grace" might be defined as worship of God, fellowship with God, obedience to God, and service for God. To properly do those things requires attention to the Word of God.) God has given the believer new and eternal life, but has left the old nature (the sin nature) resident in the flesh. The new life a believer has is a product of grace and is maintained by grace, but requires personal effort to apply that grace so as to overcome the temptation of sin.

Experiential sanctification is the believer's state before God in the world. One lives his or her life in such a manner so as to conform one's lifestyle to be godly and Christ-like. The believer makes a conscious effort to bring his state in the world to the same level of godliness, holiness, and righteousness as his standing in Christ. This is a life-long process in which the believer should steadily progress. A stairway illustrates the believers' progress in experiential sanctification. We learn, we practice what we learned (standing on a step), we progress (going up a step), sometimes we go down a step, we learn, we practice, we progress, etc. throughout life.

The work of experiential sanctification is through the spiritual empowerment of the born-again human nature to say "No" to temptation, and enforce the decision, resulting in a habitually righteous life. Saying "No" and enforcing that decision is the exercise of persevering grace. Perseverance is also the grace that causes the sinning believer to respond to conviction (or chastisement) with repentance and confession, by faith knowing God will cleanse and restore. "By faith" is a scripture term for the grace of perseverance (see Hebrews 11).

Believers may stumble in sin by choosing to commit acts of sinning in response to temptation. Persevering grace is why the sinning believer responds by faith in repentance and confession. Persevering grace given by God always puts sinning believers back on their feet, persevering grace keeps them on the path of righteousness, where by persevering grace and faith they continue their earthly walk in righteousness.

(There is a final aspect to sanctification known as Final Sanctification or Eternal Sanctification. Eternal sanctification is that transformation of soul and body that occurs in the soul at physical death and in the body at the resurrection. Eternal sanctification eliminates the sin attribute in body and soul. In eternal sanctification the believer's positional and experiential sanctification becomes identical. In every aspect of his or her life, for all eternity, the believer possesses godliness, holiness, and righteousness in every desire, every thought, and every action, sustained by God's grace.)

GOD'S COMMAND TO PERSEVERE

If perseverance in the faith is certain, then why does God command his saved people to persevere? Because that is the way of all God's graces. Grace is God choosing to bless because he wants to bless, although blessing is undeserved. Grace brings salvation, thanksgiving, knowledge, wisdom, ministry, hope, strength, justification, sanctification, and perseverance: Titus 2:11; 2 Corinthians 4:15; 1 Corinthians 1:3; 2 Corinthians 1:12; Ephesians 4:7; 2 Thessalonians 2:16; 2 Corinthians 12:9; Romans 5:17; Ephesians 1:6; Hebrews 10:30; 11:4–29 ("by faith").

However, God's grace also requires man's response. Grace does not exclude the responsibility to positively respond to the grace provided, the accountability for how the grace provided is used, and the liability for misuse. See Acts 16:31; Romans 10:11–13; 2 Corinthians 5:10; 1 Corinthians 3:11–15.

Let us look at two applications of God's grace. The first is salvation. God's gift of grace-faith-salvation, Ephesians 2:8, is the origin and source of salvation, but the exercise of saving faith, though the inevitable result of God's efficacious grace, is also the duty of the person receiving that grace, Acts 16:31; Romans 10:13. The Scripture insists God is the origin and source of salvation, "not from works, so that no one should boast." Yet the Scripture also insists the sinner must exercise saving faith in order to be saved.

> Acts 16:30–31, "Sirs, what is necessary to do that I may be saved?" 31 And they said, "Believe on the Lord Jesus, and you will be saved, you and your household."
>
> Romans 10:11–13, For the scripture says, "All believing on him will not be put to shame." 12 For there is no distinction between Jewish and Greek, for the same Lord of all is rich toward all those calling him. 13 For all that may call upon the Lord's name will be saved.

Therefore, saving faith is by God's grace through sinner's faith. Both are required for salvation. As I explained in the chapter,

"Responding to the Good News," God's grace changes the spiritual boundaries of the sinner's human nature, by removing the dominion of sin and enlivening the soul's faculty of spiritual perception, so that the unable and unwilling sinner is made willing and able to respond to God's gift with the choice to exercise saving faith.

Both God's grace and the sinner's exercise of faith are required for salvation. The one, grace, inevitably leads to the other, faith, making God the origin and source for salvation. The latter, the exercise of saving faith, is the necessary consequence of receiving God's efficacious gift of grace-faith-salvation; but God does requires the freely made choice to believe in order to be saved. God's grace and man's duty to respond to God's grace in faith may seem contradictory, but the Scripture teaches both.

By God's grace are you saved through your faith, Ephesians 2:8. "By God's grace" is God's choice, "through your faith" is the sinner's choice. Though the inevitability of God's efficacious grace working in the sinner to produce faith seems contrary to the requirement, the duty, of "through your faith," the choice to believe, agrees with God designing human nature with free will. God always respects what he created, and therefore God always requires the exercise of free will in response to God's commands.

Turning from salvation to living the Christian life, believers are saved to be *doúlos* [Zodhiates, s. v. 1401], "servants, slaves," to God, and therefore are led and empowered by God's grace to be servants. However, there is a choice to be made to behave like servants. Romans 6:13, "present yourselves to God" a choice "and your members as instruments of righteousness to God." Compare Romans 6:16–19.

The relationship of God's grace and man's duty is also seen in 1 Corinthians 3:11–15. God gives grace to grow in knowledge and understanding, grace to deny temptations to sin, grace to worship, grace to have fellowship with, obey, and serve God. The Christian's duty is to study the word, apply the Word to his life, deny temptation, obey God's commands, serve God, and worship God. If the Christian should build his life by God's grace and his or her positive response to that grace, then there will be rewards. If not, then he or she will not receive rewards, but will be saved "so as through fire," 1 Corinthians 3:11–15; 2 Corinthians 5:8.

Therefore, God's gift of the grace of perseverance requires a believer's positive response to use the grace given and act to persevere.

That raises the question, what if a believer does not use the grace of perseverance to persevere?

Why God commands perseverance is the question that troubles some Christians, so much so that they have developed a doctrine that salvation can be lost if one does not act to persevere in the faith by means of faith. Without question there are many scriptures that command perseverance through obedience to God's values.

How does one respond to that doctrine? The first response is to understand that Christ's propitiation of God for human sin was really, actually, and genuinely a complete and completed legal satisfaction (propitiation) of God's holiness, justice, and wrath against the crime sin, all sin, all past, present, and future sin. The merit powering the propitiation is limitless, because it is the merit of deity, because the one who made that propitiation of God was the God-man. I have explained this in previous chapters.

The limitless merit of Christ's propitiation is why "now there is not even one condemnatory judgment to those in Christ Jesus," Romans 8:1. Why? "The law of the Spirit of life in Christ Jesus has made you free from the law of sin and of death," Romans 8:2. What is the result? "You have received a spirit of adoption by which we cry out "Abba! Father!" Romans 8:15.

God never lets go of even one of his saved people.

> John 10:28–29, "I give them life eternal; and never no never will they perish for the age; and never will anyone take them out of my hand. 29 My Father who has given them to me is greater than all; and no one is able to take them out of the Father's hand."

I do not see an exception to "anyone" or "no one" in those Scriptures. Therefore "anyone" and "no one" includes any actions taken by the believer. A believer cannot sin and lose his or her salvation, 1 John 2:1–2; Hebrews 7:25.

The principle is this: salvation is given by God and salvation is maintained by God, given and maintained by the same means: the complete and completed legal satisfaction (propitiation) of God's holiness, justice, and wrath against the crime human sin made by Jesus Christ on the cross.

Why then the many commandments to persevere? Because sin never stops tempting, and occasionally the believer says "Yes" to temptation and commits an act of sinning.

> 1 John 2:1–2, My little children, I am writing these things to you that you may not commit acts of sinning. Now if anyone should commit an act of sinning, we have one who represents us with the Father, Jesus Christ the righteous.

Therefore, the principle that effects perseverance is this: God always acts to maintain a believer's salvation, which includes the infallibility of the grace of perseverance, and the continuous reminder to persevere. That is why the believer, despite occasional failures in his duty to persevere, will never lose the grace of perseverance, and will continuously act to use that grace in order to persevere in the faith by means of faith. Both living a righteous life, and responding to conviction of sin with repentance and confession (1 John 1:9) are characteristics of God's persevering grace acting efficaciously in the believer's soul.

What, then, is the practical application of persevering faith? Experiential sanctification. The normal Christian life is this: when a believer is confronted by a temptation, he or she, by means of the grace of perseverance, through the spiritual power effected by his or her born-again human nature, will habitually respond to the temptation with "No,' and enforce that decision by choosing to maintain a righteous life.

What if the believer responds to a temptation with a "Yes?" God's grace of perseverance maintains his faith—that is its purpose—resulting in the positive response of repentance and confession to the conviction (or chastisement) given by the Holy Spirit. In other words, the grace of perseverance powers the believer's response of faith to God the Holy Spirit's efficacious work to restore intimate fellowship between the sinning believer and God in Christ.

Let us take this to the extreme. I find nothing in Scripture to support the doctrine that the grace of perseverance may be withdrawn or may become ineffective. But what if a believer becomes so rebellious that he or she persists in acts of sinning, and refuses to respond by faith to conviction and chastisement with repentance and confession? The apostle John said this also.

> 1 John 5:16–17, If anyone should see his brother sinning a sin not tending toward death, he should ask, and he will give him life—those not sinning toward death. There is a sin tending toward death; concerning that I do not say that he should ask.

17 All unrighteousness is sin; and there is a sin not tending toward death.

Should a believer persist in acts of sinning, becoming non-responsive to conviction and chastisement, then the grace of perseverance will work though the most basic principle of salvation: God is the Savior. God will maintain the believer's salvation by removing him or her from this mortal life to heaven, where "the work of this one will be burned up, he will suffer loss—but he himself will be saved; but so as through fire," 1 Corinthians 3:15. There is, as the apostle John said, "a sin tending toward death." Physical death, not spiritual death, because God is the one who maintains the salvation of his saved people.

As I said, that is an extreme case. The balance given in the Scripture is that the Holy Spirit will correct error in his saved people, though the time and ways may (usually not) be long and complicated. The grace of perseverance keeps the believer through good times and bad, as the believer uses that grace through the means of experiential sanctification to persevere in the faith by means of faith.

To require anything other than God's grace, the sinner's faith, and Christ's merit to be saved, or to require anything other than God's grace and Christ's merit to maintain salvation, is an error repugnant to the Scripture. The merit of Christ is unlimited, the grace of perseverance is never withdrawn or ineffective.

The Basis Of Persevering Faith

Because the perseverance of the believer is often disputed by those who are certain salvation may be lost, an extended discussion is warranted.

One of the phrases the Scripture uses to identify perseverance is "by faith." Examples.

Romans 1:17, "And the righteous will live by faith."

2 Corinthians 5:7, for we conduct our life by faith not by sight.

Galatians 2:20, I have been crucified with Christ. Now I live— no longer I but Christ lives in me. But now that which I live in the flesh, in faith I live—and that from the Son of God, the one having loved me and having given himself for me.

That believers will persevere in the faith by means of faith is assumed throughout the New Testament. Hebrews 10:36–11:1, which serves as the introduction to Hebrews 11, states the need for perseverance and the basis for persevering faith.

> Hebrews 10:35–39, Therefore, do not lose your confidence, which has a great reward. 36 For you have need of perseverance, so that, having done the will of God, you may receive the promise. 37 "For yet a little while, the one coming will come, and will not delay. 38 But my righteous one will live by faith; and if he might withdraw, my soul does not take pleasure in him." 39 But we are not of those withdrawing to destruction, but of faith to preserving of the soul.

Hebrews 11 is often called the hall of faith, but actually examples persevering faith for the reader's edification and encouragement. The opening verses state the basis of persevering faith.

> Hebrews 11:1, Now faith is the title deed of the things of which we are assured, the objective evidence of the things not yet seen.

And so on, 11:3, 4, 5, 7, 8, 9, 11, 17, 20, 21, 22, 23, 24, 27, 28, 29, 30, 31, "by faith": persevering grace and persevering faith.

The "things of which we are assured" in Hebrews 11:1 are the promises God has made to believers concerning the future, 10:36.

An Analysis Of Persevering Faith

Objectively, persevering faith is itself (Hebrews 11:1) the "title deed" or "substance" (*hupóstasis*) of things "of which we are assured" (*elpízō*). Put another way, persevering faith—which is the use of God-given persevering grace—is based on the real expectation of receiving God's promises as given in the Scripture, because my God-given faith is the title deed showing me the promises belong to me.

The "things of which we are assured" in Hebrews 11:1 are the promises God has made to believers concerning the future, 10:36.

The word "hope" in Scripture, *elpízō*, means to expect with assurance; the word "expect" is the key to understanding Bible-based hope. This is not the "I hope it does (or doesn't) ... " of common speech; that brand of hope indicates uncertainty, perhaps anxiety.

The hope of Scripture is certain. For example, "I hope—I know with absolute assurance—that Jesus is returning, because he who promised is faithful" (see John 14:3). So also all that God has promised the believer is by the believer expected with the absolute assurance of

God-given faith, because God-given faith is my title deed to the promises.

How then is "faith" the *hupóstasis* (title deed; substance) of the promises? The Writer's point is that God-given faith gives certainty to the promises. What is a promise? Things of which we are assured but have not seen.

God-given faith is believing God who cannot lie. God-given faith is informed by God's word and acts of the reality described by that word. God-given faith, then, is the *hupóstasis* of the promises—their substance, their present reality, a title deed—that gives certainty to the hope—the assurance—of receiving those promises.

God-given faith is the hand of the soul receiving and holding onto the genuine reality of God's promises, thereby giving unfailing assurance (hope) of receipt of the promises. God-given faith knows God's promises will be received, and acts on the reality of that assurance. That is persevering faith born of persevering grace.

How is faith itself the *hupóstasis?* The word *hupóstasis* means the real presence.

> In general, [*hupóstasis* is] that which underlies the apparent, hence, reality, essence, substance; that which is the basis of something, hence, assurance, guarantee, confidence (with the objective sense). The ground of confidence, assurance, guarantee, or proof. [Zodhiates, s. v. 5287.]

> Moulton and Milligan [659–660], give secular examples of *hupóstasis* to describe real property, thus, faith may be seen as the "title deed" of things hoped for. A title deed is the objective proof of legal possession.

A photograph or a sculpture of a person is representation. When the person is literally, physically standing before you, that is *hupóstasis*, the real presence, as seen of Christ as the person God, Hebrews 1:3, cf. John 14:9.

In Hebrews 11:1, the Writer uses *hupóstasis* in the sense of title deed, i.e., real possession. If I have the title deed to my car, house, or any real property, I have real possession whether or not the property is literally, physically before me. So faith is the title deed (*hupóstasis*), the real possession, the objective reality, of the things promised by God but not yet received, giving assurance (*elpízo*) to the expectation of receiving the promises.

By persevering faith, engendered and empowered by persevering grace, the believer persists in the faith by means of faith, all the way through this mortal life and death into the endless, everlasting life yet to come, with the fullest assurance of the reality of that yet-future life, because he/she has as their present possession the title deed to that endless, everlasting life in the immediate presence of God.

A simple in real life example. After my parents died, as the executor of their estate I tried to sell their recreational vehicle. I could not sell it without a series of legal actions to transfer the title to me. Why? The title deed said the RV was my parent's possession, and it did not matter they were dead, because it was their name on the title deed, not mine. Your name, believer, is on the title deed to heaven. The grace of perseverance keeps the title deed secure in your hand, which is in Christ's hand, which is in the Father's hand, John 10:28–29.

Objective, Holy Spirit-given faith and understanding in God and his testimony in the Scripture is the title deed that gives us the assurance of receiving God's promises. The believer's name is on the title deed, written there by God and maintained by God. This title deed cannot be transferred or otherwise destroyed, because kept in God's hands, John 8:28–30.

On the basis of the objective reality of the promises, the believer perseveres in the faith by means of faith, knowing with the assurance of Scripture's testimony that he will receive the promises contained in the title deed. Persevering faith is therefore a grace God gives that the believer may possess an objective reality of the promises, and perseverance is the grace the believer uses to persevere in that faith by means of faith.

In More Detail

The concept of faith itself being the objective reality of the promises will be new to some readers. So I will continue with the explanation.

An example of how the Hebrews Writer intends his readers to understand *hupóstasis* is in Hebrews 1:3. There the Writer says that Jesus is the visible "exact reproduction" (*charaktér*) of the *hupóstasis* (person/essence/substance) of the invisible God. The word *hupóstasis* at 1:3 means the Person God was literally present: to see Jesus was and is to see God. Jesus Christ was not a sculpture of God, not a photograph, not a hologram, not an appearance or manifestation; he was God in person, face-to-face.

As Jesus said to Philip, "The one having perceived me has perceived the Father," a statement indicative of both mental and sensual perception; compare the heard, seen, and touched of 1 John 1:1. The literal, physical presence of the incarnate God-man, Jesus the Christ, revealed the transcendent reality of the Father. Jesus the Christ is the *hupóstasis* of God: the physical, visible, audible, actual, genuine presence of the reality of God in our universe, 1 John 1:1; John 14:9. Returning to Hebrews 11:1, the presence of faith is itself the real presence (*hupóstasis*) of the things anticipated with the certainty of their appearing.

Another example of the Writer's use of *hupóstasis* is Hebrews 3:14. The Writer exhorted the believer to "hold the beginning of our *hupóstasis* (confidence) steadfast to the end." The word in the context of 3:14 could be translated "title deed," proof of possession of the property. When a believer has faith in the promise, faith is itself the title deed providing proof of possession of the promise. This is because genuine faith—title-deed kind of faith—cannot exist without conviction from the Holy Spirit.

Therefore, in Hebrews 3:14, *hupóstasis* refers to that certain reality in which one's faith is resting confident and assured. As the messenger of the confession of faith, 3:1, Jesus Christ is the real presence of the reality of God (1:3) in which believers share, 3:14 [Kittel, 8:587]. So just as Jesus Christ is the real presence of the reality of God, 1:3, so 3:1 is a description of the reality on which faith rests "from the beginning unto the end," 3:14. Even so faith in the promise, 11:1, is the reality of receiving the promise. Persevering faith is based on the objective reality of the promises and the objective certainty of receiving the promises.

In Hebrews 11:1 faith is the *hupóstasis*. This is the kind or quality of faith in which the believer perseveres. When a believer has genuine God-given faith in the promises, then the reality of those promises is always present with the believer—his faith is his title deed to the promises. Not promises wished for or wondered about, nor an anxious "I hope so," not even an expectation desiring to be fulfilled, but the steadfast assurance that the promises are real, genuine, imminent. God knows the doubts sin injects into our confidence, weakening our resolve to believe and persevere. He has given us promises, and given us faith as the title deed to the promises, to encourage us to use his grace of perseverance and persevere. By faith I am absolutely and completely assured of the reality of the things God has promised, and do in fact by the hand of faith hold them in my soul as a present reality.

In Hebrews 11:1, the word "substance," *hupóstasis*, and the word "objective evidence," *élegchos* [Zodhiates, s. v. 1650], are parallel descriptions. Faith is the *hupóstasis*, the presence of the reality, of things of which we are assured, and faith is the *élegchos*, the objective evidence, of things not seen. The Greek word *élegchos* is used in one other place in the New Testament, 2 Timothy 3:16, "All Scripture ... is profitable ... for *élegchos*," "conviction" a subjective use of the word. In Timothy *élegchos* bears the subjective meaning "means of proof with a view to refuting," thus translated "conviction," or in some versions "reproof" or "rebuke."

In Hebrews 11:1, *élegchos* is used in an objective sense. Not "faith is the means of proof and persuasion" which would be subjective. A subjective interpretation means that the more faith you have (the quantity of faith), the stronger your belief in the promises. In this view, a small or weak faith cannot hold onto the promises; a large or strong faith holds fast to the promises.

That subjective view places the burden of perseverance solely on the believer. But Scripture teaches that God gives grace to persevere, e.g., Hebrews 13:5; Romans 8:28–39, grace which the believer is to receive and put to use in his or her life, Hebrews 10:36. Moreover, the Bible never speaks of the quantity of faith, but its quality, e.g., Matthew 17:20, where a tiny amount of faith is able to resolve big problems. Jesus' point was that one has faith, or does not. Quality, not quantity, is how faith perseveres: one either has faith, or does not. The believer has faith, always.

> What is faith? Faith is inwardly believing the testimony of God through the infallible conviction given by the Holy Spirit, and faith is outwardly acting through the power given by the Holy Spirit to conform one's thoughts and actions to that conviction.

> A person is not "enabled" to believe by the Spirit's convicting power, but rather as being convicted of the truth, and on the basis of that conviction, each person appropriates and applies the truth to his or her specific circumstance, whether the spiritual issue is salvation or discipleship. That phrase, "appropriates and applies the truth," is what the Bible names "faith."

Because genuine faith is conviction given by the Holy Spirit, the faith to persevere in the faith by means of faith is maintained in the believer by the Holy Spirit.

Therefore, faith, like salvation, cannot be lost by the person who is genuinely saved.

An objective interpretation of *élegchos* is more in keeping with the use the Hebrews Writer makes of *hupóstasis*. For example, at 1:3, Jesus is not the means of proof demonstrating there is a God. Jesus is the objective presence of God. Since in Hebrews 11:1 *hupóstasis* and *élegchos* are parallel descriptions of persevering faith, then both must bear an objective meaning: the presence of faith is the objective reality (*hupóstasis*) and the objective demonstration (*élegchos*) of things *elpízō* (assurance), possessed though not seen. The fact of genuine faith is itself the tile deed to faith's promises.

An objective interpretation means God gives a believer that quality of faith which results in the steadfast assurance that the promises are genuine and imminent. An objective faith places the burden of "proof" on God and emphasizes the believer's moral responsibility to receive and use the grace God gives for perseverance.

Another reason both *hupóstasis* and *élegchos* must bear an objective meaning is that the things promised and hoped for, but not seen, are present in the spirit domain, i.e., in heaven. If the faith described in Hebrew 11 is subjective, then man is trying to discern the reality of things in heaven through his sensual and rational faculties. This is not possible. In this mortal life spiritual things are perceived through the spiritual perceptive faculty of the soul, not the sensual faculties by which man subjectively understands the material world.

The unsaved sinner cannot understand the things of God just because they are spiritually discerned (1 Corinthians 2:14), and the unsaved sinner's spiritual perception is dead (inoperative) because of sin. Nor can the saved sinner perceive spiritual things through his material senses, because those senses were designed and created to perceive the material world.

Faith is the means of perceiving the spirit domain because God the Holy Spirit is the source of spiritual perception (1 Corinthians 2:10–11). He reveals spiritual things to material man through the soul's faculty of spiritual perception employed by faith. Faith is the objective reality of things of which we are assured, the objective evidence of things not yet seen.

The Use Of Persevering Faith

Persevering faith is based on the objective conviction that spiritual realities testified to in Scripture are certain to be received. Persevering faith is possible because the believer knows by conviction God keeps the promises he has made in the scriptures. This is not a matter of human perception, nor is it a matter of feeling persuaded. I objectively know God keeps his promises, because the spiritual reality of the matter has been revealed to me by God the Holy Spirit in the Scripture.

Yes, a personal rational comprehension of Scripture is essential to perseverance, because God has created us to be rational beings whose choices are supported by reason. There is a difference, however, between being certain because of experience, and having experience validated by the certainty of faith. The certainty of faith—which must be based in spiritual understanding of Scripture—validates our experiences as genuine or false in relation to the promises of God. The certainty of faith causes us to make the choice to persevere and informs us when the practice of our faith, perseverance, is based upon spiritual reality.

However, in Hebrews 11:1 the writer is not talking about the choice to persevere, he is addressing the basis for perseverance: by faith. Holy Spirit-given conviction of faith in God's promises is itself the real presence of things hoped for, the objective evidence of things not seen. The God-given conviction "faith" is the title deed God has given me for the promises I have been given but not received.

Persevering faith begins in Scripture and is supported by God-given conviction: I know God is keeping his promises because God has convicted me that he is faithful. One may read the Scripture and deny its veracity. Holy Spirit given conviction leads to faith that accepts the veracity of Scripture. That certainty is the basis of persevering faith.

Therefore, my <u>choice</u> to persevere in my Christian life <u>must</u> be based upon that Holy Spirit-revealed knowledge and conviction of the absolute, genuine spiritual reality given in the scriptures. Worldly circumstances can discourage, but not destroy. I can endure a great struggle with sufferings because I know, from the scriptures, by Spirit-given, Spirit-convicting absolute knowledge that God who cannot lie will be faithful to his promises to me. The presence of Holy Spirit-given faith is itself the objective reality of God's promises. We can say, then, that faith itself is the substance and title deed (*hupóstasis*) of God's promises (the things of which we are assured) in the same sense in which Jesus the Christ is the literal, physical reality of the presence of God. Faith is the reality of the promises of God.

Faith is also the objective evidence (*élegchos*) of the spiritual reality of the things not seen. I can't say this more plainly: objective faith is given by God, not created by man. Man's faith is more subjective: I know, I reason, I feel, therefore I act. The biblical truth is I persevere in faith, a subjective act, because I have an objective faith in the reality of the promises. Because the believer has God-given faith, the believer has assurance in the things not seen: the presence of God-given faith is the objective evidence of the things not seen.

Human nature has the attribute of confidence, trust; in a word, faith. However, genuine biblical, scriptural faith is not natural, because genuine biblical, scriptural faith is supra-natural: it is not man-made it is God-given. If you have faith in God the Savior, you did not get there by yourself.

Because the believer is a sensual, rational creature, I will say this in a more familiar way: God-given faith gives the perception of immediate presence to spiritual realities. Put another way, perseverance is knowing that "God said it, that settles it, I'm going to believe it and do it." The objective reality, *hupóstasis*, that God gives in the promises is itself the objective evidence the believer possesses the promises, and is the assurance the believer will receive the promises, because that (kind or quality of) faith comes only from God. If one has God-given faith, then one has the certainty needed to persevere and receive the promises.

Persevering Faith By Example

For by faith the elders obtained a good testimony (Hebrews 11:2). This is the announcement of the Writer's theme for chapter 11. I will not discuss these examples of persevering faith, except to say the Writer will concern himself with the fruits and consequences which follow faith. The examples in Hebrews 11 reveal the believer's part in perseverance.

Faith in the promises provides the basis for perseverance. I have received from God that grace of perseverance that gives certainty (conviction) concerning the goal or end result of perseverance: to receive the promises God has made to me in the scriptures.

Faith is not, however, the efficient cause of perseverance. The act of persevering is a choice: I am persevering in the practice of my faith because I intend to receive the promises. If this were not true, if a decision need not be made to persevere, then the Writer would not have written 10:25–29, or 11:1–39; indeed, he could have ended his epistle at 10:25. The exhortation, "do not lose your confidence," 10:35, has its counterpart in "you have need of perseverance," 10:36. Both express the choice to be made. Having received God's grace of perseverance through faith, the believer must choose to act in perseverance by means of faith. That he will so choose (because supranaturally convicted by the Holy Spirit) does not lessen the necessity of making a choice. The grace of God doesn't work in spite of the believer, but always works through the believer's regenerated nature to accomplish God's will for the believer.

The exhortations in Hebrews 11, illustrated by the example of the elders, are intended to encourage the believer to make the right choice: to persevere in the faith by faith. Thomas Manton's commentary on Hebrew's 11 [By Faith, 51], called this faith "sanctifying faith," a typically Puritan emphasis on separation from sin and dedication to God. The testimony of the elders illustrates the experiential sanctification required of believers: what one believes one must do. Because genuine biblical belief is gained though Holy Spirit given conviction, then what one believes one will do.

Faith must influence all the parts of the spiritual life. Without faith perseverance is noble morality (or ignoble stubbornness). Perseverance by means of faith is given by grace but is also the self-motivated personal pursuit of that experiential sanctification which conforms the life to God's commandments. I can say "self-motivated" because the natural response of the born-again human nature *is* to pursue a sanctified manner of life.

In the Hebrews 11 context, to persevere is to maintain unswerving confidence in the promises God has given in Scripture, through the conviction the Holy Spirit gives to the believer concerning the promises. The choice to persevere includes the choice to use the means of grace to maintain one's faith. I am not speaking of certainty, which is conviction, but the use one makes of that certainty, which is choice: inner conviction should result in an appropriate outward action. The text in Hebrews 11:2 is *en taúta gár*, "for in this" kind of faith, which is to say, because of this kind of faith, the elders obtained, etc.

What is intended is that through the exercise of their faith the elders obtained a good report or testimony concerning their perseverance in and by their faith. Their inner conviction—that grace received—was the basis for an appropriate choice. By the <u>exercise</u> of their faith the elders <u>maintained</u> their perseverance by using the grace of perseverance they had been given: Abel offered to God, Enoch pleased God, Noah prepared as directed by God, Abraham obeyed by faith in God, etc. The choice to persevere includes the choice to use the means of grace necessary to maintain one's faith.

We must always remember that in this mortal life, in all things spiritual, there is always a God-ward side and a man-ward side. God's responsibility is convicting his people of the certainty of spiritual reality (found in the scriptures) and empowering their soul to achieve the goal of successful perseverance, which is receiving the promises proclaimed in the scriptures. Man's responsibility is to choose to make appropriate use of the means of grace God provides to strengthen, mature, and encourage the believer in his or her faith, in order to continue to live according to faith, that he/she might persevere and receive the promises. If one's faith is genuine faith, then he or she will always make that choice to persevere.

What, then, are the means by which we are empowered to persevere? The persevering faith of the elders is demonstrated in that they took action (experiential sanctification) based upon what God's Word said was true, and by the conviction of faith they held those things to be true. The Writer has not only presented the truths of the Christian faith in his epistle, he has also exhorted his readers to the practical expression of these truths.

The more immediate context is what I call the privileges and obligations, or duties, of the faith, 10:19–25. Faith is not some ambiguous feeling; faith—if it is genuine, God-given, soul-saving, persevering faith—looks toward the promised future as a solid and sure reality that demands appropriate action. The certainty of faith causes the believer to make the choice to persevere and informs the believer when the practice of faith, his or her perseverance, is based on the spiritual reality witnessed to by Scripture.

The choice and the practice are equally essential to the maintenance of faith. Although the conviction of truth is objective and absolute, the recognition and practical application of that conviction is subjective within the soul. One might liken faith to a spiritual "muscle" that requires constant exercise to maintain its tone and strength. Without constant exercise through practical application the subjective recognition of faith diminishes. The result is that one comes less often into God's presence, uses prayer and devotion less frequently, becomes apathetic toward his believing brethren, and calloused toward their suffering in the world; ultimately, one abandons gathering together with his Christian brethren (thus the exhortations in Hebrews 10:19–25). As these wrong actions become habitual, the practice of perseverance is lessened and faith is weakened. If this describes you, return to the source. The faith that saved you from sin is the same kind of faith that preserves you from sinning.

We are, in this physical frame, creatures of subjective sense and rationality, whose faith must be practiced in practical expressions to be maintained all the way through the end of life to the promised reward; hence the necessity of experiential sanctification. The certainty of faith causes us to make the choice to persevere, and informs us when the practice of our faith, perseverance, is based upon spiritual reality. No wonder, then, the Writer of Hebrews energetically exhorted his readers to press forward to spiritual maturity by putting their faith into practice, as did their spiritual ancestors. We too, in this modern day and age, as we wait for the soon-appearing of Christ, must persevere in the faith as they did, both spiritually and practically.

To persevere in the faith is to continue in the faith by means of faith all the way through life and death. Perseverance is a grace God gives the believer to overcome all spiritual and physical obstacles to faith and thereby continue in the faith, and persevering faith is the believer using the means of grace God has provided for him or her to continue in the faith. God tells his saved people to persevere, and he gives his saved people every grace and spiritual power necessary to be able to persevere. By means of the grace of perseverance every believer will persevere in the faith by faith all the way through life to the end of physical life and into eternity. Believers are overcomers; when they fall down they get up; they persevere.

Chapter Summary

The chapter begins with an introduction briefly defining both experiential sanctification and perseverance. Unlike positional sanctification, which is a complete and completed act of God for the believer, experiential sanctification is the work of the Holy Spirit and the believer to conform the believer to be like Christ during this mortal life. Persevering faith comes from the persevering grace God has given the believer to use through the means of grace (worship, fellowship, obedience, service, Scripture) to continue in the faith by means of faith.

Experiential sanctification is defined in depth. Then follows a detailed explanation of all the aspects of the grace of perseverance. The commandment to persevere, and the believer's response is explained. The command to persevere is contrasted with the belief salvation may be lost if one does not persevere. The conclusion of that discussion is this: salvation is given by God and salvation is maintained by God, given and maintained by the same means: the complete and completed legal satisfaction (propitiation) of God's holiness, justice, and wrath against the crime human sin made by Jesus Christ on the cross.

The many commandments to persevere are explained. Because sin never stops tempting, and occasionally the believer says "Yes" to temptation and commits an act of sinning, God never stops reminding his saved people to use the grace of perseverance. The principle is this: God always acts to maintain a believer's salvation, which includes the infallibility of the grace of perseverance, and the continuous reminder to persevere.

The basis of persevering faith was explained. The grace of perseverance is seen in the repeated biblical expression "by faith." That believers will persevere in the faith by means of faith is assumed throughout the New Testament. Hebrews 11 is an exhibition of that principle.

Then follows an extensive and in depth analysis of persevering faith, using the Book of Hebrews as the source. Greek words and relevant scriptures are explained. The conclusion of that lengthy discussion is perseverance has two aspects. One, God gives the believer the grace of perseverance by which the believer is infallibly maintained in the faith by means of faith. Two, the believer uses the grace of perseverance as commanded by God.

The consequence of the grace of perseverance has two aspects. One, the security and assurance of salvation. Two, the objective conviction that spiritual realities testified to in Scripture are certain to be received.

The chapter concludes with a brief look at persevering faith by example in Hebrews 11.

Physical Death, Soul Transformed, Intermediate State

Because this book is about the Ordo Salutis, I will not address the normal Christian life, other than what I have written about security, assurance, experiential sanctification, and perseverance. Instead, I will move along to the end of life. This chapter is about the conscious active life of the soul (the person) between physical death and resurrection of the body.

Most New Testament believers will experience physical death versus rapture. All persons who experience physical death must be somewhere in the interim between physical death and resurrection. Why? Because the Scripture teaches the human soul is naturally immortal, Genesis 2:7; Matthew 17:3; Luke 16:23; 23:43; 2 Corinthians 5:8.

The Natural Immortality Of The Human Soul

At Genesis 2:7 the Holy Spirit teaches us the human soul is naturally immortal. God formed a human body from dirt, a body that was without life. All the parts were there, nothing was functioning. God created the human soul from nothing (*ex nihilo*), and placed that human soul into that inert body, thereby animating the body. How did the human soul animate the body?

The human soul is the person, with essence, life, nature, and personality. I think of the human soul as a container composed of the three essentials of sentient life: the essence that makes us human (created *ex nihilo*) and not some other kind of being; the human nature (also created *ex nihilo*); the immaterial essence "life," which is the animating principle.

Personality develops from human nature and experience. Adam and Eve alone were created (Adam) and formed (Eve) with personality. In their descendants personality develops over time after birth through experience.

God created the human soul and human nature *ex nihilo*, but God did not create "life" *ex nihilo*, because God himself is the origin and source of life. God has life in himself, John 5:26. "I am he who exists," said God at Exodus 3:14, meaning there is no cause for God's existence, he exists because he exists. The origin and source of life in every living being is God.

From Genesis 2:7 it should be apparent the immaterial essence which we (and the Scripture) identify as "life" is independent of the material body. The material body was formed out of existing non-living material things. The body existed as an inert, non-living, non-functional material form. The human soul with the essence life, of which God alone is the origin and source, was created separate from the body.

God placed the soul (the person) into the material body, thereby animating the material body: the immaterial essence life made the material body alive. The union of non-living material body with the living soul created a fully functional human being soul and body: Adam, 'ādām ["man," in the sense of humankind, and specifically this one man] became a living person.

Because the origin and source of human life is God's life-in-himself, the soul is naturally immortal. (Only human and angel souls are naturally immortal.) God made the immaterial human soul alive by placing the animating principle life into the immaterial soul. We know this because by observation we know the difference between life and death. Life is when the person is in the body; death is when the person leaves the body.

Scripture recognizes the dissolution of the human body, but there is no known dissolution of the human soul in Scripture. The biblical view is once the person comes into existence, that personal existence continues endlessly. "I am," said God at Exodus 3:15, "the God of Abraham, the God of Isaac, and the God of Jacob"; "He is not," said Jesus, "God of the dead but of the living," Mark 12:27, quoting Exodus 3:15. Physical death means the body becomes non-living, but the person continues living, because the soul is naturally immortal and the soul is the person. As Genesis 2:7 has taught us, by showing the creation of the person independent of the body, a person does not require a body to be a person.

Several scriptures tell us the disembodied person is conscious and active after the death of the body.

> Luke 23:43, And Jesus said to him [the saved thief on the cross], "Truly I say to you, today you will be in Paradise with me." [Paradise is heaven, 2 Corinthians 12:1–4.]

> 2 Corinthians 5:8, Now we are full of confidence and are pleased, rather, to be absent away from the body and to be at home with the Lord.

> Philippians 1:23, I am constrained between the two, having the

desire to depart and to be with Christ, for that is much better.

Luke 16:23, Then also the rich man died and was buried. 23 And in Hades, having lifted up his eyes, being in torment, he sees Abraham from afar, and Lazarus in his bosom.

Therefore, the Scripture teaches the human soul is naturally immortal.

What Is Physical Death?

As previously discussed, the animating principle "life" is in the soul, not the body. The Woman was formed from Adam's soul and body, and therefore she was alive because the animating principle "life" is in the soul. In the propagation of Adam and the Woman (now known as Eve, Genesis 3:20), the male and female gametes carried the animating principle (gametes are living cells, and therefore possess life) and by the union of the gametes—fertilization resulting in conception—the newly conceived person is alive. Procreation does not create life it transmits the life that God gave Adam.

Every living cell in the material body is living because infused with the soul. In a mundane illustration, think of the soul as water and the body as a washcloth. The water makes the washcloth wet, but the water and the cloth remain separate things. Remove the water and the cloth is no longer wet. Remove the soul and the body is no longer living. Just as both water and cloth continue independently, whether in union or not in union, even so the soul and body. Without the water the cloth is dry; without the soul the body is lifeless.

Therefore, material life, the living body, is alive because the immaterial soul in the body communicates life to the body. The material body becomes lifeless when the living soul separates from the body. That separation of immaterial soul from material body is what is known as physical death.

The Transformation Of The Believer's Soul

During this mortal life and at the moment of physical death, both soul and body are infused with sin. The sin attribute resides in the soul, the body is corrupted by the effect of mortality caused by sin. Both soul and body must be transformed to be sinless. The body is transformed by death and resurrection, removing all the effects of mortality. What of the soul?

We know at physical death the soul continues in active conscious life whether a person is unsaved or saved. How do we know? Above I gave scriptures indicating the person continues in active conscious life after physical death. Above I gave scripture showing the human soul is immortal. Therefore, Scripture teaches the human soul, the person, is active and conscious after death. I will explain as we continue.

Every human being is conceived in a state of spiritual death. In the scripture, separation is the defining characteristic of death, whether physical death or spiritual death. The person, from the moment the person comes into existence at fertilization of the ovum, is separated from God, spiritual death, because every person has the sin attribute in his or her human nature. That is the inheritance received from sinful Adam, Genesis 5:3; 1 Corinthians 15:22.

Salvation makes the saved person spiritually alive. The believer's human nature is transformed by regeneration (born-again) to be a new creation (2 Corinthians 5:17; Galatians 6:15). However, God has chosen to leave the sin attribute of the old sinful human nature resident in the saved regenerated human nature. The sin attribute in the saved person no longer dominant, Romans 6:14, but it unceasingly tempts to acts of sinning, 1 John 1:8–10.

The reason God has left the sin attribute resident in the saved soul during this mortal life is not clearly explained in the Scripture. Nor does the sovereign God owe anyone an explanation, "Yes Father, because doing so was good in your sight," Matthew 11:26.

However, in his mercy and grace God provides a partial answer. "And he said to me, 'My grace suffices you, for the power is perfected in weakness.' Most gladly, therefore, rather will I boast in my weaknesses, so that the power of the Christ may rest upon me" (2 Corinthians 12:9). As those whose work it is to be Christ's ambassadors of reconciliation, 2 Corinthians 5:20, God's grace is manifested through our weakness, so that salvation is seen by our faith, not by sinlessness.

The saved person is spiritually alive, but has the sin attribute. Therefore the saved person, though habitually choosing to live righteously, occasionally chooses to respond to temptation and commit an act of sinning (1 John 1:8–10). Every act of sinning committed by a saved person is an act of spiritual death, however temporary, because sin separates the saved person from fellowship with God. Not separated from the salvific relationship, but from fellowship (praise the Lord for 1 John 1:9; 2:1–2). The saved person needs the transformation of the soul that removes the sin attribute from the regenerated human nature. That transformation of the soul occurs at the physical death of the body, or at the rapture, when the immortal soul becomes incorruptible, which is to say, becomes sinless and is given the grace of indefectability.

Let us discuss the removal of the sin attribute in more detail.

Why The Sin Attribute Is Removed

The sin attribute in the saved human soul must be removed before the believer can go to heaven. Paul wrote, 1 Corinthians 15:50, "Now this I say, brethren, that flesh and blood is not able to inherit the kingdom of God, nor the decay inherit the incorruption." The saved continue to bear the image of the earthly man during this mortal life because they are descendants of Adam. To enter heaven the saved must bear the image of the heavenly person, Jesus Christ, 1 Corinthians 15:49. Being conformed to the image of Christ is ongoing during the believer's mortal life, completed at physical death or rapture, Romans 8:29.

Salvation initiates that transformation to the image of Christ through the regeneration of the saved person's human nature. During this mortal life the believer is being conformed to the image of Jesus Christ. That process is completed when the sin attribute is removed. The sin attribute is removed from saved human nature at physical death or rapture. That is when, as Paul says in 1 Corinthians 15, the corruptible shall have put on incorruptible: the person has become sinless. Having been transformed to sinless, the corruptible has put on incorruption. The transformation of the soul into the image of the Son begun at salvation is completed at physical death, or rapture.

We know the sin attribute is with us, the saved, during this mortal life, 1 John 1:8–10. How do we know it is removed at physical death or rapture. Two reasons. One, the saint who dies goes to heaven, 2 Corinthians 5:8, as does the saint who is raptured, 1 Thessalonians 4:17. Two, "flesh and blood is not able to inherit the kingdom of God, nor the decay inherit the incorruption," 1 Corinthians 15:50, compare 15:53. Therefore the sin attribute is removed at physical death or rapture.

The Grace Of Indefectability

Scripture does not mention the grace of indefectability by name, but it examples that grace. To be indefectible means "not subject to failure or decay." We see this grace in action in the angels who did not sin and have never sinned. The grace of indefectability works with their sinless nature to maintain their sinless state. So also the saved in heaven, the grace of indefectability will work with their sinless nature to maintain their sinless state.

An example of the grace of indefectability is seen in Jude 9. "Michael the archangel, when contending with the devil in a dispute about Moses' body, did not presume to bring against him a judgment of slander, but rather said, 'The Lord censure you.'" Certainly the angel was tempted, but temptation is not sin. Temptation could not find as much as a toehold in his sinless nature to create an act of sinning. The holy angels have neither the tendency nor the inclination to sin. The grace of indefectability works with the sinless angelic nature in such a way that there was no response to the temptation.

An illustration. You might tempt me, offer to me, an alcoholic beverage. I have a tendency to sin (the sin attribute is in my born-again human nature), but I do not have an inclination to sin in that particular manner: drinking alcohol is not a sin, but drunkenness is a sin; I have no inclination to either. There is zero response in my soul to say "yes" to that particular temptation; in fact the opposite, I am repulsed.

Even so, in heaven both tendency and inclination to commit any act of sinning will be gone because the sin attribute will have been removed, and the believer will have the grace of indefectability.

Adam was created sinless. He did not have a tendency to sin, because he did not have the sin attribute in his human nature. But Adam was capable of experiencing an inclination to sin when tempted, because he had free will, and he was created mutable. To be mutable is to be susceptible to change. God gave Adam's human nature mutability so he could grow in his relationship with God, and grow in fulfilling his stewardship responsibilities (Genesis 1:26–28) toward the earthly creation and its creatures. When Adam was tempted, his free will chose to respond to the temptation, and his mutability allowed that change, and thereby his human nature gained the tendency to sin. Now Adam is in heaven, and he is still mutable (we will always grow in grace, knowledge, and understanding), but he is sinless in heaven, and has the grace of indefectability to work with his sinless nature and maintain his sinless state.

The humanity of Jesus Christ the God-man was always being tempted during his time on this earth, but he had zero response to say "yes" to temptation. His deity couldn't sin. His humanity had no tendency to sin—he was conceived without the sin attribute—and he had zero inclination to commit an act of sinning, because his deity nature and human nature worked together in harmony to deny temptation.

Sin repulsed Jesus Christ, it was a contradiction against his sinless nature. Look at his responses to the temptations Satan offered. He experienced temptation, but temptation is not a sin. He always said "No" to temptation. He had the grace of indefectability. He experienced being tempted, but never experience a positive response to temptation.

The saved in heaven, having been freed from the presence of sin, are able to maintain their sinless state through God's gift of the grace of indefectability.

The Location of the Believer During The Intermediate State

In physical death the body returns to the ground out of which it was taken (Genesis 3:19) until resurrection, whether saved or unsaved. What of the person, the soul?

The definition of the intermediate state is the location of the soul—the disembodied person—between physical death and resurrection of the body. Let's examine the details.

What happens to the material body and the immaterial soul of every human being when soul and body are separated by physical death? The body, being lifeless, experiences the normal decay and decomposition that affects all biological matter, Genesis 3:19. The soul, which is the person, enters what is known as the intermediate state. W.G.T. Shedd [*Endless*, 59–60] stated the biblical doctrine, (my comments in brackets to show the context preceding the statement).

> The substance of the Reformed view, then, is, that the intermediate state [between death and resurrection] for the saved is Heaven without the body, and the final state for the saved is Heaven with the body; the intermediate state for the lost is Hell [*hádēs*] without the body, and the final state for the lost is Hell [*géenna*; lake of fire] with the body."

Shedd's definition incorporates resurrection ("with the body"), which will be discussed in the next chapter. Between death and resurrection, "the intermediate state for the saved is Heaven without the body ... the intermediate state for the lost is Hell [*hádēs*] without the body."

In other words, both saved and unsaved continue in conscious active life between physical death and resurrection of the body. Because this book is about the Ordo Salutis, I will not address the intermediate state of the unsaved (see Luke 16:19–26, and my commentary on Luke's Gospel).

Heaven

The intermediate state for the saved person between physical death and resurrection of the body is heaven. What does the Scripture say about heaven? The disembodied soul (the soul is the person) will have a defined presence in heaven: because human beings are finite the disembodied person must be somewhere in time as well as space. That defined presence in time and space is a body suited for life in the immaterial domain.

The disembodied person will be incorruptible (sinless) and be given the grace of indefectability to maintain that sinless state. The believer in heaven will worship God and the Savior directly—as the hymn says, "nothing between my soul and my Savior," because faith will have become sight, and sin is no more within the believer in heaven.

The person in heaven will have a greater understanding, though will continue to learn and grow spiritually. He/she will probably perceive the passage of time differently, because immortality will no longer be perceived through the mortal body.

I have a feeling Revelation 5 gives us a glimpse into life in heaven. i.e., unhindered and spontaneous acts of worship. We will have social interaction with other believers and the angels. I believe this kind of life will continue after resurrection.

The kind of life we will live in the new heavens and earth, Revelation 20:1–22:5, seems to be similar, although the location will be different, because in the new heavens and earth there will not be a separation between the material and the immaterial.

Beyond those things I do not believe the Scripture says more.

....

The rest of this chapter focuses on two incorrect views of the intermediate state of the saved. The first I will discuss is the doctrine of "soul sleep." The second is an intermediate location for the Old Testament saved prior to Christ's crucifixion.

The Doctrine Of Soul Sleep

The doctrine of soul sleep teaches that between physical death and resurrection the person—saved and unsaved—is without all sensibility, feeling, or perception until the Great White Throne judgment, Revelation 20:11–15, at which time the body, saved and unsaved, is resurrected and the person awakened. Those holding to the doctrine believe the location of the person (the soul) during this sleep is either (a) unconscious in some kind of undefined spiritual limbo until resurrection of the body, or (b) the soul is unconscious in the grave inside the dead body until resurrection, or (c) the soul ceases to exist, to be recreated at the resurrection of the body.

Those holding to (c) the soul ceases to exist doctrine, are Physicalists: the only life is biological, there is no soul or spirit, the soul is not substantive but is only apparent because it is a consequence of biological activity. When the biological activity stops at physical death the thing we think of as a soul ceases to exist.

Some Conditionalists (the doctrine of Conditional Immortality) are Physicalists. Other Conditionalists believe the soul sleeps in the intermediate state. (A few Conditionalists believe the soul is conscious and active in the intermediate state.) The Scripture's teaching of the natural immortality of the soul denies Physicalism and soul sleep. Not all who believe in physicalism or soul sleep are Conditionalists, but the Conditionalist's doctrine of the annihilation of the unsaved person in the lake of fire attracts persons holding to those doctrines. (See my book *Against Physicalism, Annihilationism, and Conditionalism* for additional scriptural argument.)

Wherever the person might be after the death of the body, the Scripture teaches the conscious active existence of the person continues after physical death. I will examine that statement in detail.

Those holding to an unconscious, but existing and alive, state of the person during the physical death of the body, soul sleep, base their doctrine on the Scripture's use of the word "sleep" for physical death.

The English word "sleep" occurs about seventy-four times in Scripture, of which eighteen are in the New Testament. The vast majority of those uses in both testaments refer to natural physical sleep. In the New Testament, eight uses refer to natural sleep, six uses refer to being spiritual alert, Romans 13:11; Ephesians 5:14; 1 Thessalonians 5:6, 7, 10. Four uses refer to physical death, 1 Corinthians 11:30; 15:51; 1 Thessalonians 4:13, 14. I have highlighted the word "sleep."

1 Corinthians 11:29–30, For the *one* eating and drinking [the Lord's Supper] *irreverently*, judgment on himself eats and drinks, not distinguishing the body. 30 On account of these things many among you *are* weak and infirm, and many are fallen <u>asleep</u>.

1 Corinthians 15:51, Behold, something hidden I tell to you. We will not all <u>sleep</u>, but we will all be changed.

1 Thessalonians 4:13–14, Now we do not want you to be ignorant, brethren, about those having fallen <u>asleep</u>, so that you should not be grieved, even just as the rest—those not having hope. 14 Because if we believe that Jesus died and rose again, so also God will bring with him those having fallen <u>asleep</u> through Jesus.

The 1 Corinthians 11:29–30 use obviously means physical death. If, as is the case, "weak and infirm" refer to the body, then sleep must refer to the body. So also 1 Corinthians 15:51, Paul is speaking of the transformation of soul and body at the rapture, when "this the corruptible to put on incorruption, and this the mortal to put on immortality," 15:53. We understand Paul is also speaking of the physically dead body, for he says at 15:52, "For the trumpet will announce, and the dead ones will be raised incorruptible, and we [the physically living saved] will be transformed." Sleep is a euphemism for physical death.

Why is "sleep" used as a euphemism for physical death? Two reasons. One the fact of bodily resurrection. The body "sleeps" in death until awakened to life by rejoining the living soul in resurrection. Two, physical death has no terror for the believer. The body sleeps, the person moves on.

In 1 Thessalonians 4:13–18, Paul is answering a question about the state of those believers who have died. The subject is physical death. In the Greek culture the Thessalonians were saved out of (most of the saved in Thessalonica were gentiles), no one returned from physical death. Paul is teaching them about the resurrection, one of the essential doctrines of the Christian faith. The dead are currently with Jesus in heaven—he will bring them with him when he comes.

How do we know the dead in Christ are in heaven, not soul sleep? Because Christ brings the physically dead believers with him—not the dead body but the conscious active soul before the dead body is resurrected. See the order:

(1) 4:14, God will bring with him those having fallen asleep through Jesus;

(2) 4:16, the Lord himself, by a loud command, by the voice of an archangel, and by the trumpet of God, will descend from heaven, and the dead in Christ will rise first.

(3), 4:17, Then we the living remaining, together with them, will be caught up in the clouds for the meeting of the Lord in the air.

In soul sleep the soul is unconscious in some kind of undefined spiritual limbo until resurrection of the body, or the soul is unconscious in the grave inside the dead body until resurrection. But in the Thessalonian passage, the soul is with Jesus when he returns, to be reunited with the body at the resurrection. There is no scriptural basis for the doctrine of soul sleep.

There is an event in the New Testament that definitely denies the doctrine of soul sleep. At the transfiguration of Jesus on the mountain, the physically dead Elijah and Moses appeared and spoke with Jesus. One might also add 1 Samuel 28:11–14.

Intermediate Location Of The Old Testament Saved

As stated above by Shedd, the doctrine of the Christian church is, "the intermediate state for the saved is Heaven without the body." That is all the saved, Old Testament and New Testament.

However, in the development of Judaism between the Old and New Testaments—Judaism is a man-made religion of traditions, it is not the YHWH-ism God gave to Israel through Abraham, Moses, and the prophets. Judaism developed the concept of a two-compartment "hell" in the Jewish apocrypha. (See Apocalypse of Baruch, 52:1–3; 2 Esdras 2:16-31, 34–35; 6:31–35. Also 4 Esdras 14:9; Enoch 10:12–13; 100:5; 103:7.)

A little scriptural background and a few definitions are necessary. In the Old Testament, all persons who died, righteous and unrighteous, went to Sheol. In the Old Testament, the most frequent use of Sheol (Hebrew: *she'ôl*) is to identify physical death or the grave. The frequent use of the word Sheol to indicate physical death or the resting place of the dead body is not questioned by any serious student of the Bible.

Sheol occurs in sixty-four Old Testament verses. The KJV translates

Sheol with "grave" thirty-one times; "hell" thirty times; and "pit" three times. The NIV uses "grave" footnoted with Sheol. The HCSB avoids the issue by transliterating *sheʾôl* to Sheol, as did the RV and ASV.

In my book, *Life, Death, Eternity,* chapter, "The Doctrine of Sheol," I examine each of the sixty-four occurrences of *sheʾôl* in its particular context. In every literal use the meaning is the grave as the resting place of the dead body. The Old Testament view of where the soul lives between physical death and resurrection is not defined by Sheol, because Sheol is never used in contexts defining or describing the condition or location of the soul between physical death and resurrection of the body. In the Old Testament, the location of the soul after physical death is either with God, not with God, or gathered to his people, a phrase meaning alive and conscious in the same location as those believers who previously died.

The way the Old Testament deals with the intermediate state is seen in Ecclesiastes 12:5, 7.

12:5, For man goes to his eternal home.

12:7, Then the dust will return to the earth as it was, And the spirit will return to God who gave it.

One part of the person, "the dust," returns to the dirt from which it was made. This is the physical body. The other part of the person, the "spirit" (*rûah*) returns to "God who gave it." But the actual location of "his eternal home," 12:5, is not defined, except as "the spirit will return to God," and the location of that return is defined no more closely than "God who gave it." God is everywhere at once at the same time, but the spirit, being finite, must be in one place at any one time. Where is that place? The Old Testament doesn't say.

Daniel 12:13 is another example (my comments in brackets). "You [Daniel] go on to the end [physical death], then rest [from your labors]. You will stand [resurrection] in your lot [receive your inheritance] at the end of the days." Where Daniel's soul will be located while awaiting resurrection is not explained."

So the Old Testament teaches an intermediate state. But it was not Sheol. In the Old Testament, the body went to the grave, to Sheol, after physical death, but a specific location of the soul after physical death is not stated. The Old Testament believer was "gathered to his people" (all occurrences), Genesis 25:8, 17; 35:29; 49:33; Numbers 20:24, 26; Deuteronomy 35:20; see also Judges 2:10. This phrase presumes a conscious afterlife: the physically dead person is with his ancestors. But a specific location for that afterlife is never stated in the Old Testament Scripture.

The Jews, lacking a definite revelation from God on this subject, did in the apocrypha (written during the intertestamental period) supplement God's Word by developing a location for the unrighteous and righteous dead.

> The unrighteous dead went to a place of misery awaiting final judgment.

> A few perfect believers went directly to heaven upon death.

> All the other righteous went to a place of peace to wait for the Messiah.

The place for the unrighteous and the righteous was the same place, but two different "compartments" in that place. The compartment for the unrighteous went by various names. The compartment for the righteous was a lesser paradise, i.e., not the paradise that was known as "Abraham's Bosom," aka: heaven.

The Old Testament revelation locates Old Testament believers as "with God" after physical death, and Old Testament unbelievers as "not with God" after physical death. The Jews understood the location of souls after death was not specified as other than "with" or "not with" God. They created names for the "with God" place: Abraham's Bosom, Paradise.

For a discussion of Judaism's development of a two-compartment "hell," see S.D.F Stewart, *The Christian Doctrine of Immortality*, book three, chapter 5, "The Intermediate State."

That is the origin of the two-compartment hades. In post-apostolic times a Christianized rationale was developed to apply this view to the Old Testament saved.

Before moving to the early Christian (post-apostolic) era, what does the New Testament teach? For the New Testament believer the intermediate state is clearly in heaven with Jesus. The saved thief was to be "in paradise" with Jesus when he died. Paul said to be absent from the body was to be present with the Lord. The New Testament teaches the same was true for the Old Testament believer. How did the saved thief understand "paradise?"

Schurer, *A History of the Jewish People in the Time of Christ*

[2.2.183] reports on the Jewish (Judaism's) concept of paradise during the period 175 BC to AD 135.

> The righteous and godly are received into paradise, and dwell in the high places of that world, and see the glory of God and of His holy angels. Their countenance will shine like the sun, and they will live forever (Daniel 12:3; Baruch 51:3, 7–14; Ezra 6:1–3, 68–72. Compare also Assumption of Moses 10:9, 10.)

The book of 2 Esdras, ca. 100 BC, reflects the belief the home of the righteous is in the paradise of God.

> 7:36, And the lake of torment will appear, and over against it will be a place of rest; the furnace of the Pit will appear, and over against it the Paradise of joy.

> 8:52, For it is for you that Paradise is opened, the tree of life is planted, the age to come is prepared, a city is built, a rest is ordained.

By the first century AD, paradise was associated with the third heaven in Jewish apocalyptic literature.

> Apocalypse of Moses, 37:4-6, And he stayed there three hours, lying down, and thereafter the Father of all, sitting on his holy throne stretched out his hand, and took Adam and handed him over to the archangel Michael saying: "Lift him up into Paradise unto the third Heaven, and leave him there until that fearful day of my reckoning, which I will make in the world." Then Michael took Adam and left him where God told him.

The believing thief, Luke 23:43, would have understood paradise as present with Jesus in the home of the righteous. In a word: heaven.

We might also think of Moses and Elijah. Elijah went up into heaven, 2 Kings 2:11, and was later seen with Jesus, Matthew 17:3 (Mark 9:4), accompanied by Moses (who was not translated into heaven, Deuteronomy 34:5–7), at the Transfiguration of Jesus on the mountain. Did God give Elijah and Moses a day-pass out of lesser paradise (as it was known in Judaism) that was not heaven?

(I will discuss below the belief Elijah and Moses were in a "good" compartment of Hades, until after Jesus' ascension.)

The apostle Paul—an expert in Old Testament doctrine and what Judaism had made out of Old Testament doctrine—is very clear paradise is heaven, 2 Corinthians 12:2–4. "I have known a man in Christ, fourteen years earlier—whether in body I know not or out of the body I know not; God knows—this person being <u>caught up into the third heaven</u>. 3 And I have known such a man—whether in body or out of the body I know not; God knows—4 that he was <u>caught up into paradise</u> and he heard words not possible or lawful to be spoken—not permissible to man to speak."

Jesus, in Luke 16:22–23, clearly describes two locations in the intermediate state.

> Luke 16:22, Then it happened the poor man died, and he was taken away by the messengers into the bosom of Abraham.

> Luke 16:22–23, Then also the rich man died and was buried. 23 And in Hades, having lifted up his eyes, being in torment, he sees Abraham from afar, and Lazarus in his bosom.

This is the only mention of Abraham's Bosom in the Scripture. The location was the opposite of Hades, the same location as paradise: heaven.

The word some Bible versions translate "hell" is actually Hades, Matthew 11:23; 16:18; Luke 10:15; 16:23; Acts 2:27, 31; Revelation 1:18; 6:8; 20:14.

The true hell is the lake of fire, the place of endless imprisonment for unsaved human beings and fallen angels. The word for the true hell, *géenna*, appears in Matthew 5:22, 29, 30; 10:28; 18:9; 23:15, 33, Mark 9:43, 45, 47; Luke 12:5; James 3:6. The words "lake of fire" appear four times: Revelation 19:20; Revelation 20:10, 14, 15. There is also a description of the lake of fire in Mark 9:44, 46, 48, and Matthew 8:12; 13:42, 50; 22:13; 24:51; 25:30; Luke 13:28.

What does the New Testament teach about Hades? Hades is a location in the spirit domain where the souls of unsaved human beings go after physical death to await resurrection and final judgment.

In an illustration: Hades is the county jail for unsaved souls (persons) awaiting execution of the sentence of endless imprisonment in the lake of fire. There are no angels in Hades, only unsaved human beings.

Now we jump to the early Christian (postapostolic) era.

In the earliest centuries of Christianity, an understanding of the intermediate state began to reflect the beliefs of Judaism. The unsaved went to a compartment in Hades, the martyrs went directly to heaven [Roberts, *ANF*, 3:576 (Tertullian *On the Resurrection of the Flesh*, 43)], all the other saved went to a separate compartment of Hades, a "good side," than the one where the unsaved went.

We can see the development of the idea of a two compartment Hades in the Apostles' Creed. There are sixteen versions of the Apostles' Creed. Three say Jesus descended into Hell. [See Schaff, *Creeds*, 2:40–41, 52–55, showing the development of the Apostolic Creed.] In the list below, "not present" means the "descended into hell" statement is not in that version of the creed.

Ignatius, AD 170, not present

Irenaeus, ca. AD 170, not present

Tertullian, AD 200, not present

Cyprian, AD 250, not present

Novatian, AD 250, not present

Origin, AD 230, not present

The Roman church, AD 340, present

Marcellus, AD 341, not present

Sacramentarium Gallicanum, AD 350, present

Nicene-Constantinopolitan, AD 381, not present

Rufinus, AD 390, two versions, present and not present

Augustine, AD 400, not present

Necetas, AD 450, not present

Gallus, ca. AD 550, not present

Pirminius, AD 750, present

The Nicene or Nicene-Constantinopolitan version of the creed (variously dated AD 325, AD 381, AD 451), does not have the "He descended into Hell" statement.

The reason three versions of the Apostles' Creed say Jesus went to hell is a misunderstanding of Ephesians 4:8–10. The belief is Jesus went the "good compartment" of Hades to take the Old Testament saved to heaven. Here is a statement of that belief.

> To complete the salvation of the Old Testament saved, and take the Old Testament saved residing in the paradise compartment of hell, out of paradise into heaven, because he had made his

propitiation, thereby effecting a full and complete salvation for the Old Testament saved.

As we saw above in Shedd's statement of the Reformed doctrine, the belief in a good compartment of hades is not the Reformed doctrine of the Christian church. Nor was that belief expressed by any of the seven ecumenical councils (AD 325–787), see Schaff and Wace, *NPNF*, second series, vol. 14, index of subjects.

The primary problem with the belief in a good side of Hades is this: "to complete the salvation of the Old Testament saved." No. There is no such thing in the Scripture as a partial salvation. One either is, or is not, saved, and if saved the scripture principle is "absent from the body, present with the Lord." Going to Hades before going to heaven would mean the Old Testament saved were only partially saved; in fact, not saved at all, but in a kind of purgatory. The "good side of Hades" belief says Jesus went to Hades after his death to take the Old Testament saved out of Hades and into heaven. In other words, he completed their salvation by taking them to heaven. I will discuss below why the "good side of Hades" believers teach a partial salvation.

Many in the early church opposed the idea Jesus went to Hades to complete the salvation of the Old Testament saved and take them into heaven. For example, Justin Martyr (AD 100–165), *Dialogue with Trypho*, 80, Cyprian (AD 210–258), Treatise 5.25, Gregory Nazianzen (AD 329–390), *Panegyric on His Brother S. Caesarius*, 21.

As we saw earlier, in the statement by Shedd, a good side of Hades is not the doctrine of the Reformed faith. The concept has been around for centuries, but the descent of Jesus into Hades to remove the Old Testament saved is not the Reformed doctrine of the faith, although some Reformers did teach it. For example, Martin Luther believed in Christ's descent into Hades (Small Catechism, AD 1529, Part II, The Creed, second article, "Of Redemption.").

Others did not. Calvin wrote the idea of a descent into Hades "is nothing but a story" containing "childish" elements with no basis in the biblical narrative [Calvin, *Institutes*, 2.16.9]. So also the Westminster Confession of Faith, AD 1647, Chapter 32.1; London Baptist confession, AD 1689; Free Will Baptists, 1834, 1868; Methodist Articles or Religion, AD 1784; Reformed Episcopal Articles of Religion, AD 1875.

Of the moderns who reject Christ's descent into Hades, a sampling: Charles Hodge [2:619, 621], 1797–1878; R. L. Dabney [823], 1820–

1898; Louis Berkhof [342], 1873–1957; Wayne Grudem [281, 586, 590], 1948–Present,. We have already seen Shedd's view.

The Biblical View of the Intermediate State

The biblical view of the intermediate state of the saved is stated in 2 Corinthians 5:8, "Now we are full of confidence and are pleased, rather, to be absent away from the body and to be at home with the Lord." This principle applies to all the saved, Old Testament and New Testament.

How can we know the principle of 2 Corinthians 5:8 applies to all the saved? Because there is no such thing as a partial salvation. One is either saved or unsaved. If saved, the intermediate state is in heaven with Christ waiting for the resurrection. If unsaved, the intermediate state is in Hades waiting for the Great White Throne judgment.

There are seven reasons variously given by the "Christ went to Hades" believers.

1. To complete the salvation of the Old Testament saved, and take the Old Testament saved residing in the paradise compartment of Hades, out of paradise into heaven, because he had made his propitiation, thereby effecting a full and complete salvation for the Old Testament saved.

2. To announce to the Old Testament saved and unsaved he had completed his propitiation.

3. To preach his advent and to proclaim remission of sins for all who believe in him." [Robert, ANF 1:499 (Irenaeus, Against Heresies, 4.27.2)].

4. Proclaim to the unsaved (residing in the torment compartment of Hades) that they would remain there awaiting a final judgment yet to come.

5. Christ descended into Hades as a triumphant king to proclaim his victory over sin, death, and the devil to the saints who had died before him.

6. The "Progressive Revelation" explanation. Because the Old Testament saved did not have a completed revelation about heaven, they had to go to Sheol, or Hades (or paradise, or Abraham's Bosom), until the revelation was completed.

7. The Intermediate Heaven Explanation. the Old Testament

saved went to an intermediate state, Hades (Sheol, paradise, Abraham's Bosom), and then were taken to heaven, another intermediate state, later to be sent to their final state, a new heaven and earth, Revelation 21:1.

See Quiggle, *Did Jesus Go To Hell?* 23–24, 36 ff., 39 ff., for a discussion of all seven. Here I will discuss reason one, but the discussion applies to all but four and five.

There are good biblical reasons an intermediate state in a good side of Hades is biblically wrong. I have already stated one, the principle in 2 Corinthians 5:8. Psalm 6:5 (YLT) gives another, "For there is not in death your memorial, in Sheol who does give thanks to you?" If, as the "good side" proponents maintain, Sheol was not the grave but Hades with a bad and good side, would there not be saved in the good side giving thanks? But Sheol is the grave, and there is not a good side in Hades.

I also alluded to another reason, there is no such thing as a partial salvation. More plainly, the Old Testament saved waiting in Hades for their salvation to be completed requires us to believe the merit of Christ's propitiation was not available to fully and completely save sinners until after his death on the cross in a moment of time. But Noah was given grace, Genesis 6:8, and was perfect in his generations and walked with God, 6:9. Was Noah partially saved? Abraham is given as example of saved by grace through faith—all who are saved Old and New Testament, are sons of Abraham, and justified by faith as was Abraham, and blessed with believing Abraham, Galatians 3:6–9. Was Abraham partially saved?

In this theory, because every Old Testament believer before the crucifixion was not completely saved by their faith (says this doctrine), God decreed the souls of all the Old Testament believers, beginning with Adam, must spend time in a sort of waiting room until Christ accomplished the propitiation (a theory that eventually led to the Roman Catholic Church doctrine of Purgatory). The name of this waiting room is usually given as Abraham's Bosom, or Paradise. No biblical evidence supports this theory.

What was the propitiation made on the cross?

Propitiation is the satisfaction Christ made to God for sin by dying on the cross as the sin-bearer, 2 Corinthians 5:21; Romans 3:25; Hebrews 2:17; 1 John 2:2; 4:10, for the crime of sin committed by human beings, suffering in their place and on their behalf. Christ's propitiation fully satisfied God's holiness and justice for the crime of sin.

A propitiation for sin is a complete satisfaction for sin. At 1 John 2:2 we are told by the inspired inerrant Scripture, "Now he is propitiation for our sins—but not for ours only but also for all the world." On the cross, when Jesus who did not have any sin became sin for us, 2 Corinthians 5:21, the judicial guilt of every sin from Adam to the end of this present world was imputed to Christ, and he made a complete satisfaction, a propitiation, to God for those sins. Does that mean there was no salvation before the propitiation was completed? Or a partial salvation (which is the same thing as no salvation)?

Was that propitiation of God for human sin effective to save sinners before that moment in historical time when Jesus paid the penalty on the cross? Yes. God works within time, but he is not bound by time. Time is a mechanism God created to manage the universe he created. At Ephesians 1:4, before the foundation of the world—before anything was created—God decreed Christ's propitiation would be the only basis for salvation: "He chose us in him before the beginning of the universe."

A decree made in eternity is an eternal decree effective throughout all eternity. Every saved sinner in every age is saved by Christ's merit at the moment saving faith is exercised; isn't the salvation principle "saved by grace through faith"? Or is it partially saved by grace through faith? No, not partially saved, not an incomplete salvation, but fully saved by Christ's merit at the moment saving faith is exercised. That is the Reformed doctrine.

How can we know there was no such thing as a partial salvation for the Old Testament believer? God's sovereign omnipotence, omniscience, and omnipresence. What God has decreed is certain to occur. The God who calls those things which do not yet exist as though they did exist (Romans 4:17) has no problem applying the merit he had decreed to those who believed, regardless of their temporal relationship to Christ's act of propitiation at a particular moment in time. The certainty of the moment made the merit of the moment available to save any sinner at any moment in time.

The effectiveness of Christ's propitiation in the Old Testament was and is the Reformed doctrine, review Shedd's definition of the intermediate state, above.

A simple, common sense question. How was God able to forgive the sin of Adam and Eve, if forgiveness was required to wait until after the propitiation on the cross? How did Abraham's confession of faith save him (Genesis 15:6; Romans 4:2), if the limitless merit that forgives sin was not available until after the propitiation on the cross?

The historical doctrine of post-apostolic New Testament church, and the historical doctrine of the Reformed, Dispensational, and Arminian traditions, is the limitless merit of Christ's propitiation has been available to save sinners from the beginning of humankind. For example, see the Canons of the Synod of Dort (AD 1619), First Head Of Doctrine, Of Divine Predestination, Article 7. There is no room in that statement for a partial salvation.

The decrees of God are certain; there is no "what if" with God. The God who "calls those things which do not exist as though they do" (Romans 14:17) has always applied the merit of Christ's propitiation, an act that occurred in a moment of historical time, to every person throughout time, who by God's grace and their faith in God's testimony accessed the merit—Christ's limitless merit in his propitiation of God on the cross—required to forgive the eternal punishment due sin.

From eternity past into eternity future only the merit of Christ's propitiation saves; and it does so at the moment saving faith is expressed, in every dispensation, under every covenant, at any moment in the history of redemption. The salvation of the Old Testament saints was just as full, just as complete, and just as efficacious to save pre-crucifixion, as is the salvation of the New Testament believer post-crucifixion. The Old Testament saints did not wait in some kind of spiritual purgatory or intermediate Hades—name it what you will—until Christ came to rescue them. There is no scripture passage stating Christ completed their partial salvation and removed the Old Testament saints from a good side of Hades.

Someone, somewhere, asks, what about Ephesians 4:8–10? That passage says Christ descended into Hades. The passage reads,

> Therefore He says: "When He ascended on high, He led captivity captive, And gave gifts to men." (Now this, "He ascended"—what does it mean but that He also first descended into the lower parts of the earth? He who descended is also the One who ascended far above all the heavens, that He might fill all things.)

Only by bringing the interpretation to the passage can "descended into the lower parts of the earth" be made to mean *hádēs*.

Paul, focusing on Christ, states, "Now this, 'he ascended,'" implying that Christ must first descend before he could ascend (note the parallel with John 3:13). The "lower parts of the earth" is not specifically a reference to the grave, nor to a supposed descent of Christ into hell. The phrase "lower parts of the earth" is in parallel with, and the opposite of, "far above all the heavens."

When Christ ascended, Acts 1:9, he ascended above the material heavens, above the spirit domain second heaven, and into the spirit domain third heaven where God manifests his throne (Revelation 4). Christ, who ascended into heaven, first descended out of heaven to the earth. The phrase "the lower parts" indicates his condescension to assume humanity to himself, and his subjection to mortality, which is the opposite of his exaltation "far above all the heavens."

Just as the word "ascended" indicates his exaltation, the opposing "descended" indicates his coming to earth. Just as "ascended" incorporates all the eternal results of his exaltation, "descended" looks to his entire earthly life, his incarnation-death-resurrection-ascension. Christ came to earth, and when he had completed his mission, and had triumphed over his enemies, he ascended in exaltation leading captivity captive. Who were the captives? Sin, death, hell, and all evil powers, because Christ triumphed over all that made men captive to eternal judgment.

For an exposition of the entire passage see my work, *A Private Commentary on the Bible: Ephesians*.

Conclusion

The descent into Hades theory doesn't agree with the biblical uses of Sheol or Hades, nor agree with the biblical or cultural use of Paradise or Abraham's Bosom.

The theory of the descent into Hades that began in ancient Judaism in the Apocalyptic books, and was adopted by early post-apostolic Christianity, grew out of a misunderstanding of the relationship between the intermediate state [in heaven without the body] and resurrection, and was supported by the view only the martyrs were worthy of immediately going to heaven.

The descent into hell theory was not accepted in post-apostolic

Christianity until the AD 750 Apostles Creed replaced former expressions of the creed without the statement. However, it was not adopted by all as some today use the similar Nicene-Constantinopolitan Creed that does not have the statement. (Oddly, both creeds are used by some denominations.)

Reformed theologians past and present reject the descent into Hades theory. The theory contradicts the doctrine of the eternal sufficiency, availability, and efficiency of the merit of Christ's propitiation. Other explanations are inconsistent with biblical doctrine, especially the biblical principle "absent from the body, present with the Lord."

None of the verses used by the descent into Hades theory support that theory. Scripture never names or identifies a separate compartment in Hades, never names or identifies a separate location in Hades named Paradise/Abraham's Bosom, in which the Old Testament saints waited for Christ's propitiation. Every believer, from Adam and Eve to the last person saved, when absent from the body is present with the Lord in heaven, waiting for the resurrection of their body.

Chapter Summary

This chapter begins where mortal life ends, with physical death, the transformation of the soul at physical death, and the intermediate state of the soul (the person) between physical death and resurrection.

The chapter begins with the natural immortality of the person, i.e., the human soul. The soul was created ex nihilo independent of the physical body, and therefore is capable of existence separated from the human body. That separation is what we know as physical death. The soul might be compared to a container with the three elements of sentient life: the essence that makes us human (created *ex nihilo*) and not some other kind of being; the human nature (also created *ex nihilo*); the immaterial essence "life," which is the animating principle.

Scripture, e.g., Luke 24:43; 2 Corinthians 5:8; Philippians 1:23; Luke 16:23, tell us the disembodied person is conscious and active after the death of the body. Physical death is defined: when the living soul separates from the body.

The next section describes the transformation of the believer's soul immediately after physical death: sin attribute removed from human nature, thereby transforming changing corruption into incorruptible.

Then follows a discussion of why the sin attribute is removed at physical death: to enter heaven the saved must bear the image of the heavenly person, Jesus Christ, 1 Corinthians 15:49.

The grace of indefectability is discussed. Scripture does not mention the grace of indefectability by name, but it examples that grace. To be indefectible means "not subject to failure or decay." In heaven the grace of indefectability will work with the sinless nature of the saved person to maintain their sinless state.

Then follows a long discussion of the intermediate state. The Reformed doctrine is stated: for the saved the intermediate state is Heaven without the body. A brief description of heaven is given.

The remainder of the chapter focuses on two incorrect views of the intermediate state of the saved. the first is soul sleep for all physical dead believers. The second is the common belief the Old Testament saved did not go to heaven, but went to a sort of Protestant purgatory (or limbo), usually described as a "good" compartment of Hades, where the Old Testament saved waited until Christ's propitiation of the cross to complete their salvation and take then to heaven.

The soul sleep concept is disproven with scripture: sleep is a euphemism for physical death. The "good" side of Hades argument for the Old Testament saved is disproven with Scripture, the history of the doctrine, and two principles: there is no such thing as an incomplete salvation; absent from the body is to be present with the Lord, the principle stated in 2 Corinthians 5:8. The "good" compartment of Hades view is contrasted with the biblical teaching.

The discussion of the "good" compartment of Hades/incomplete salvation view ends with a summary of the relevant arguments, including the fact Reformed theologians past and present reject the descent into Hades theory. The theory also contradicts the doctrine of the eternal sufficiency, availability, and efficiency of the merit of Christ's propitiation, and the fact no scripture supports the theory.

Transformation and Reanimation of the Body

Introduction

This mortal Christian life has an end for every believer. Almost every saved person will physically die and be physically resurrected. Not every saved person will die, some will be transformed and translated by rapture, even as Enoch and Elijah were transformed and translated by rapture.

Paul the apostle teaches that some saved persons of the New Testament church will be transformed without passing through physical death, 1 Thessalonians 4:17; 1 Corinthians 15:51–52. That is, out of all the New Testament church from AD 33 to the Rapture, only those living at the time of the rapture—a tiny part of the whole—will not pass through physical death.

Jesus taught that the saved who live through the Tribulation will enter into the Davidic-Messianic Kingdom, Matthew 25:31–34, a time when human physical life is prolonged. Those saved persons alive at the end of that kingdom (Revelation 20:9) may be transformed and translated—raptured—into the Eternal Kingdom that is in a new heaven on a new earth, Revelation 21:1–22:5. Like Enoch (Genesis 5:24; Hebrews 11:5) and Elisha (2 Kings 2:11), they will be transformed without passing through death, when this present heavens and earth are destroyed, Revelation 20:11; 2 Peter 3:10.

The conclusion is all but a tiny number of the saved will experience physical death and resurrection; so also all the unsaved will experience physical death and resurrection (those killed at Revelation 20:9 may pass directly to the Great White Throne judgment, Revelation 20:11–15, resurrected, without entering Hades).

Whether by transformation of the soul through death and of the body by resurrection, or transformation of the soul and body by rapture, for every saved person "it is necessary this the corruptible to put on incorruption, and this the mortal to put on immortality," 1 Corinthians 15:53, because "flesh and blood is not able to inherit the kingdom of God, nor the decay inherit the incorruption," 1 Corinthians 15:50. The mortal body needs to put on incorruption and immortality to inherit the kingdom of God.

I discussed the transformation of the soul in the previous chapter. This chapter will focus on the transformation of the body to make the believer fit for God's presence in heaven as immortal and incorruptible soul joined to immortal and incorruptible body.

The Transformation Of The Believer's Body

Why must there be a transformation and a resurrection of believers? There are three reasons.

The First Reason

Scripture says so. Although the word "resurrection" appears only in the New Testament, both Old and New Testament speak of resurrection. Job 19:26; Psalm 16:9–10 (in context, David speaks of himself); Daniel 12:2, 13; Ezekiel 37:1–14; John 5:28–29; 1 Corinthians 15:50–52; 1 Thessalonians 4:13–18; Revelation 20:4–6, 12.

The Second Reason

The second reason is the body is mortal and corrupted. The mortality and corruption of the body is demonstrated by several scriptures. For example, Romans 6:23, "the wages of sin is death." Romans 5:12, "death came upon all persons, in that all sinned." First Corinthians 15:22, "in Adam all die." The mortal, i.e., "flesh and blood, is not able to inherit the kingdom of God, nor the decay inherit the incorruption," 1 Corinthians 15:50.

The believer's body is not the source of sin, although acts of sinning are committed in mind and body. The Scripture clearly teaches the mind and body are not the source of sin.

> Romans 6:12–13, Therefore, do not let sin rule in your mortal body, for obedience to its desires. 13 Neither present your members to sin as instruments of unrighteousness, but present yourselves to God as living out from the dead, and your members as instruments of righteousness to God.

The location of sin is in the soul, in the human nature. In Paul's letters the phrase, "the flesh," is a euphemism for sin acting out through the material mind and body. Only a few times is "the flesh" used literally, e.g., Jesus Christ is come in the flesh, 1 John 4:2 Most of the time the phrase is used in a morally evil sense, e.g., 2 Peter, 2:10. "those who live after the flesh with lust of that which defiles, and who despise authority."

To be "in the flesh," Romans 7:5, is to be unsaved. That is why "the ones being in the flesh are not able to please God," Romans 8:8. The saved are no longer "in the flesh," but retain the sin attribute in their human nature. Therefore believers are to "not let sin rule in your mortal body, for obedience to its desires. Neither present your members to sin as instruments of unrighteousness" as quoted above, Romans 6:12–13. This is done through obedience to God's "Do this, Don't do that" rules for Christian living.

The source of sin is the corrupt human nature, corrupted from the original "image and likeness" of God by the addition of the sin attribute. When Adam sinned, his mutable human nature gained that principle of rebellion against God, Genesis 2:17; 3:6ff, the Scripture names "sin." When Adam procreated, that sinful human nature was inherited by his children, Genesis 5:3. The result of the sin attribute in the immaterial human nature is separation from God, which is spiritual death, and the eventual separation of the soul (the person) from the body, which is physical death.

At physical death (or rapture), as discussed in the previous chapter, the human nature of the saved person is cleansed from the sin attribute, to continue endlessly in that sinless state in the presence of God.

God has made clear his intent to resurrect the body. A sinless soul—immortal, incorruptible—requires an immortal, incorruptible body.

> 1 Corinthians 15:50, flesh and blood is not able to inherit the kingdom of God, nor the decay inherit the incorruption.

> 1 Corinthians 15:54, Now when this the corruptible shall have put on incorruptible, and this the mortal shall have put on immortality, then will come to pass the word having been written, "Death has been swallowed up in victory."

The immortal incorruptible body is formed by the resurrection of the deceased body, or the living body transformed at the rapture.

> 1 Corinthians 51–53, We will not all sleep [physically die], but we will all be changed [soul and body], 52 in an instant, in the twinkling of an eye, at the last trumpet. For the trumpet will announce, and the dead ones will be raised incorruptible, and we [the living] will be transformed. 53 For it is necessary this the corruptible to put on incorruption, and this the mortal to put on immortality.

The yet-future transformation or resurrection of the body is a fact. 1 Corinthians 15:12–13, "Now if Christ is proclaimed, that he has been raised out from dead ones, how say some among you that there is not a resurrection of dead ones? But if there is not a resurrection of dead ones, neither has Christ been raised."

The Third Reason

The third reason for the resurrection is seen in the original creation of the person Adam. God created Adam and then formed a body for Adam, Genesis 2:7. God formed the Woman soul and body from Adam, Genesis 2:22–23. Adam and the Woman procreated children who were soul and body, Genesis 4:1–2; 5:3. All in Adam are soul and body.

Looking to the future, God rewards his saved people for the good works done in the body, 1 Corinthians 3:11–15, when his saved people stand before the judgment seat of Christ, 2 Corinthians 5:10. God will punish the unsaved in the mind and body that was the instrument for the sinful works, Revelation 20:11–10.

God's Intent In Transformation And Resurrection

After looking at the Scripture evidence—the teaching of the Scripture as a whole—the reason for the transformation or resurrection of the body to immortal and incorruptible is God created humankind as soul and body, God intends his saved people to serve him in soul and body, and God intends to punish the unsaved in soul and body.

The transformation of the believer's body from mortal to immortal, from corruptible to incorruptible, will take place in one of two ways: resurrection of the dead body or transformation of the living body.

There will be the transformation of the living saved at the rapture.

1 Corinthians 15:51, We will not all sleep [physically die], but we will all be changed [soul and body], 52 in an instant.

An "instant" means immediately, a precise moment in time. There are many examples of "an instant" in the four gospels, because that is how long it took Jesus to heal a person from a disease. So also the transformation of the living believer's soul and body at the rapture.

In an earlier letter to another local church, 1 Thessalonians 4:16–17, Paul described the order of transformation and resurrection. "the dead in Christ will rise first [resurrection]. Then we the living remaining, together with them, will be [transformed and] caught up in the clouds for the meeting of the Lord in the air."

Paul's order is not different in 1 Corinthians 15:52. "For the trumpet will announce, and the dead ones will be raised incorruptible, and we will be transformed." Transformed how? "For it is necessary this the corruptible to put on incorruption, and this the mortal to put on immortality," 1 Corinthians 15:53.

> Now we implore you brethren, by the coming of our Lord Jesus Christ and our gathering together unto him, behold, something hidden I tell to you. We will not all sleep, but we will all be changed. Because the Lord himself, by a loud command, by the voice of an archangel, in an instant, in the twinkling of an eye, and by the trumpet of God will descend from heaven—for the trumpet will announce, and at the last trumpet, the dead in Christ will rise first; and the dead ones will be raised incorruptible. Then we the living remaining, together with them, we will be transformed. For it is necessary this the corruptible to put on incorruption, and this the mortal to put on immortality. And we will be caught up in the clouds for the meeting of the Lord in the air. And so always with the Lord we will be. (Combining 1 Corinthians 15:51–53; 1 Thessalonians 4:16–17; 2 Thessalonians 2:1)

There will be the re-creation of the believer's body at the resurrection.

> Resurrection. God reforms the physically dead decomposed body from existing materials and gives that body endless immortal physical life, and God causes the disembodied soul originally propagated with that body to unite with it and animate it. The united soul and resurrected body will continue endlessly in that reunited state.

> In the saved, the death of the body frees the immortal soul from the presence of sin, and the immortal saved soul is immediately transformed and glorified to be endlessly incorruptible. Then, when the body of the saved person is resurrected, it is reformed free from the presence of sin and transformed and glorified to be endlessly immortal and incorruptible. The saved live endlessly in the state of reunited body and soul without sin or corruption.

Then, about 1,000 years later.

> In the unsaved, resurrection reunites the immortal sinful soul with a body reformed to be immortal and corruptible to endure judgment and endless punishment. The unsaved live endlessly

in the state of reunited body and soul with sin and corruption.

I said the unsaved dead will be resurrected about 1,000 years after the transformation of the living and dead saved. There are several resurrections in Scripture, and there is an order to those resurrections. 1 Corinthians 15:23, "each in their own order: *the* firstfruit Christ, then those of Christ at his coming."

Christ was the first person to be resurrected. I understand this is not what most have been taught. Most are taught Christ resurrected persons out from the dead during the times of his earthly ministry. Those were healings of the physical condition death, not resurrections out from the dead.

In the definition above, I defined the resurrection of the saved as "the body of the saved person is resurrected, it is reformed free from the presence of sin and transformed and glorified to be endlessly immortal and incorruptible." But those whom Christ raised (the Scripture never says they were resurrected but were raised) out from the dead were not transformed to be immortal and incorruptible.

Christ is the "firstfruit" of the coming resurrections. The "firstfruit" was literally that first-ripening grain, a token of the full harvest, offered to God as a statement of gratitude for blessing the planting with a harvest. Christ as the firstfruit was a token of the full harvest of the resurrected saved. We see that in two rituals of the Mosaic Law.

Christ resurrected on the day of the wave offering of the firstfruits. In ancient Israel there were two offerings of literal firstfruits. The first was known as the sheaf of the firstfruits or the wave offering of the first fruits. The second was the firstfruits offered on the more familiar Day of Pentecost, also known as Feast of Harvest or the Feast of Weeks.

The wave offering of the firstfruits was from the barley harvest. This firstfruits was waved (literally waved) before the Lord on day of the week one (Sunday) following the Sabbath after the Passover.

Passover Nisan 14, Leviticus 23:5.

Wave sheaf of the Feast of First Fruits offered the tomorrow after the Sabbath after the Passover (Leviticus 23:9–14). The Feast of Unleavened bread would be in progress (Leviticus 23:6–8).

The second literal wave offering was made for the wheat harvest, seven weeks later, Leviticus 23:15, at what we think of as the Day of

Pentecost. Pentecost serves as an illustration of the greater resurrection yet to come after Christ the firstfruit.

After Christ the first fruit, each would be resurrected in their own order. First the New Testament church at the rapture, prior to the second advent (I am not setting a time. Whether pre-, mid-, or post-tribulation the rapture is prior to the second advent). Then the Old Testament saved will be resurrected at the second advent, Daniel 12:2, "many sleeping in the dust of the earth will awake," the context being the Tribulation, Daniel 12:1. The saved who were martyred during the Tribulation will be resurrected at or immediately following the second advent, Revelation 20:4, 6.

Physical death is not the enemy of the Christian. One might have anxiety about the means, but death is a friend. Through physical death and resurrection this corrupted body will become incorruptible, this mortal body will become immortal. Surely that is good news.

Chapter Summary

As noted in the previous chapter, most New Testament believers will experience physical death versus rapture. For those raptured there will be a transformation of the body from corruptible to incorruptible and immortal. For those experiencing physical death there will be a resurrection and transformation of the body from corruptible to incorruptible and immortal, and reanimation of the body.

Indeed, every believer who has died—Old Testament, New Testament, Tribulation, Millennial Kingdom—will experience the resurrection and transformation of the body from corruptible to incorruptible and immortal, and reanimation of the body. How is the body reanimated? The animating principle life is in the soul, the soul will be reunited with the resurrected body, restoring life to that incorruptible and immortal body.

The substance of this chapter is why and how the resurrection, transformation, and reanimation take place.

Endless Life Body and Soul in the Presence of God

Introduction

This chapter will discuss the believer's endless life in the final state after resurrection or rapture. When discussing the believer's life in the presence of God, the term "endless life" is preferred over "eternal life," not because the believer does not have eternal life (believers do have eternal life). Why?

In a previous chapter I defined eternal life as duration and quality of life. The duration is endless, not actually eternal, because eternal is without beginning as well as without end. The believer has a beginning, conception in the mother's body. The believer has no end to that life, because the human soul is naturally immortal, and the resurrected body is re-created to be immortal. Therefore the believer has endless life in the presence of God.

The Scripture clearly states that immediately after physical death the believer is present with his Lord and Savor Jesus Christ.

> 2 Corinthians 5:8, Now we are full of confidence and are pleased, rather, to be absent away from the body and to be at home with the Lord.

This principle applies to all the saved, Old and New Testament. This is the disembodied intermediate state between physical death and resurrection. As discussed in the two prior chapters, the intermediate state ends with the resurrection and transformation of the body, and the rejoining of the immortal incorruptible soul with the immortal incorruptible body.

The Scripture does not "fill in the blanks" with a description of the intermediate life in heaven. If Revelation 4, 5 gives any understanding of that life, it is filled with recurring acts of worship.

Active, Conscious Endless Life In Heaven Post-Resurrection

What then is the nature of the active, conscious endless life in heaven after resurrection? The period of life after the resurrection will be discussed under three broad categories:

> The life of the resurrected New Testament church during the Tribulation.

> The life of the saved during the Davidic-Messianic-Millennial Kingdom.

The life of the saved during the Eternal Kingdom.

A brief discussion of the life of the unsaved after their resurrection will conclude this chapter.

The Life of the New Testament Church During The Tribulation

My personal eschatology is a pre-tribulation rapture of the New Testament church (one chapter in my book *Rapture* discusses this view; see also my book *Dispensational Eschatology*). Several scriptures and doctrinal principles can be brought to bear on the subject, but Revelation 3:10 seems conclusive (see my book *A Private Commentary on the Bible: Revelation 1–7*).

I am aware of differing views on the rapture, including the Postmillennial and Amillennial views there is no rapture and no Tribulation. Those views do not affect the goal of the Ordo Salutis, the endless life body and soul in the presence of God. For those who do believe, this section will be helpful toward understanding that goal of the Ordo Salutis.

In 1 Thessalonians 4:17 Paul tells us almost all we can know about the New Testament church during the Tribulation. "And so always with the Lord we will be." However, we may glean a little more from other scriptures.

During the Tribulation, the New Testament church is watching the events described in Revelation 4:1–18:24. The New Testament church is not mentioned in association with those events, because the Tribulation is the fulfillment of the Old Testament Day of the Lord leading to the Davidic-Messianic Kingdom on earth after the second advent.

However, the Revelation does give some information in chapters 2–3, concerning the state of the church both during and after the Tribulation. (Comments on the scriptures are from my book, *A Private Commentary on the Bible: Revelation 1–7*, and *A Private Commentary on the Bible: Revelation 17–22*.)

> 2:7, To the one who is prevailing I will give him to eat out of the tree of life, which is in the paradise of God.

To "prevail" means to understand and act on what Jesus has said by means of faith. To prevail is to continue in the faith by means of the faith against every obstacle to the faith. By faith we understand Jesus Christ's judgment is right. By faith we repent and confess our sins. By faith we receive cleansing from our sins and our fellowship with Christ is restored. By faith we do the works in his name, by his power, for his glory.

The "tree of life ... in the paradise of God" is a promise of location as well as quality of life. The believer has a place in heaven, the genuine paradise of God, where he will eat of the fruit of the tree as part of his inheritance in Christ, 1 Peter 1:4. The tree is not only in the heavens of the here and now, but in the new heaven and earth, Revelation 22:2, that will replace this current universe, 20:11; 21:1, and thereby this scripture assures the reader of a place with God in the here and now, and in the eternal state that is God present with his people, 21:22–23. The tree and the location symbolize the believer partaking of and enjoying all the benefits of an endless life spent with God. The fruit of the tree of life is exactly what the name implies, the duration and quality of eternal life.

> 2:11, You be faithful unto death, and I will give to you the crown, the one of life.

To be faithful unto death is our cause: it is to exercise toward Christ unswerving adherence; it is to use all he has entrusted to us for his glory.

To be faithful "unto death" does not mean until death, but through death, enduring death, embracing the loss of life for the sake of his glory. To live a life of faithfulness the Christian must live for Christ to the very end of life, and persevere through death, until having gained his or her eternal inheritance, and put on the crown of life. One of my core values is this: I will continue active in my faith until Christ takes me home to heaven.

What this crown and the other crowns mentioned in the New Testament are is unknown. Like all other rewards, re: 1 Corinthians 3:12, gold, silver, precious stones, a crown is probably not material, or even some kind of outward display, but rather some kind of spiritual capacity or function to further one's ability to serve and glorify the Lord

> 2:17, The one who is prevailing, I will give to him the manna, the one hidden. And I will give to him a white stone, and on the stone a new name has been written, which no one knows except the one receiving.

The meaning of the hidden manna is not in Exodus 16, the origin of manna, but in Jesus' explanation of manna in John 6. Jesus is the Christian's manna. Jesus said, John 6:58, referring to himself as the spiritual "food" that gives eternal life, "This is the bread having come down out of heaven. Not as your fathers ate the manna and died. The one eating this bread will live forever." The point of the "reward" passages at the end of each of the seven letters of the Revelation is eternal life, fellowship, and service with Jesus. The hidden manna represents these things in the believer's salvific relationship with God in Christ. The Lord is speaking of himself, not a hidden jar of manna.

When a "new name" is given to a believer it reflects a new purpose given to the person by God, or a new relationship established between the person and God. The new name indicates something "new" about the person in character, quality, attribute, relationship, or purpose. Abram became Abraham because he was to be the father of the faithful. Jacob became Israel because from him would come a new nation dedicated to serving the Lord. Saul the destroyer became Paul the evangelist and apostle.

In the letter to Pergamos, the new name reflects the renewed relationship of the repenting and prevailing believer. The white color of the stone is a reminder of the righteous character and purpose the believer has in his relationship with Jesus. In relation to eternity, one might think of the white stone with the new name as an identifying badge one wears in heaven, where we will be known by our relationship, our character, and our purpose.

> 2:26, 28, And the one who is prevailing and keeping my works until the end, I will give to him authority over the nations ... 28 And I will give to him the morning star.

The one who prevails will in some manner participate in Christ's rule of the coming Davidic-Messianic-Millennial kingdom. The New Testament believer is a joint-heir with Christ, Romans 8:17. Whether directly participating in his rule, or participating representatively (Christ is the believer's representative in all things), the one prevailing will participate in Jesus' authority over the nations. The allusion is to Psalm 2, the psalm of Messiah-King, and specifically 2:9.

In the kingdom the believer may have the authority to affect lives for good and the power to punish: the shepherd's rod keeps the sheep on the right path and it chastises the sheep that stray, Matthew 19:28; Luke 22:30 may have meaning for entire New Testament church, because the Twelve apostles also represent the New Testament church.

The morning star speaks of spiritual communion and fellowship between the believer and Christ. Jesus arises morning by morning in the heart and mind of the believer after each night's journey through life; his presence is the reward of daily perseverance.

> 3:5–6, The one who is prevailing, in this manner will be clothed in white garments. And never no never will I blot his name out of the book of life. And I will confess his name in front of my Father, and in front of his messengers.

The reference to "clothing' is a metaphorical reference to character, e.g., Zechariah 3:1–5. Another example, Matthew 7:15, false prophets come in sheep's clothing: an outward display of harmless intent, humble disposition, and solicitous care; inside they are like ravening wolves. Undefiled clothing in this verse similarly speaks to character. Performing dead works defiles the believer's soul (perhaps a figurative allusion to Leviticus 11, 21; Numbers 6, 19). Undefiled clothing indicates certain believers continued to seek the Lord's guidance and do works through his power. They were a singular witness of the power of Christ in a church full of dead programs and ineffective ministries.

To "live with me in white" must be interpreted in this same context, i.e., these are the believers who possess spiritual power and continuing fellowship with Jesus. Their worthiness is the result of their association with Jesus: their perseverance in spiritual fellowship; good works done by him in them. To "live with Jesus in white" means to live undefiled by the world in a vital and intimate fellowship with him through his Word and with his Spirit.

Jesus confesses believers before the Father because their names are in the book of life. The name represents the person. Jesus' confesses the person before the Father because of the certainty of eternal life.

The Book of Life is a figure of speech for Jesus himself. The saved are "in Christ." They have a vital, living, intimate, endless, everlasting salvific relationship with God because they are saved. Every believer is in a spiritual union with Christ. No believer can ever be "blotted out" of the book. These words from Jesus are an assurance of everlasting salvation, not a threat of loss of salvation. No one who is in the book will ever be removed from the book. One characteristic of a saved person is he or she will prevail in the faith by faith. That is the doctrine of perseverance. The book of life symbolizes the everlasting relationship believers have with God, as does a similar symbol, Isaiah

49:16, "See, I have inscribed you on the palms of My hands."

> 3:12–13, The one who is prevailing, I will make him a pillar in the temple of my God. And never no never might he go out anymore. And I will write upon him the name of my God, and the name of the city of my God, the New Jerusalem coming out of heaven from my God, and my new name.

The literal temple in heaven is the immediate presence of God, that is, the manifestation of himself in heaven, Revelation 4:2–11. I believe that manifestation is continuously maintained by God in heaven. That "temple" seems to consist of the manifestation of God on a throne and the sea of glass before the throne. The sea of glass is mentioned at 4:6 and 15:2. In both mentions worship is taking place.

The pillar in the temple is a figure of speech. God is not going to transform the believer into a literal pillar. The figure of speech is intended to communicate permanence. The believer will never depart from God because of sin. The believer will "never no never" go out from God's presence—he/she will never commit an act of sinning. Naturally believers, like the holy messengers, will leave the temple area as assigned works in the universe by God. But the temple, which is the presence of God, is their permanent home until the end of this present universe. Then, Revelation 21:22, which states that there is no temple in the New Jerusalem, means the entire city is the temple and the believer is a living enduring memorial to the grace of God.

In the phrase, "I will write on him," Christ is conveying a three-fold assurance of eternal life. By writing these names upon the believer, he has assured him or her that God has owned and identified the believer as his child. The believer is a citizen of the New Jerusalem (Revelation 21:2); Christ in his full and complete revelation of himself (the new name), has owned and identified himself with the believer. What greater assurance of eternal life could the believer need?

> 3:21, The one who is prevailing, I will give to him to sit with me on my throne, as I also overcame and sat down with my Father on his throne.

When Jesus Christ ascended to heaven he sat down "at the right hand of God." Christ is currently seated "at the right hand of God," Colossians 3:1; Hebrews 10:12. He is not seated on a separate throne, but on the same throne, side-by-side, so to speak, with the Father and the Holy Spirit. Jesus Christ is the God-man, he is God the Son incarnate in Jesus of Nazareth. The Son is the same one deity essence as the Father and the Spirit. There is one throne of God on which sit God Father-Son-Spirit.

But there is another throne that is specifically Jesus Christ's throne.

2 Sam 7:12–14a, 16, When your days are fulfilled and you rest with your fathers, I will set up your seed after you, who will come from your body, and I will establish his kingdom. He shall build a house for My name, and I will establish the throne of his kingdom forever. I will be his Father, and he shall be My son.

And your house and your kingdom shall be established forever before you. Your throne shall be established forever. (NKJV)

Ps 132:11–12, The Lord has sworn in truth to David; He will not turn from it: "I will set upon your throne the fruit of your body. If your sons will keep My covenant And My testimony which I shall teach them, Their sons also shall sit upon your throne forevermore. (NKJV)

Luke 1:30–33, And the messenger said to her, "Do not fear Mariam. For you have found favor with God. Look now, you will conceive in your womb, and will bear a son, and you will call his name 'Jesus.' He will be great, and will be called 'son of Most High.' And the Lord God will give him the throne of David, his father. And he will reign over the house of Jacob to the ages, and of his kingdom there will not be an end."

The throne of Jesus Christ, the "my throne" of Revelation 3:21, is the throne of the Davidic-Messianic Kingdom.

The New Testament believer will not sit beside Jesus on this throne; that would imply equality. Jesus Christ represents the believer in this matter just as he represents the believer in all things concerning his saved people. The New Testament believer will be part of Jesus Christ's administration of his Davidic-Messianic-Millennial Kingdom.

Revelation 19:7, We should rejoice and should leap for joy, and will give the glory to him, because the wedding supper of the Lamb has come, and his bride has made herself ready.

The bride is not the New Testament church, as this group is so often misidentified. The New Testament church is part of the bride, but also part of those "having been invited to the wedding supper of the Lamb."

In the context of the Revelation—in the context of this 19:7–9 moment—what is in view is the promise of the Davidic-Messianic Kingdom that was given to national ethnic Israel, not to the New Testament church. The New Testament church is joint-heir with Christ in all things, Romans 8:17. As he inherits the promised kingdom, those he represents, the New Testament church, inherit with him, not directly, but by representation.

Who then is the bride at Revelation 19:7? The Davidic-Messianic kingdom itself is the restoration of national ethnic Israel, through whom King Jesus Christ will rule the world. So, at least in this context, the bride cannot be the New Testament church. The raptured, resurrected church is present, but another people group is being identified as the bride.

The "wedding supper" is a not a literal supper but a figure or symbol for the fulfillment of the promises. In this sense the prophecies were a betrothal: 2 Samuel 7:13, 16; Psalm 2; and passages in Psalm 72; Isaiah 2; 9; 11; 25; 65; Zechariah 14; and in the New Testament Matthew 5:5; 19:28; 25:11; Luke 21:31; Acts 1:6; Revelation 5:10; and many others. In Revelation 19:9 we see the fulfillment of those promises celebrated in a symbol, a wedding, The wedding supper is a symbol indicating the fulfillment of the promises: the Old Testament prophecies of the coming kingdom were the betrothal; the wedding supper is the fulfillment.

Every saved person who is in heaven at the time of the "wedding supper" will experience the literal fulfillment of the promises of an earthly Davidic-Messianic Kingdom. Who, I ask, will be left out of the Kingdom? The Davidic-Messianic Kingdom is in part a fulfillment of the authority God gave to Adam, Eve, and their descendants over the earthly creation, Genesis 1:26–28, a responsibility in which they failed. The second Adam, Jesus the Christ, will assume and properly execute that authority. All the redeemed, Old Testament and New Testament, are represented in the second Adam, 1 Corinthians 15:22.

So none are left out, all those redeemed who are in heaven—out of every dispensation, out of every people group—in this moment just before the advent—will participate in the kingdom. All will participate in the fulfillment of the "betrothal" promise of the kingdom prophecies. All the redeemed in heaven will participate in the kingdom.

Who, then, is the bride receiving the kingdom with Christ. As the heir of David, the Christ will inherit the kingdom promised to national ethnic Israel through David's heir, 2 Samuel 7:13, 16. As the Messiah he will rule the nations, Psalm 2. The bride is the people of David, for whom the Christ receives the kingdom. The bride is national ethnic Israel, the nation to whom the promises were made.

> Revelation 19:14, And the armies who were in heaven were following him upon white horses, being clothed in fine linen, white, pure.

Not one army, but more than one. All the members of these armies are, in the context of the passage, in the third heaven, because they are leaving the third heaven with Christ. Who is in the third heaven? The army of holy messengers (angels; the Hebrew and Greek words mean messenger). The army that is all saved persons from Adam to Christ's crucifixion-resurrection. The army that is the New Testament church. The army that is the martyred, resurrected Tribulation saints. It seems reasonable the armies of the redeemed are in their resurrected form, because they are leaving the spirit domain returning to the earth, which is the material domain.

The Life of the Saved During the Davidic-Messianic-Millennial Kingdom

The Scripture states Christ has made his New Testament church "kings and priests," Revelation 1:6; 5:10. The function of the New Testament church during the Davidic-Messianic-Millennial Kingdom will be to act as kings and priests. In some way Christ's rule will be administered through the New Testament church (cf. Matthew 19:28; Luke 22:30). As priests, the New Testament church may in some way assist in the evangelization of those unsaved children born during the Millennial Kingdom.

The Life Of The Saved During The Eternal Kingdom

The Eternal Kingdom is in a new heaven on a new earth. At the end of the Millennial Kingdom, this present heaven and earth will be destroyed.

> Revelation 20:11, the earth and heaven fled, and no place was found for them.

> 2 Peter 3:10, But the day of the Lord will come as a thief in the night in which the heavens will pass away with a rushing noise, and elements will be unbound with burning fire, and earth and the works in it will be burned up.

God will create a new heaven and a new earth. Revelation 21:1,

"And I saw a new heaven everlasting and a new earth, for the first heaven and the first earth they had gone away; and there is no more sea."

The new earth in the new heaven will have a dwelling place for all the saved out of all the ages. Revelation 21:1–4, "And the holy city, New Jerusalem, I saw coming out of heaven from God, prepared as a bride adorned for her husband. 3 And I heard a great voice from the throne, saying, 'Look, the tabernacle of God amid humankind. And he will dwell with them, and they will be his peoples, and God himself will be with them. 4 And he will wipe off every tear from their eyes. And death will not be anymore, nor sorrow, nor wailing, nor pain. They will not be anymore because the first things have gone away.'"

The new earth and new heaven will be a place of worship and service toward God with no sin.

> 21:7, The one prevailing will inherit all things, and I will be his God, and he will be my son.

> 21:8 But to fearful, and to unbelieving, and to having become abhorrent, and to murderers, and to sexually immoral, and to sorcerers, and to idolators, and to all liars, their portion is in the lake burning with fire and sulfur, which is the second death.

> 21:27, And never no never may enter into it anything defiling, and those practicing anything detestable to God, and a lie; only those being written in the book of life of the Lamb.

Conclusion

The life of the saved—of every person saved in every age of humankind—after physical death and after resurrection, will endlessly be conscious, active, sinless, incorruptible service and worship toward God. We know because God said so.

The Conscious, Active life Of the Unsaved

The Scripture does not have much to say about the unsaved after physical death. That is because the intent of the biblical writers was to tell the unsaved how to be saved (evangelism), and tell the saved the nature, practice, and future of their salvation (discipleship). Evangelism of the lost and discipling the saved are the mission and duty of the New Testament church.

However, the Holy Spirit and the New Testament writers did not leave us in doubt as to the nature of the life of the unsaved after physical death. In the remainder of this chapter I will address the conscious active life of the unsaved in the intermediate state and after resurrection.

The Scripture presents two locations for the unsaved after physical death. Referring again to Shedd (chapter, "Physical Death and the Intermediate State").

> the intermediate state for the lost is Hell [*hádēs*] without the body, and the final state for the lost is Hell [*géenna*; lake of fire] with the body.

I have inserted the words *hádēs* and *géenna* because this is the way the Scripture distinguishes between the two locations for the unsaved after physical death. The relationship between the two locations may be illustrated: Hades is like the county jail where the convicted sinner is held before being moved to the permanent prison of Gehenna (*géenna*) which is the lake of fire, Revelation 20:11–15.

Hades

Hades is the word the New Testament consistently uses to describe the place where unsaved souls are located between physical death and resurrection. The word *hádēs* appears ten times in the New Testament: Matthew 11:23; 16:18; Luke 10:15; 16:23; Acts 2:27, 31; Revelation 1:18; 6:8; 20:14.

The Bible is also consistent in its testimony that saved souls do not go to *hádēs* after physical death but immediately go to God's presence, e.g., Exodus 3:6; Matthew 22:32; 2 Corinthians 5:8; Philippians 1:23; 1 Thessalonians 4:13–14.

Jesus spoke about *hádēs* four times. In the gospels Jesus used *hádēs* as a metaphor for death and eternal damnation in three out of four uses. This is not to say *hádēs* is not a literal place in the spirit domain. Non-literal language is based on something literal and communicates something literal. *Hádēs* is the literal place in the spirit domain where the unsaved dead go after physical death. Therefore a metaphorical use communicates a literal truth: the truth of a place of just punishment for unsaved souls.

Jesus used *hádēs* in a figure of speech known as a merism in Matthew 11:23. Jesus is upbraiding the people who had rejected him and his message. This verse reads, "And you, Capernaum, who will be lifted up to heaven, will be brought down to Hades." Hades is being used as the opposite of "heaven." The city had obviously not been literally exalted to heaven by God, but metaphorically by the people. Heaven was being used as a figure of speech to communicate Capernaum's worldly success. But in rejecting the Messiah the people of Capernaum had gained the opposite: they had condemned themselves to spiritual death and endless punishment, in a word *hádēs*, because there is no salvation in any name but Jesus.

Matthew 16:18, "Now I also say to you, that you are Peter, and on this the rock I will build my church, and the gates of Hades will not prevail against it." The "gates" are a biblical metaphor for the strength of a city, a combination of military, economic, and political might. The metaphor is based on something literal. Most biblical cities had walls and a gate. The gate kept out the enemy. The walls at the gate housed the government. The marketplace was just within the gates, so the gates were also the economic center of the city. Through these literal customs the word "gates" acquired a metaphorical meaning.

The "gates of *hádēs*" speaks of the power of *hádēs*. Now *hádēs* is a location in the spirit domain where the unsaved dead are imprisoned until the Great White Throne judgment, Revelation 20:11–15. As such it has no power to threaten the church. So the use here is metaphorical, it represents something else. The most common and likely interpretation is that "gates of *hádēs*" represents Satan and his fallen angels. The close connection of Matthew 16:23, where Jesus said to Peter, "Get behind me Satan," supports the interpretation.

Now, Satan does not rule in *hádēs*, an idea gained from Milton's epic poem *Paradise Lost*. *Hádēs* is for human souls, not fallen angels. Because *hádēs* is the place for lost sinners, and Satan is the originator of sin, through sin Satan may be said to have the power of death, and so by a turn of the figure Satan's strength may be said to be *hádēs*, because that is where all his victims are kept.

Satan doesn't really have the power of death. All persons belong to God, and he is the only one who decides life and death, eternal life or endless punishment. But since Satan originated sin, and thereby activated God's penalty against sin, which is death, then in a figure Satan as the originator of sin may be said to have the power of death. Moreover, since through temptation to sin Satan brings death to human souls, then he may also be said to have the power of death through his power of temptation. And since the result of a sinner's death is confinement in *hádēs*, then as the place where his victims are confined the strength of Satan may be said to be the gates of *hádēs*, i.e., his strength is shown in the damnation of his victims.

So this verse is a metaphorical use of the literal place *hádēs*. As such it shows the strength of sin and the strength of death: all unsaved sinners go to *hádēs* from which there is no escape. Sin and death—*hádēs*—shall not prevail against the church, because Jesus is Lord over life and death, and he has given the church eternal life.

Other uses of *hádēs* are in Luke 10:15; Acts 2:27, 31 (where it is used as the Greek equivalent of Sheol; Jesus went down to the grave). In the Revelation passages the unsaved dead are in view. In Revelation 20:14, the reason "death" is said to be cast into the lake of fire is because at this point in eschatological time the only dead are the unsaved dead; the saved were resurrected to incorruptible eternal life a thousand years or more earlier.

"Dead" in Revelation 20:14 does not mean physical death, because the unsaved previously suffered their physical death, went to *hádēs*, and are now resurrected to immortal corruptible life. "Dead" means the second death, which is eternal spiritual death: eternally separated from God. Because all the unsaved go into the lake of fire there is no death outside that lake.

There is a current view among some that even the unsaved in the lake of fire cannot be separated from an omnipresent God. That may or may not be true. God may exclude himself from the lake of fire. However, what is in view is permanently endlessly separated from spiritual life: the second death. The lake of fire is a place of Gods' unremitting justice and wrath against those endlessly separated from him by spiritual death. The unsaved person has received what he or she wanted, a life without God, resulting in a life without love, mercy, compassion, kindness, and grace.

The reason *hádēs* is cast into the lake of fire is because this is the "second death." The first death is physical death, when the unsaved go to Hades. The second death is endless spiritual death and endless punishment for sin. Death and *hádēs* are being used metaphorically (personification) and literally: all the occupants of *hádēs*, which is all the unsaved from the first unsaved death to the last, were cast into the lake of fire.

A literal use of *hádēs* is Luke 16:19–26, Jesus told the story of the rich man and Lazarus. Deciding whether this text is a parable or a fact-based narrative is not essential to understanding *hádēs*. A narrative relates historical facts and a parable always includes literal elements, e.g., a sower sowing seeds, a mustard seed, weeds (tares) and wheat. A parable's point is drawn from the use of literal elements in the story.

In Luke 16:19–26 some of the literal elements are: life; death; a righteous person; an unrighteous person; a place of torment; a place of ease; a "great gulf fixed"; the desire for a witness to others needing to be saved from the place of torment. The visual and verbal communication between persons in *hádēs* and heaven is probably non-literal, i.e., the characters speak for the narrator (Jesus) in order to carry the narrative forward and communicate the truth concerning *hádēs*.

The key text for the immediate purpose is 16:23, "And in Hades, having lifted up his eyes, being in torment, he sees Abraham from afar, and Lazarus in his bosom." Whether a parable or a narrative the rich man's soul had to be somewhere—he had died, 16:22, and *hádēs* is where Jesus said his soul was located. Whether or not the rich man was a real person, death is a real event that happens to all persons. And having died, the soul of the rich man went to *hádēs*. Since the human soul is literal, and death is literal, it is reasonable the location of the rich man's soul after death is literal; deity (Jesus the God-man) would know the truth of these things. *Hádēs* is a real place in the spirit domain where unsaved souls go after physical death.

In addition to telling us where unsaved persons end up after death, Jesus says some things about *hádēs*. It is a place "with torments." The word is in the dative case, answering the (unspoken) question "What is happening to the rich man in *hádēs*." The word "torments" is in the plural, indicating either great and severe torment, or many different kinds of torment. The word translated "torments" is *básanos* [Zodhiates, s. v. 931]. To the Greeks the word literally meant a "touchstone," which was a black siliceous stone used to test the purity of gold, silver, and other metals. From there the word came to mean a test or criteria by which the qualities of a thing are tried. Metaphorically it meant an instrument of torture used to force a person to reveal the truth, and came to mean an examination, trial by torture. The New Testament writers used *básanos* to describe torment, pain from disease (e.g., Matthew 4:24), and in Luke 16:23, 28, punishment. *Hádēs* is a place of punishment for unsaved souls.

The unsaved soul from any age of humankind suffers painful punishment in *hádēs* because he or she rejected God's love by rejecting

God as Savior. They had no faith in God the Savior and therefore died unsaved and unforgiven. When God's love in salvation is rejected, what remains to the unsaved person is God's justice and wrath.

There is no escape from *hádēs*. The rich man saw Abraham and Lazarus and requested Lazarus be sent to provide him some relief from the pain. Abraham responded that there was a great gulf fixed between heaven and *hádēs*, 16:26, so that no one could pass from one location to the other. That "great gulf fixed" is physical death. Hebrews 9:27, "it awaits for men to die once, then after that judgment." The power of physical death is to fix the spiritual state of the unsaved soul: endlessly unsaved. The truth is there is no escape from *hádēs*.

The sum is that *hádēs* is the place where unsaved souls go to wait in torment for the Great White Throne judgment. Why are the unsaved dead tormented in *hádēs*? God is the origin and source of all that is loving, good, kind, merciful, compassionate, and the like. When sinners reject God as their savior they reject everything loving and good. All that remains to them is God's wrath and every negative thing that accompanies his wrath.

Gehenna

Gehenna (*géenna*), the lake of fire, is the place where the unsaved spend eternity. The lake of fire, or *géenna*, is the true hell. The word *géenna* appears twelve times: Matthew 5:22, 29, 30; 10:28; 18:9; 23:15, 33, Mark 9:43, 45, 47; Luke 12:5; James 3:6. The words "lake of fire" appear four times: Revelation 19:20; Revelation 20:10, 14, 15. There is also a description of the lake of fire in Mark 9:44, 46, 48, and Matthew 8:12; 13:42, 50; 22:13; 24:51; 25:30; Luke 13:28.

The lake of fire is the second death, Revelation 20:6, 14. The first death is physical death, which confirms their spiritual state of unsaved: endlessly separated from the spiritual life given only through faith in Christ. The second death is endless imprisonment in the lake of fire. Only the soul goes to Hades. After the unsaved are resurrected the reunited body and soul are cast into Gehenna.

How do we know the unsaved dead will be resurrected? John 5:28–29, "Do not marvel at this, because an hour is coming in which all those in the grave will hear his voice 29 and will come forth: the ones having practiced good, to resurrection of life; the ones habitually doing evil, to resurrection of judgment."

Revelation 20:10 with 19:20 confirm that sinners will be punished but not annihilated by the lake of fire. In 19:20 the beast and false prophet are cast into the lake of fire. In 20:10, after one thousand years (20:7), the beast and the false prophet are still alive in the lake of fire and with the fallen angels and the unsaved will continue to be tormented day and night forever and ever.

Why is the punishment of the unsaved endless? There are many reasons, of which I will give a few. The first is that sin is a crime committed against an infinite being: God. The crime itself is committed by a finite being but the evil of sin is an infinite evil requiring endless punishment because it is committed against an infinite being. We understand the principle value, fining a man who kills a dog, executing a man who kills another man.

Another reason is that unsaved sinners never stop sinning. They go to *hádēs* and *géenna* because they are unsaved sinners and they will forever be unsaved sinners. They receive no grace to control their tendency and inclination to sin (as they do receive during this mortal life). Their natural enmity against God continues in the lake of fire because they are unsaved sinners. For eternity they will blaspheme God for punishing their sin. If the crime and guilt are endless then the punishment must also be endless.

The sinner's crime is both moral and legal. The moral crime is that the sinner is not in the moral and spiritual image of God in which he created mankind. The legal crime describes the problem the sinner has with the moral crime. The sinner disobeys God's laws and has no desire to be obedient. Therefore he has no desire to be in God's image. Because the unsaved are not redeemed their human nature remains infected with sin, and thus they will never be—and do not want to be— in God's image or obey God's laws. Since their sinful condition is endless, and their judicial guilt is endless, then their punishment is endless.

The sinner has no holy resources with which to pay the debt of his judicial guilt for the crime. A perfect life, from conception to physical death, could pay the debt, but all are born sinners, except Jesus, and no one is intrinsically righteous, except Jesus. The sinner has no moral or spiritual resources with which to pay his or her debt to God's violated laws and holiness. God's justice demands a person receive what is due in an amount equal to the debt owed. The debt is a crime against the infinite and holy God. The debt is unpayable—the sinner has no means to pay for his or her crime of sin—so endless punishment is just.

234

The life, reward, and joy of the saved is endless; so also must be the punishment of the unsaved. If the punishment of the unsaved is not endless, then the blissful life of the saved is not endless.

God has promised the saved endless eternal life and promised the unsaved endless punishment. If the one promise has a limit to its duration, then the other must also. But since the saved do have endless eternal life with God, the unsaved must endure endless separation from God. Unless God breaks his promise to the saved, the unsaved will endure endless punishment. God does not break his promises.

Annihilationism

In recent years the doctrine of annihilationism has made a resurgence. The doctrine of annihilationism arose from the Greek doctrine of physicalism—an obscure doctrine never accepted by the majority in the ancient world—that human beings are material only; that what we think of as a "soul" is merely a by-product of biology, not real but only apparent. In Physicalism, all thoughts, all emotions, any sentient sense of self are merely and only the result of biological processes. In Physicalism, when the body dies the human being ceases to exist.

A doctrine known as Conditional Immortality took annihilationism and physicalism, sprinkled in a little Christianity, and said human beings have a soul, but the soul can be destroyed, made non-existent, just as if the person never existed.

What the ambiguous phrase "conditional immortality" means is all persons ever born will appear at the GWT (Great White Throne, Revelation 20:11–15) to be judged worthy of continuing life, or worthy of annihilation. In the doctrine of conditional immortality there is no salvation until the GWT, where every person will be judged worthy, or not, of immortality or annihilation. For those not judged worthy some unknown duration will be spent suffering in the lake of fire, then annihilation of body and soul.

Scripture is opposed to conditional immortality, physicalism, and annihilation. The Scripture clearly teaches the dissolution and subsequent resurrection of the physical body, but the Scripture never teaches the dissolution of the human soul. The soul once conceived continues endlessly, because the source and origin of the life in the soul is God who has life-in-himself. Surely what Jesus said is a sufficient answer to this false doctrine. Matthew 22:31–32, "... have you not read that having been spoken to you by God, saying, 'I am the God of Abraham and the God of Isaac and the God of Jacob?'" God established a salvific relationship with Abraham, Isaac, and Jacob during their mortal life, and because God is "not the God of the dead but of the living," that salvific relationship continued after their physical death.

The human soul once conceived in the womb continues endlessly. The body once resurrected from physical death continues endlessly. The beast and false prophet are the exemplars of those scriptural facts.

Modern annihilationism depends on the Greek word *apóllumi* [Zodhiates, s. v. 622] (and the word from which it is derived, *ólethros* [Zodhiates, s. v. 3639], 2 Thessalonians 1:9) Their key verse is Matthew 10:28, "And do not be afraid of those killing [*apokteínō*] the body, but are not able to kill [*apokteínō*] the soul; but fear rather the one being able to *apóllumi* both soul and body in Gehenna."

Most Bible versions translate *apóllumi* as "destroy." In most uses, *apóllumi* means destroy in the sense of physical death. However, at Matthew 9:17 the word means destroy in the sense of ruin, "Nor do they pour new wine into old wineskins; but if it is the wineskins burst and the wine is spilled and the wineskins *apóllumi:* not annihilated but ruined. At Matthew 15:24 the word means unsaved, "But answering he said, "I was not sent except to the lost (*apóllumi*) sheep of the house of Israel." The unsaved person is in a state of spiritual ruin.

The biblical use of *apóllumi* is the same as the secular use. Moulton and Milligan example from the papyri: the loss of money, the loss of clothing, the loss of life of two pigs [Moulton, s. v. 622]. Gerhard Kittle shows in Greek secular literature the word was used "to destroy or kill in battle; to suffer loss of money." In other uses, "to trifle away one's life ... thereby bringing themselves to destruction" i.e., to ruin [Kittel, 1:394].

We turn to Silva [*NIDNT*, 1:357]. *Apóllumi* was used in Homer of slaughter in war. To "disappear, be lost, be ruined (financially), perish, die ... injury, destruction, final end of earthly existence ... sickness in body, rot in wood, rust in iron." In a specific theological sense in the New Testament, "definite destruction, not merely in the sense of extinction of physical existence, but rather of an eternal plunge into Hades and a hopeless destiny of death ... Over against life with God there stands the terrible possibility of eternal perdition." (Eternal: unending; Perdition: a state of endless punishment and damnation into which a sinful and un-penitent person passes after death.)

The use at Matthew 10:28 conforms to all other Scripture uses and all secular uses. *Apóllumi* "is not annihilation, but endless punishment in Gehenna (the real hell)" [Robertson, 1:83]. Looking to the verse in context, "men should fear, i.e., all human beings should reverence-respect-worship God, 10:28, because he can *apóllumi* the soul and the body in hell, i.e., endless punishment in the lake of fire" [Quiggle, *Matthew*, 183]. 'Destroy' is not annihilation (a concept foreign to Scripture) but endless ruin through endless separation from God in the lake of fire.

Chapter Summary

This final chapter discussed the believer's endless life in body and soul in the presence of God. When discussing the believer's life in the presence of God, the term "endless life" is preferred over "eternal life," not because the believer does not have eternal life (believers have eternal life) but eternal means without beginning or end.

In a previous chapter I defined eternal life as duration and quality of life. The duration is endless, not actually eternal, because eternal is without beginning as well as without end. The believer has a beginning, conception in the mother's body. The believer has no end to that life, because the human soul is naturally immortal, and the resurrected body is re-created to be immortal. Therefore the believer has endless life in the presence of God. (So also the resurrected unsaved person has endless life, but not incorruptible life.)

This chapter discusses all phases of the saved person's life post-resurrection. Various aspects of that endless life are discussed using Christ's seven letters to seven churches, in the Revelation, chapters 2 and 3, the "wedding super" Revelation chapter 19, and the second advent in Revelation 19–20.

The life of the saved during the Davidic-Messianic-Millennial Kingdom is discussed. Aspects of life in the eternal kingdom on the new heaven and earth, Revelation 21:1–22:5, are explored.

The conscious active life of the saved and unsaved is discussed, with an extended exploration of the meaning of Hades as the intermediate state of the unsaved dead. Then, the state of the unsaved is Gehenna (lake of fire) is presented.

The state of the unsaved brings up the recent reintroduction and rising popularity of the doctrine of Annihilationism. This subject is briefly explored and disproven as a valid Christian doctrine. Alongside that discussion, the recently revived doctrines of Physicalism and Conditional Immortality are discussed and proven to be heresies when added to the orthodox Christian faith.

The human soul is naturally immortal because God created the human soul with the animating principle life as one of its constituent components. No scripture or scripture passage teaches the dissolution of the human soul.

Therefore, every human being lives on after physical death, in conscious active life. The immortal soul of the saved is transformed at physical death to be sinless and given the grace of indefectability to remain incorruptible. The immortal soul of the unsaved remains sinful and corruptible.

Every human being continues after physical death in an intermediate state. For the saved, that intermediate state between death and resurrection is heaven. For the unsaved, that intermediate state between death and resurrection is Hades.

The physical body of every human being will be resurrected, and the soul reunited to the recreated body. The body of the saved will be resurrected immortal and incorruptible, to be reunited with its soul and live endlessly in the presence of God. The body of the unsaved will be resurrected to be immortal and corruptible, to be reunited with its soul to live endlessly in the lake of fire.

My friends, the simple fact is this, life never ends. Yes, there is a pause in physical life, but Your life will continue after physical death because the source of life, the animating principle God designed into the human soul, cannot be annihilated or put to sleep. That same source of life will reanimate the resurrected body.

What you need to consider is quality and location. Will you have endless immortal incorruptible life in the presence of God? Or will you have endless immortal corruptible life separated from God. Only those who during this mortal life have faith in the risen Jesus Christ as Savior from the penalty due sin will continue endlessly immortal and incorruptible in the presence of God in this universe and the next.

Appendix: Discussion Of The Lapsarian Views

The Gross Error Of Supralapsarianism

"Your critique of supralapsarianism is particularly noteworthy. You strongly—and rightly—oppose the notion that God created some humans for damnation, advocating for a view that upholds God's justice and mercy. This is a significant departure from the supralapsarian perspective, which makes God appear unjust and arbitrary" (theologian J. Neil Lipscomb, in a letter to the author).

The supralapsarian order was not created by Theodore Beza (1519–1605), but he revived and refined the doctrine. (Gottschalk of Orbais, ca. AD 808–867, seems to have created supralapsarianism.) Beza's intent in the supralapsarian order of God's pre-creation decrees was to prevent any possibility of synergistic salvation, which I define as both God and the sinner make significant contributions to the sinner's salvation. Arminianism is synergistic: God gives grace but the sinner must choose to accept or deny salvation. Roman Catholic Church is synergistic: good works activate God's grace. Synergistic concepts were present during (and before) Beza's time, and long discussed by the New Testament church. Synergistic soteriology had long before Beza been developed by the Roman Catholic Church, and was confirmed by the Council of Trent (1545–1563) before Beza's death.

Beza accomplished his objective (to prevent any possibility of synergism) by elevating God's sovereignty above all other attributes, even to the exclusion of some attributes. The problem with that approach is God's attributes cannot be divided. God is one essence. No one attribute operates apart from all other attributes. God's attributes are not joined in a union, they are in a state of oneness: "the whole essence is in each attribute and the attribute is the essence" [Shedd, *Dogmatic*, 1:254; see also Dolezal, 43]. Supralapsarianism created an unjust God, a God who is a monster, a God who exercises arbitrary sovereignty to condemn the righteous.

Supralapsarianism Has Several Serious Problems

Problem one, men who are not contemplated as sinners are ordained to eternal punishment.

In the supralapsarian order, God decided the eternal fate of men before the decree Adam must sin (the decree making Adam sin is another false aspect of supralapsarianism), which means God

Discussion of the Lapsarian Views

specifically created some men to eternal damnation without a just reason for their damnation.

Put bluntly, in the supralapsarian view, those whom God created in order to elect them to eternal damnation were viewed as righteous when he damned them. That is arbitrary sovereignty, that is unjust, that is monstrous.

> Problem two, God decreed Adam must commit his act of disobedience.

In the supralapsarian doctrine, God did not permit or allow Adam's exercise of free will to choose to disobey. In the supralapsarian doctrine God took away Adam's free will, God decreed Adam must sin. The supralapsarian doctrine makes God the culpable (criminally responsible) author of sin. Put bluntly, God created human sin by making Adam sin.

> Problem three, the supralapsarian cannot give the gospel.

The supralapsarian cannot say "God loves you and sent his son to die for you and save you from your sins." In the supralapsarian doctrine God loves only his elect. The supralapsarian does not know who are God's elect. His gospel says, "Christ died to save his elect people from their sins." Scripture such a Romans 10:13; Revelation 22:17 are not in the supralapsarian's gospel.

> Problem four, attributes like love and mercy are not extended to all humankind.

In the supralapsarian doctrine, God loves only the elect. One modern supralapsarian, Dr. David Engelsma, in *Common Grace Revisited*, wrote, "God is not kind ... to all unthankful and evil people" and the idea of God loving all is "absurd, if not blasphemous." Supralapsarian doctrine rules out any act of the Lord to show and display grace or mercy to those who never believe.

In the supralapsarian doctrine, when Jesus gave us the exhortation in Matthew 5:44–45, he did not really mean it.

> Love your enemies, and pray for those persecuting you; bless those cursing you, do good to those misusing you and hating you, 45 so that you may be sons of your Father in the heavens. Because he makes his sun rise on evil and good, and sends rain on righteous and unrighteous.

In the supralapsarian doctrine, God makes the sun rise and the

240

rain fall on the elect, and if those things happen to affect the non-elect, that is just an accident, an unhappy coincidence, because the benefits of Christ's propitiation are only for the elect.

The supralapsarian doctrine was rejected by several synods when originated by Gottschalk, and 800 years later was rejected by the Synod of Dort.

More importantly, supralapsarian doctrine is opposed by scriptural concepts and teaching of God as just, e.g., Genesis 18:25, "Shall not the Judge of all the earth do right?" The supralapsarian doctrine sees God as electing righteous persons to eternal condemnation—righteous because not yet fallen in the order of God's decrees according to the supralapsarian doctrine. This view also contradicts scriptural ideas concerning the treatment of the innocent, and relieving misery (an aspect of mercy).

When Christ said, "disciple all the peoples (Matthew 28:19), and "Go into all the world, proclaim the Good News to all the creation," (Mark 16:15), in the supralapsarian doctrine he meant only go to the elect. When Christ said, "the one thirsting, the one desiring—let him come, let him take freely the water of life" (Revelation 22:17), and Paul said, "all that may call upon the Lord's name will be saved," in the supralapsarian doctrine Jesus and the Holy Spirit meant only the elect.

The supralapsarian doctrine seems to be the dominant view today. It isn't, it is just the one with the loudest supporters. Many only superficially understand. The supras gained the upper hand in the debate when the TULIP was invented in 1905 [Stewart, *Ten Myths,* appendix], and then popularized in 1934 by Boettner's book, *The Reformed Doctrine of Predestination*. Since then the supras have been the loudest and most obnoxious voice in the room; many follow the loudest voice without examining the content.

Excursus: John Owen, A Loud Proponent of Supralapsarianism

One who did understand the supralapsarian doctrine was John Owen (1616–1683), its most well-known supporter. Owen was three years old when the Canons of Dort were published, and grew up with the continuing debate of lapsarian views.

Owen viewed the infra and sublapsarian doctrine of "sufficient for all," as a form of Universalism (universal salvation), conveniently ignoring the latter half of that statement, "efficient to salvation only for the elect." His argument against Universalism is long and complex, and here I will only give his summary of six previous points. [*Works*, 10:264. Reprinted in *The Death of Death in the Death of Christ*, 152].

> This, I say, being that reconciliation which is the effect of the death and blood of Christ, it cannot be asserted in reference to any, nor Christ said to die for any other, but only those concerning whom, all the properties of it, and acts wherein it doth consist, may be truly affirmed; which, whether they may be of all men or not, let all men judge.

Owen made two errors. The first is he denies the efficacy of faith. The unlimited merit of Christ's propitiation of God for sin must be applied by faith to be efficacious unto salvation. No faith, no salvation. In a mundane illustration, electricity is always at the electrical outlet, but nothing happens until one plugs into the outlet. So faith must plug into Christ's merit for there to be salvation.

Owen's other error is he made Christ's propitiation man-centered instead of God-centered. His argument is Christ died only for the elect. No, Christ died to propitiate God for the crime of human sin, thereby fully satisfying God's justice and holiness. Owen assumes a propitiation of God for all human sin must mean all sinners must be forgiven of their sins. But throughout the Scripture, Old Testament and New Testament, the merit that forgives—the merit of Christ's propitiation—must be applied by God's grace through the sinner's faith, else there is no forgiveness. The limitless merit of the propitiation is applied only by God's grace through the sinner's faith. No faith = no salvation.

Therefore, the right premise is God applies the limitless merit of Christ's propitiation according to his eternal decrees: temporal benefits for all humankind, eternal benefits for the elect.

A Discussion Of Infralapsarianism

According to the infralapsarian view, the decree of election followed the decree permitting the fall. Sin was the background in which God viewed all human beings, and from which he chose to save some. None were innocent because the fall was permitted (not decreed) before the election.

In the infralapsarian doctrine, there is no election to reprobation. In deciding who to elect God contemplated all as sinners. God in mercy chose to rescue some from sin. God in justice chose to take no action toward those not chosen but to leave them as they were, sinners, taking no action to either help or to hinder their salvation. Election guarantees salvation, nothing more, nothing less, saying nothing about those not elected.

In the supra order, God took away Adam's free will and decreed Adam must sin. In the infra and sub orders, God permitted-allowed Adam's freely made choice to sin. Looking back to a previous discussion of foreordination, out of all Adam's possible choices concerning the forbidden fruit, God chose to effectuate from possible to actual Adam's freely made choice to disobey and eat the fruit. Whether or not there was a different possible choice is irrelevant. Adam's choice was freely made within the historic context of his life, not decreed, and therefore Adam is criminally responsible for human sin. (For a discussion as to why the sinless Adam could chose to commit an act of sinning [his mutability and his free will are involved], see my book, *Adam and Eve, A Biography and Theology.*)

In the infralapsarian order man is the author of his endless punishment, God the author of endless salvation. This view agrees with Scripture, e.g., those who are saved were chosen out of the world in which all are sinful. All men are viewed as they are in sinful Adam, made out of the same lump of sinful clay, Romans 9:21, out of which God took some clay and fashioned it into vessels of honor.

The debates in the Synod of Dort concerning the extent of Christ's propitiation were long and difficult, infamously at one point resulting in a challenge to a dual over competing positions. All agreed salvation was monergistic (God alone is origin, source, and initiator of salvation). All the monergistic concepts of the extent of the propitiation had been present in the history of the New Testament church since at least the beginning of the Reformation; longer if we include Augustine and other church fathers.

Yet, in the end, a consensus was reached among the participants, which did not satisfy all, but was agreeable to most. Nor did that consensus agreement fully answer all the issues posed by each competing view. The majority of the Synod declared for the infralapsarian order of decrees as the official Reformed doctrine of soteriology: sufficient for all, efficient for the elect. The loud and obnoxious supralapsarian doctrine stands outside the official statement of Reformed doctrine.

Comparing The Sublapsarian And Infralapsarian Views

The sublapsarian doctrine reverses two of the items in the

infralapsarian order.

Infralapsarian: to elect; to provide a redeemer for the elect

Sublapsarian: to provide a redeemer; to elect.

The difference is this. In the Infralapsarian order Christ is the redeemer only for the elect; This is the strictest interpretation of Dort's "sufficient for all, efficient for the elect" doctrine.

The sublapsarian order takes the "sufficient for all, efficient for the elect" doctrine to its logical and scriptural conclusion: Christ is a redeemer for all upon the condition of faith. More plainly, God's foreordained gift of grace-faith-salvation guarantees the salvation of the elect, but a) there are also temporal benefits to the non-elect, and b) because Christ is a redeemer for all then any non-elect may be saved if he meets the condition for salvation: faith in God and God's testimony as to the way of salvation.

Election guarantees the salvation of some, it does not prevent the salvation of any. To repeat from a previous discussion, "God would have all persons to be saved (1 Timothy 2:4), but he wills for certain persons to believe (Ephesians 1:4; 2 Thessalonians 2:13), thereby guaranteeing the elect will believe, without any kind of decree preventing any from believing (disbelief is what sin does)."

Appendix: Arminian Soteriology

Arminian soteriology originates in two philosophical principles.

Divine sovereignty is not compatible with human freedom, and therefore not compatible with human responsibility.

Ability limits obligation.

Therefore, says Arminian soteriology, faith cannot originate in God, but is a free and responsible human act exercised independent of God, and since the Bible regards faith as obligatory, then the ability to believe must be universal.

To understand the error of Arminian soteriology, one must understand the exercise of free will is not the error, but rather the error is making free will the determining factor between saved or unsaved. Faith is freely exercised, but the determining factors are God's foreordination, Ephesians 1:4, God's gift of grace-faith-salvation, Ephesians 2:8, and Christ's propitiation, Romans 3:21–26; Hebrews 2:17; 1 John 2:2; 4:10.

The salvation principle, at its most basic, is by God's grace through the sinner's faith by Christ's propitiation. God's grace does not enable a sinner to choose between No or Yes. The sinner's faith is the consequence of God's grace, and is the God-ordained means by which the sinner accesses the unlimited merit of Christ's propitiation. Without God's grace there is no faith; without Christ's propitiation there is no merit to overcome the demerit of sin. The faith expressed by the sinner as a consequence of God's gift (Ephesians 2:8) is the empty hand of the soul reaching out to receive God-given salvation.

Divine Sovereignty And Human Freedom

Divine sovereignty is compatible with human freedom. This is not the place to discuss foreordination (see my book, *God's Choices*), but succinctly, before God created anything, God omnisciently knew within himself all the possible consequences that could arise from his decision to create. That omniscient knowledge included all possible freely made choices that might be made by the sentient creatures he would create. God foreordained certain possible freely made choices from possible to actual, such as fit his purpose in creating, and his plans and processes to fulfill that purpose. God's choice of which to effectuate from possible to actual was not based on prescience (foresight) but his omniscient wisdom as to which freely made choices fit his purpose in creating.

Omniscience is what God knows within himself without input from any source outside himself. Omniscience is that attribute of God which is the perfection of his knowledge and wisdom. His knowledge and wisdom are without limitation. God knows all things, including himself and everything actual or potential in his creation.

Therefore all freely made choices are certain, because foreordained, but not necessary, because freely made by the person within his or her circumstances.

The orthodox doctrine is this. What God knew in himself is that he chose (foreordination) to effectuate Adam's freely made choice to sin: permission to sin, not a decree mandating sin. Whether or not there were other possible choices is hypothetical and irrelevant. Perhaps all of Adam's possible choices led to his act of disobedience? We may be certain at least one of Adam's possible choices was to disobey God's command. That is the freely made choice God chose to effectuate from possible to actual.

Adam, not God, is culpable (criminally responsible) for his sin, because in the historical moment Adam's choice was freely made. In relation to human freedom and responsibility, the choice to sin originated in Adam, both in relation to God's foreordaining decree, and in the historical moment. God did not decree Adam would sin (contra supralapsarianism), God effectuated Adam's freely made choice to sin. Therefore, Adam's choice was not necessary, because freely made, but it was certain, because foreordained.

By God's foreordaining decree Adam was appointed the legal representative of all his descendants. By God's Law of Biological Reproduction Adam was made the seminal head of the human race. By Adam's freely made choice to sin, and by Adam's propagation after he sinned, all in Adam, the entire human race, became sinners, 1 Corinthians 15:22.

God therefore, by his sovereign choices, in the timelessness before God created anything, knew that all human beings who would exist in the universe God would create, would be sinners by reason of Adam's freely made choice to sin. That meant without God's intervention none would be saved. On the basis of his internal knowledge, God chose (foreordination) to give some sinners his gift of grace-faith-salvation, thereby changing the boundary of sin's rebellion to willingness, so the sinner receiving the gift would freely and willingly choose to believe and be saved. God's electing choices does not prevent faith, that is what sin does. God's grace in salvation is so completely and perfectly efficacious the sinner's human nature will be changed, the sinner will inevitably freely choose to believe, and thereby will be saved.

Therefore, God's act of foreordination of human freely made choices is compatible with human freedom and responsibility, having been sovereignly designed to be compatible in the timelessness of eternity before God's act of creating the universe. Out of all possible freely made choices, God chose to effectuate some freely made choices from possible to certain, because those freely made choices were agreeable to his purpose in creating.

Obligation And Ability

The second Arminian principle is, "ability limits obligation." This was a response to the Reformed doctrine that sin renders human beings unable to freely respond to the obligation to believe and be saved. However, Reformed theology overstates the case for inability, and Arminian theology misunderstands inability.

There are two effects of inability caused by the indwelling sin attribute. The first is stated in 1 Corinthians 2:14, "But a natural person does not accept things of the Spirit of God, for they are absurd to him, and he is not able to know them, because they are discerned spiritually." The unsaved person lacks spiritual perception. What is spiritual perception?

> Spiritual perception. A faculty of the human soul that allows man to perceive, understand, and communicate with God. The ability of the soul to receive and understand spiritual things. A faculty of the soul through which man has communion with God. The ability of the soul to receive, understand, and appropriately apply biblical knowledge to live godly in this present world. In the unsaved soul the sin attribute has rendered spiritual perception grossly insensitive, such that the unsaved person does not have the spiritual discernment to receive or understand the things of the Spirit of God, 1 Corinthians 2:14. [Quiggle, *Dictionary.*]

The unsaved sinner's inability to perceive spiritual things leads to a second effect of inability. Ephesians 2:1, "... dead in your trespasses and your sins." Some (too many) of Reformed theology compare "dead" to physically dead. Such is not the case. The unsaved person is spiritually dead. The practical implications of spiritually dead and lacking spiritual perception are simple: constant, willing, freely made choices to act in unremitting rebellion against and rejection of God and his salvation. The fact that rebellion is freely chosen means sin does not create inability, but gives the wrong kind of ability: to freely choose to reject God and God's salvation.

The unsaved sinner is spiritual dead in relation to God, spiritually active in relation to his freely made choices to commit acts of sinning.

The sinner's inability to receive spiritual things generates a freely chosen response of rebellion and disobedience to the obligation to positively respond to God's call to believe and be saved. Therefore, inability does not limit obligation, because the sinner does respond, by acting in obligation to his sinful human nature. A negative response reflects the ability to respond as much as a positive response. And whether or not we agree that God's sovereignty is compatible with human freedom, the human freedom to choose rebellion versus belief is compatible with human responsibility.

Let us return to the definition of free will (previous chapter). "Free will is the moral authority God designed into his sentient creatures to make choices within the physical, moral, and spiritual boundaries of their nature, as further influenced by internal and external motivations and consequences." The sinner is making choices. The internal motivation is the "fence" set by the sin attribute allowing negative choices, but not positive choices, in relation to the obligation to believe.

When the sinner is confronted by the obligation to believe, God is not preventing the sinner from choosing a positive response. The sinner's sinful human nature chooses to make a negative response. Because the negative response is a freely made choice, the sinner is culpable for his or her wrong choice. The issue is not inability but culpability. Ignorance of the law is a legal principle holding that a person who is unaware of a law may not escape liability for violating that law merely by being unaware of its content. So also God and his laws.

However, the sinner is without the excuse or ignorance, because God designed into the human conscience God's moral principles of right and wrong. The sinner knows the right choice concerning faith and salvation, but rejects that choice because it is absurd to him. Through God's design of human nature the sinner knows the right choice. Because the sinner knows the right choice, the sinner is culpable for his or her freely made wrong choice.

How do I know a sinner is aware of right and wrong? Because God designed a conscious into human nature, informed by God's moral laws.

> Romans 1:18–21, For the wrath of God from heaven is revealed upon all ungodliness and unrighteousness of humankind, by unrighteousness suppressing the truth, 19 because the known of God is revealed in them, for God has revealed it to them. 20 For that which cannot be seen visibly of him are perceived, being understood from the creation of the world by the things made, both his eternal power and deity, for them to be without excuse. 21 For having known God, they did not glorify him as God, or were thankful, but were without real wisdom in their reasonings, and their foolish heart was darkened.

> Romans 2:12–16, For as many as sinned without Law also without Law will perish. And as many as with Law sinned according to Law will be judged. 13 For not the hearers of Law are righteous with God, but doers of Law will be justified. 14 For when gentiles not having Law by nature do the things of the Law, these not having Law are to themselves a law, 15 who show the work of the Law written in their hearts, their conscience testifying, and between one another the reckoning accusing or else defending, 16 in that day when God will judge the secrets of men, according to my Good News, by Christ Jesus.

Ability does not limit obligation, because all know, and all are culpable. No one sins unwillingly, every act of sinning is a freely made choice.

Arminian Soteriology

Biblically, free will is the empty hand of the soul reaching out to receive salvation from God. The soul freely extends its hand—willingly exercises saving faith—because the gift of God has changed human nature so efficiently (efficacious grace) that the former rebel against God now willingly desires salvation.

The main issue in Arminian soteriology, seldom identified by others, is prevenient grace. The word "prevenient" means goes before. Prevenient grace means grace goes before salvation. Every soteriology, including Arminian, believes in the prevenient grace of Ephesians 2:8. The difference among the competing soteriologies is when and how prevenient grace is applied.

Reformed and Dispensational soteriology view prevenient grace as applied individually by God through his foreordained gift of grace-faith-salvation, Ephesians 2:8, thereby electing certain individuals to receive the gift. That gift is individually efficacious in changing the spiritual boundaries of the person receiving the gift, so the person freely, willingly, and inevitably chooses to exercise saving faith.

Arminian soteriology believes prevenient grace is applied universally by God to every human being through his gift of grace-faith-salvation, Ephesians 2:8. Arminian soteriology views prevenient grace as God giving every sinner the grace needed to freely decide for him or herself whether or not to believe the gospel and be saved: a neutral free will neither disinclined by sin nor inclined by God's efficacious grace. In Arminian soteriology, the way in which prevenient grace is efficacious is to enable any sinner to choose to believe and be saved, or chose to remain a sinner. God gives this prevenient grace to all because of Christ's work on the cross, so that all people are capable of hearing and responding gospel as they may choose. (A few Dispensationalists accept Arminian soteriology.)

The history of the Arminian view is instructive.

> In the original Arminian view, the sinner is in bondage to sin until he/she hears the gospel, and the hearing of the gospel is itself the application of prevenient grace, by which the sinner is enabled to exercise saving faith, or not, as he/she may choose.

> In the second Arminian view, the sinner is in partial bondage to sin, but God is always indiscriminately drawing sinners to Christ, and this act of drawing is the prevenient grace which, as the gospel is heard, makes the sinner capable of hearing and responding gospel as he or she may choose to believe and be saved, or not.

> The third, and modern, Arminian view (developed by Charles Wesley) is that because of the first coming and atoning work of Christ, God has dispensed a universal prevenient grace that fully negates the depravity of every person. This prevenient grace places sinners in a neutral spiritual state, so when the gospel is presented they may freely choose to believe unto salvation, or not. Wesleyan prevenient grace is universal in its scope (every human being) and effect (completely freed from the effects of sin).

Reformed and Dispensational soteriology say God's gift of prevenient grace is the consequence of God's foreordaining action to give the gift of grace-faith-salvation to select persons, thereby electing those persons to salvation by reason of the efficacious action of God's gift to change the unwilling and unable to able and willing.

Arminian soteriology separates election from prevenient grace. Arminianism says everyone gets God's prevenient grace. But Arminian soteriology says election to salvation is by prescience, i.e., by foresight. The Arminian doctrine of foresight election God says looked outside himself into the history of the universe he would create, saw who would believe and who would not believe after receiving prevenient grace, and elected to salvation those he foresaw would believe. God acted because of what he learned.

How could God look outside himself throughout all of time and space? That is the doctrine of God's omnipresence. Arminian foresight election is based on God's omnipresence: God knows and decides because he looked outside himself and learned. Calvinistic election is based on God's omniscience: God knows within himself and decides based on what he knows without looking outside himself.

(One of the more serious problems with the prescient (foresight) election view is God learns by consulting persons and events outside himself. Biblically, either God knows by looking within himself, the attribute of omniscience, or God is not omniscient and must learn from others.)

Reformed and Dispensational soteriology say election to salvation is by foreordination. God looked inside himself and decided to whom of those he knew would create he would give prevenient grace for salvation. Those individuals to whom God decided to give prevenient grace are identified as elected to salvation, because of the infallible efficacy of the gift.

In both Reformed, Arminian, and Dispensational soteriology, salvation is "saved by God's grace through the sinner's faith without personal merit from the sinner but by Christ's merit alone." The choice to exercise saving faith is not meritorious whether viewed from the Reformed, Dispensational, or Arminian perspectives of prevenient grace. For Arminianism prevenient grace makes the exercise of saving faith possible. For Reformed and Dispensational prevenient grace makes the exercise of saving faith certain. Election is a second order doctrine because election is not an essential doctrine of the faith. (How

God knows is an essential doctrine of the faith.)

Arminian soteriology does not concern itself, as do Reformed and Dispensational soteriology, with how the Old Testament sinner understood the means to salvation. That is because in the Arminian system, universal prevenient grace resolves that issue. Whatever the Good News might be at any time in the history of the world, however the sinner might gain understanding of the means to salvation, the Arminian view of prevenient grace places the sinner in a neutral spiritual state, so when the Good News is presented any sinner may freely choose to believe unto salvation, or not. Because Wesley came out of a Reformed background, I suspect his use of the word "gospel" focused solely on faith in Christ, and therefore he probably believed with Reformed soteriology that Christ was both the object and content of saving faith for the Old Testament sinner.

Appendix: Terms And Definitions

The following terms and definitions used in this book are from my book, *Dictionary of Doctrinal Words* (some definitions given here are explained in greater detail in *Dictionary*).

Adoption. Adoption is that spiritual state in which God places the believer as an adult son and heir of God, making them "sons of God." God has one natural child, the Son, who is heir of all things. God takes those who are not his natural children, sinners, saves them by his grace through their faith, and adopts them into the position of a natural born child (Ephesians 1:5). Adoption and son-ship are not gender-specific terms but a position of relationship and inheritance applicable to every believer. See "Sons of."

Aeviternity. The state that logically lies between the timeless state of God and the temporal state of the things and creatures God created. God's pre-creation decisions as to what kind of universe to create were made in Aeviternity.

Arminianism. A gospel that teaches Christ by suffering on the cross restored to all human beings what was lost in Adam, resulting in God dispersing a measure of prevenient grace to all human beings so they are not pre-disposed by sin to rebel against God. Any unsaved sinner, through this universal prevenient grace, can now hear the gospel, evaluate and examine its claims, and make a decision based on their own free will to follow Christ or not. More simply, the Arminian concept of prevenient grace initiates the possibility of saving faith in every human being.

Atonement. Atonement is not redemption. Atonement is propitiation (complete satisfaction) of God's justice for the crime of sin through a suitable vicarious sacrifice suffering the judicial penalty against sin. Atonement/propitiation equals legal satisfaction.

Believer. A sinner who has become born-again by exercising saving faith in Jesus Christ.

Born Again. Salvation is an instantaneous act with several results, which may be separated for the purpose of discussion. The unbeliever is unable to understand the things of the Spirit of God (1 Corinthians

2:14), because his/her faculty of spiritual perception is "dead," which is to say, grossly dulled, unable to perceive spiritual things (Ephesians 2:1, 5). The first part of "born-again" is the believer's faculty of spiritual perception is brought to life, thus enabling the spiritual understanding required to be convicted of sin, the Savior, and salvation. This is accomplished through God's gift of grace-faith-salvation (Ephesians 2:8) by the work of the Holy Spirit to accomplish the salvation decreed by God (Ephesians 1:4; 2 Thessalonians 2:13; 1 Peter 1:2). The exercise of saving faith is the sure and certain outcome of God's gift of grace-faith-salvation.

Upon the exercise of saving faith by the sinner, God imparts to him/her eternal life, John 10:27–29; 17:2–3; Romans 6:23b; 1 John 2:25, which is God sharing (in a participatory way) the communicable aspects of his eternal life, creating communion with God and spiritual understanding. To be born-again, or regeneration, is the result of God sharing the communicable aspects of his eternal life. The attributes of human nature, which were jumbled and wrongly prioritized by the sin attribute, are normalized, which is to say, godliness is restored to human nature through the godly attributes of holiness, righteousness, love, mercy, etc. The believer is given new wants and new desires. His/her human nature is re-prioritized toward God.

Upon the exercise of saving faith, God imputes the righteousness of Christ to the now-believing sinner, freeing him or her from the judicial guilt and penalty of sin (justification) because Christ has satisfied God's law on behalf of the sinner, Romans 6:23. The now-saved sinner has been reconciled to God, 2 Corinthians 5:18–19. This brings peace with God, Romans 5:1, because with sin forgiven (Ephesians 1:7), and the judicial penalty satisfied through Christ's propitiation (1 John 2:2), there is no more enmity between God and the believer.

Upon the exercise of saving faith, the Holy Spirit accomplishes the sanctification of the believer, which is to set the believer apart from the defilement caused by sin and dedicate him to God, Ephesians 1:4; 1 Corinthians 1:30; 1 Peter 1:2. In the act of sanctification sin loses its dominating power, Romans 6:14–23, and a new principle of life, holiness, is added to the believer, Ephesians 4:24, becoming the dominating principle in his human nature, 1 Thessalonians 4:7; 1 Corinthians 3:17b; Colossians 3:12; 1 Peter 1:15.

The believer now stands before God in Christ as forgiven, justified, sanctified, regenerated, and filled with eternal life. He is freed from the penalty, power, and pleasure of sin, with absolute assurance of the future transformation and glorification of human nature and body that frees the believer eternally from the presence of sin. The believer is empowered to resist sin's temptations, live a holy life, understand the Scripture, worship, obey, fellowship with, and serve God. God hears and answers his prayers, and he (or she) perseveres in the faith to lead a holy life, looking toward resurrection and an eternal life in God's presence.

The Holy Spirit is always present with his saved people in any age of humankind, but the Old Testament believer was not indwelt by the Holy Spirit. The New Testament believer is indwelt by the Holy Spirit. In this age of the NT church, when the human nature has been regenerated by the work of the Holy Spirit, the Holy Spirit then takes up permanent residence in the believer's soul, John 14:17; Acts 10:44–48; 1 Corinthians 6:19.

Content of Faith. A term in Dispensational Theology that describes God's testimony in history, as the means by which God's grace in salvation is accessed. The sinner is always saved by God's grace through the sinner's faith in God, through God's historically current testimony as given in the progressive revelation of truth.

The content of faith changes as God progressively gives new revelation and changes the economies (dispensations) through which he administers his affairs in the world. As faith is the means by which God's grace in salvation is accessed, the content of faith (God's testimony), was the historical means whereby God's grace was accessed in the various dispensations.

Conviction. The work of the Holy Spirit in the individual to infallibly reveal right and wrong according to the testimony of Scripture.

Effectuate. To effect; to bring about; to cause to come to pass; to cause a potential event to pass from possible to actual. In the decree of foreordination God effectuated certain events out of all possible events to become actual events. See Foreordination.

Election. The choice of a sovereign God (Ephesians 1:4), (1) to give the gift of grace-faith-salvation to effect the salvation of some sinners (Ephesians 2:8), and (2) to take no action, positive or negative, to either effect or deny salvation to other sinners (Romans 10:13; Revelation 22:17). The decree of election includes all means necessary to effectuate salvation in those elected.

Faith. Faith is belief, trust, confidence. All human beings have faith as an attribute of their human nature. However, natural faith is not the same as the living, saving, empowering faith the Scripture requires of sinner and believer. Biblical living, saving, empowering faith is belief, trust, confidence plus a commitment to God as the Savior from the penalty due sin through the infallible conviction given by the Holy Spirit. See Conviction.

The kind of faith that saves and empowers the Christian's life is inwardly believing the testimony of God through the infallible conviction given by the Holy Spirit, and faith is outwardly acting through the power given by the Holy Spirit to conform one's thoughts and actions to that conviction. A person is not "enabled" to believe by the Spirit's convicting power, but rather as being convicted of the truth, and on the basis of that conviction, each person appropriates and applies the truth to his or her specific circumstance, whether the spiritual issue is salvation or discipleship. That phrase, "appropriates and applies the truth," is what the Bible names living, saving, empowering faith.

Faith, Saving. The conformity of thought and action to the infallible conviction of the Holy Spirit through volitional simple trust or confidence in the testimony of God that the risen Jesus Christ is the only Person who is able to save the sinner from the penalty of sin. See Sin, penalty.

A sinner is not enabled to believe, he or she is convicted through the work of God the Holy Spirit of the truth of personal sin, the judicial guilt and punishment of sin, the need for salvation by faith not works, and the all-sufficiency of the propitiation made by Jesus Christ the Savior required to save his or her soul. On the basis of that conviction the sinner personally appropriates these truths to satisfy his or her spiritual need for salvation. That personal appropriation of truth to satisfy the spiritual need for salvation is the exercise of saving faith.

Fellowship, God with the Believer. When God enjoys our presence within his presence and we are counted as his friend. Fellowship is by holiness in one's heart and mind and righteous actions in one's Christian life.

Foreknowledge. God's knowledge of what will happen, based upon his decrees of what will happen. More simply, God's foreknowledge is based on his foreordination.

Foreordination. The decree of God occurring between his decision to create and his act of creation as to which agents, events, and outcomes, out of all possible agents, events, and outcomes potential in the decision to create, would pass from possible to actual, in which the liberty or contingency of secondary causes is established, in which God is not the author of sin, and in which no violence is done to the free will of his creatures.

Free will. The moral authority God designed into his sentient creatures to make choices within the physical, moral, and spiritual boundaries of their nature, as further influenced by internal and external motivations and consequences.

God's Omnipresence. God is fully and immediately present in every possible aspect and dimension, spatial and temporal, in all created domains. God interpenetrates all created domains but his essence remains separate from all created domains and all that is in those domains.

God's omniscience. God has all knowledge and all understanding within himself without requiring knowledge or understanding outside himself. There are no exceptions to God's knowledge. There are no exclusions to God's understanding. Because God is all-knowing and all-understanding, God is all-wise. Through the exercise of his omniscience God sovereignly determined a perfect purpose and the perfect means and ends to fulfill that purpose.

God's Sovereignty. God's omnipresent authority, omnipotent power, absolute holiness, and omniscient wisdom to govern himself and his creation and creatures as seems best to himself, without experiencing effective opposition, in complete agreement with his essence and character as God.

Good News. The "good news" is salvation in the risen Jesus Christ. The good news consists of the accusation of sin with the proclamation of the risen Jesus Christ the only Savior. The word "gospel" is a man-made term for what the Scripture says is the *euangélion*, literally the "good news."

Grace. God choosing to bless because he wants to, although blessing is undeserved.

Grace, efficacious. God's grace working effectively with the sinner's human nature to free the will from the dominion of sin, and inform the sinner of his or her spiritual guilt and spiritual need, so that the unwilling sinner is made willing to choose to act in agreement with the command to believe and be saved. Efficacious grace is the work of the Holy Spirit in applying God's gift of grace-faith-salvation to effect salvation. Efficacious grace enlivens the sinner's faculty of spiritual perception (2 Thessalonians 2:13; 1 Peter 1:2), infallibly leading to the exercise of saving faith.

Grace-faith-salvation. A term derived from Ephesians 2:8 indicating the complete salvation principle: saved by grace through faith. The gift of God in the salvation of sinners is grace-faith-salvation.

Hope. The assurance the believer has in the promises of God. "Hope" is the assurance that the thing promised will be received; thus, hope always refers to the thing embraced in hope, not to the basis or character of hope.

Indefectibility. A grace God gives after this mortal life that will endlessly preserve the believer from defecting from God through sin. The grace of perseverance keeps the believer in the faith by means of faith during this mortal life. After death, the grace of indefectibility will work though the believer's sinless human nature to endlessly preserve the believer from sin. This is the grace God gave the unfallen angels to preserve them in their choice to not defect from God and follow Lucifer.

Immortality. Created personal existence continuing without foreseeable end. All sentient beings were created to be immortal. In regard to human beings, the soul was created naturally immortal, the body will be resurrected immortal.

Justification. God's declaration that the believing sinner is "Not Guilty" of his or her crimes of sin against God. The reason a sinner may be declared "Not Guilty" for the crime of sin is someone else paid the penalty for the crime. That someone else was Jesus the Christ. The limitless merit of Christ's propitiation is applied by God to remit the judicial guilt of the person God is saving.

Justification, positional. The believer's permanent standing of "justification" before God in Christ. God sees the believer in a salvific relationship with himself in Jesus Christ, and imputes Christ's righteousness to the believer. A believer's standing is as permanent as the salvific relationship

Lapsarian. A word used to describe the lapse of Adam from sinless to sinful, resulting in all humankind's lapse into sin. There are three lapsarian views in Reformed theology.

Supralapsarian. The order is:

To elect to eternal life some of the persons who were to be created, and to elect (condemn) to destruction the other persons who were to be created.

To create.

To decree the fall of mankind into sin.

To send Christ to redeem the elect.

To send the Holy Spirit to apply this redemption to the elect.

The first decree in supralapsarianism is also known in Reformed theology as double predestination: an election to salvation and a corresponding election to reprobation.

Infralapsarian. The order is:

To create.

To permit the fall.

To elect some out of this fallen mass to be saved, and to leave the others as they were.

To provide a redeemer for the elect.

To send the Holy Spirit to apply this redemption to the elect.

Sublapsarian. The order is:

To create.

To permit the fall.

To provide a redeemer

To elect some out of this fallen mass to be saved, and to leave the others as they were.

To send the Holy Spirit to apply this redemption to the elect.

My lapsarian order

God's decision to manifest his glory.

God's decision to manifest his glory in a particular manner by creating a universe populated with sentient creatures.

God's exercise of his omniscient knowledge and wisdom to understand all possible agents, events, and outcomes in the proposed universe that could fulfill his purpose.

God's decree of foreordination: to create a particular

universe by choosing to effectuate certain agents, events, and outcomes (out of all possible) that <u>would</u> fulfill his purpose.

God's foreordaining decision to permit the fall of humankind into sin.

God's decree to satisfy his justice and holiness against sin through a propitiation for sin.

God's decree to give both temporal and eternal benefits to humankind out of Christ's propitiation.

> God's decree to justly leave some sinful persons as they were (the non-elect), taking no action to either hinder or aid in their salvation.

> God's decree of mercy to give some sinful persons the gift of grace-faith-salvation (election) to be saved.

God's decree to send the Holy Spirit to effect the redemption of the elect.

God's decree of predestination to conform the saved person to the image of Christ, and to adopt him or her as a son of God and joint-heir with Christ.

God's omnipotent act of creating the universe.

After the universe came into existence, then God's providence worked and is working to effect his pre-creation decrees, according to his purpose in creating.

Life. The principle of animation. Life is an immaterial spirit essence originating in God that when placed into non-living physical material causes that non-living material to possess the qualities we recognize and describe as alive. Life is a necessary component of the soul, which all living beings possess. See: Soul.

Life, eternal. Both the duration of life and quality of life God gives to the saved. The duration is endless, forever. The quality is God sharing his communicable attributes in a measure suitable to a finite being, so the believer is conformed to the likeness of Jesus Christ.

Life, spiritual. The result of salvation is participation in God's spiritual life. Spiritual life has two components. One, the soul's faculty of spiritual perception is relieved from the gross dullness caused by sin and is enlivened for conscious communion with God. Two, participation in the life of God in all the fullness possible for a finite being: God communicates the communicable attributes of his eternal life to the saved person.

Mercy. Mercy has two aspects. The first aspect is the delay of deserved justice. The second aspect is relieving misery.

Obedience. Faith in exercise, responding to the divine will, directed by the divine authority, energized by divine power.

Perseverance. To persevere in the faith is to continue in the faith by means of faith throughout life and through physical death into eternity. Perseverance is a grace God gives the believer to overcome all spiritual and physical obstacles to faith. Persevering faith is the believer using the means of grace God has provided for him or her to continue in the faith by faith. God tells his saved people to persevere, and he gives his saved people every grace and spiritual power necessary to be able to persevere. By means of the grace of perseverance every believer will persevere in the faith by faith all the way through life to the end of physical life and into eternity.

Predestination. God's decree to conform the believer to be like Christ according to certain aspects of Christ's spiritual character and physical form (Romans 8:29–30; 1 John 3:2), and to place the believer in the legal position of God's son and heir (adoption) (Ephesians 1:5, 11), so that the believer has an inheritance from God and is God's heritage. (Note: In Reformed theology, the term "predestination" smashes together four distinct biblical doctrines: foreordination + election + predestination + providence.)

Prevenient Grace. The theological and biblical concept that God gives grace to enable the sinner's faith. Prevenient means "coming before."

Progressive Revelation. The doctrine of progressive revelation is the simple observation God does not reveal all things at the same time, but over time God's revelation is completed.

Propitiation. The satisfaction Christ made to God for sin by dying on the cross as the sin-bearer, 2 Corinthians 5:21; Romans 3:25; Hebrews 2:17; 1 John 2:2; 4:10, for the crime of sin committed by human beings, suffering in their place and on their behalf.

Providence. That which God's foreordination effectuated in eternity-past, God's providence accomplishes in historical-present. Providence is a term used to describe God's unceasing works by which he maintains and preserves the universe and all his creatures, and governs its operations and their actions, so as to accomplish his plans and eternal purpose.

Reprobation. To be disqualified from heaven and subject to judgment and eternal punishment.

Resurrection. God reforms the physically dead decomposed body from existing materials and gives that body endless immortal physical life, and God causes the disembodied soul originally propagated with that body to unite with it and animate it. The united soul and resurrected body will continue endlessly in that reunited state.

Salvation. The remission of sin's penalty by the application of the merit of Christ's propitiation of God on the cross to the sinner's spiritual need. The merit of the propitiation is applied to the sinner's spiritual need by God's grace through the means of the sinner's personal faith in God and God's testimony as to the way of salvation.

Saving faith. A sinner is not enabled to believe, he or she is convicted through the work of God the Holy Spirit of the truth of personal sin, the judicial guilt and punishment of sin, the need for salvation by faith not works, and the all-sufficiency of the propitiation made by Jesus Christ the Savior required to save his or her soul. On the basis of that conviction the sinner personally appropriates these truths to satisfy his or her spiritual need for salvation. That personal appropriation of truth to satisfy the spiritual need for salvation is the exercise of saving faith.

Sanctification. Sanctification is the right standing before God resulting from the salvific experience. Sanctification has three aspects: positional, experiential, and eternal.

Sin. The moral violation of God's holiness by failure to conform to the image and likeness in which he created human nature and sin is the legal violation of God's laws by disobedience. At its most basic, sin is the failure to conform fully to God's image and likeness. In the final analysis, sin is any thought or action that does not conform to the essence, personality, character, attributes, or purpose of God. Scripture uses the word "sin" to (1) refer to the evil life principle disobedience, aka the sin attribute in human nature, 1 John 1:8, and (2) to refer to human nature as influenced by the sin attribute, aka acts of sinning, 1 John 1:10.

Sin, act of. Sin is actions in thought, word, or deed that express the sin nature's rebellion against God through disobedience to his commandments. An act of sin is the volition resulting from an illicit desire of the will positively responding to temptation. The unsaved person sins as a habit of life. The believer commits occasional acts of sin. In the believer an act of sin causes a dulling of the soul's faculty of spiritual perception (reversed by conviction, confession, repentance, restoration, 1 John 1:9). The time to stop an act of sin is during temptation, when the believer says to him or herself, "I choose to obey God."

Sin attribute. An evil life-principle (attribute) that is part of fallen human nature which, through constructive interaction with other life-principles (attributes) in one's human nature, influences a person to self-determine his or her course in the world in opposition to God's holy character and revealed will, whether that will of God is discovered in Scripture, or in that revelation of himself God has made in human conscience. Sin is accomplished in acts of rebellion against God and disobedience to his commandments.

Sin, dominion of. Sin has authority (dominion, rule) over the sinner, not as some invincible overlord, but as an innate part of human nature constructively working with all the other attributes of human nature to persuasively incline the will to choose an act of sinning. The evil attribute sin influences every other attribute with the inclination to sin, and in that sense sin can be said to dominate the will. The sinner freely chooses sinning because his will is of itself always inclined to choose sinning, and as being rebellious and disobedient toward God never desires to change its inclination to choose sinning to rebel against God, disobey his commandments, and seek a path in life apart from God.

Sons of. A description of character. The biblical terms "seed of," "offspring of" "sons of," or "daughters of," are, when speaking metaphorically, those persons whose characteristics are like the person of whom they are a "seed of," "offspring of," "son of," or "daughter of."

When used symbolically neither "sons of" nor "daughters of" is a gender specific term. The term "sons of" means a person possesses the characteristics of the person or thing he or she is a "son of." The "sons of rebellion," at 2 Samuel 23:6 were the rebellious. The "sons of the prophets," 2 Kings 2:3, were those men who were faithful to God and preached his Word. The sons of fools, and the sons of vile men, Job 30:8, were fools and vile.

The term "sons of God" (Hebrew: *benê 'ĕlōhîm;* Greek: *huiós theós*) is used in Genesis 6:2, 4; Job 1:6; 2:1; 38:7; Matthew 5:9; Luke 20:36; Romans 8:14, 19; Galatians 3:26. In every use it refers to persons who are like God because they are in a faith-based relationship with God. No fallen angel and no unsaved human being are ever characterized as a son of God.

Soul. An immaterial substance that gives life and governs behavior in all living things. The soul is composed of the animating principle life, the human essence, and the human nature composed of that complex of attributes which with life experience synergistically determine the personality of living beings.

The human soul is naturally immortal, having been created *ex nihilo* by God, Genesis 2:7, apart from the human body. The soul's natural immortality comes from the animating principle "life," that God gave the soul when created, and is propagated in each human being through the processes of biological reproduction, as the animating principle life in the gametes is continued in the newly conceived zygote. That the animating principle is intrinsic to the human soul is seen in Genesis 2:7, God placed the soul into the inert physical body and the body was animated.

The immaterial soul is in union with the material body, but is able to exist independently apart from the material body. God will reunite the soul that was disembodied through the death of the body with the resurrected body. See Death, physical.

When in the disembodied state, the human soul has a form defined by time and space—for lack of a better term, a body suited for life in the spirit domain.

Soul sleep. The doctrine the human soul is unconscious, or "sleeps" when separated from the human body between physical death and resurrection of the body. The doctrine misunderstand scriptures referring to physical death as "sleep." In those scriptures the word "sleep" refers to the death of the body not a condition of the soul. The body "sleeps" while awaiting resurrection. The use of "sleep" to refer to physical death is a euphemism intended by the Holy Spirit to communicate the believer is not to fear physical death.

Sovereignty. That attribute of God wherein his authority to act is determined by his own counsel, is uninfluenced by anything or any being, and is without limitation.

Spiritual Death. Separated from a relationship with God and in the spiritual condition of active rebellion against God. Spiritual death, or "dead in trespasses and sins," does not mean the unsaved sinner is inactive, but means he/she is actively in rebellion against God, always making the spiritual decision to reject God and salvation in Christ.

Standing. A person salvific state as he or she stands before God in his office as the righteous Judge. Standing indicates the relationship one has with God: either a salvific relationship with God in Christ, or no relationship and condemned because of sin and awaiting judgment. The standing of the believer is sanctified: forgiven, regenerated, possessing eternal life, judged as holy and righteous, placed into an eternal relationship with God.

State. A term referring to how the believer lives his or her daily life on the earth. God gives the believer the gift of grace and through personal effort the believer uses the means of grace to apply grace so as to overcome the temptation of sin in order to conform his manner of living (thoughts and actions) to be more like Christ. The believer's preferred state is to live his or her life in such a manner so as to conform one's lifestyle to be godly and Christ-like. The believer makes a conscious effort to bring his state in the world to the same level of godliness, holiness, and righteousness as his standing.

Spiritual perception. A faculty of the human soul that allows man to perceive, understand, and communicate with God. The ability of the soul to receive and understand spiritual things. A faculty of the soul through which man has communion with God. The ability of the soul to receive, understand, and appropriately apply biblical knowledge to live godly in this present world. In the saved soul spiritual perception has been enlivened by the work of the Holy Spirit (the soul becomes born-again).

Sources

Alexander, Archibald. *Evidences of the Authenticity, Inspiration, and Canonical Authority of the Holy Scriptures.* 1830. Reprinted, 2021, West Linn, OR: Monergism Books, n.d.

Ames, William. *The Marrow of Theology.* 1648. Reprinted, Durham, PA: The Labyrinth Press, 1983.

Berkhof, Louis. *Systematic Theology.* London: Banner of Truth Trust, 1959.

Brenton, Sir Lancelot, C. L. *The Septuagint with Apocrypha: English.* London: Samuel Bagster & Sons, 1851. Reprinted http://ecmarsh.com, 2010.

Buswell, J. Oliver. *A Systematic Theology of the Christian Religion.* Grand Rapids, MI: Zondervan, 1962.

Calvin John. *Calvin's Commentaries.* 1847. Reprinted, Grand Rapids, MI: Baker Book House, 1996.

_____. *Institutes of the Christian Religion.* 2 vols. 1559. Reprinted, Grand Rapids, MI: Eerdmans Publishing, 1971.

Dabny, R. L. *Lectures in Systematic Theology.* 1927. Reprinted, Grand Rapids, MI: Baker Book House, 1985.

Dolezal, James E. *All That Is In God.* Grand Rapids, MI: Reformation Heritage Books, 2017.

Grudem, Wayne. *Systematic Theology.* Grand Rapids, MI: Zondervan, 1994.

Harris, R. Laird; Gleason L. Archer, Jr.; and Bruce K. Waltke. *Theological Wordbook of the Old Testament.* 2 vols. Chicago, IL: Moody Press, 1980.

Harrison, Everett, F., ed. *Baker's Dictionary of Theology.* Grand Rapids, MI: Baker Book House, 1960.

Hodge, Charles. *Systematic Theology.* 1871–1873. Reprinted, Grand Rapids, MI: Eerdmans Publishing, 1981.

Hoehner, Harold W. *Ephesians, an Exegetical Commentary.* Grand Rapids, MI: Baker Academic, 2002.

Kittel, Gerhard, and Gerhard Friedrich. *Theological Dictionary of the New Testament.* 10 vols. Translated by Geoffrey W. Bromiley. Grand Rapids, MI: Eerdmans Publishing, 1967.

Lipscomb, J. Neil. *From Ancient Wisdom to Modern Understanding, A Historical Survey of Systematic Theology.* Independently published, 2023.

MacArthur, John. *1 Timothy.* MacArthur New Testament Commentary. Vol 24. Chicago, IL: Moody Publishers, 1995.

_____. *The Love of God.* Nashville, TN: W Pub Group, 1996.

Manton, Thomas. *An Exposition of the Epistle of James.* 1693. Reprinted, Marshallton, DE: National Foundation for Christian Education, n.d.

_____. *By Faith, Sermons on Hebrews 11.* 1873 ed. Reprinted, Carlisle, PA: The Banner of Truth Trust, 2000.

Moulton, J. H., and G. Milligan. *Vocabulary of the Greek Testament.* 1930. Reprinted, Peabody, MA: Hendrickson Publishers, 1997.

Murray, Ian. *Spurgeon versus Hyper-Calvinism.* Carlisle, PA: The Banner of Truth Trust, 2010.

Owen, John. *The Works of John Owen.* 1850–1853. Reprinted Carlisle, PA: The Banner of Truth Trust. 1965.

Quiggle, James D. *A Private Commentary on the Bible: John's Epistles.* Amazon/KDP, 2016.

_____. *A Private Commentary on the Bible: Matthew's Gospel.* Amazon/KDP, 2016.

_____. *Adam and Eve, A Biography and Theology.* Amazon/KDP, 2011.

_____. *Against Annihilationism, Physicalism, and Conditionalism.* Amazon/KDP 2024.

_____. *Dictionary of Doctrinal Words.* Amazon/KDP, 2018.

_____. *Did Jesus Go To Hell?* Amazon/KDP, 2021.

_____. *Dispensational Soteriology.* Amazon/KDP, 2023.

_____. *God's Choices, The Doctrines of Foreordination, Election, and Predestination.* Amazon/KDP, 2012.

_____. *Life, Death, Eternity.* Amazon/KDP, 2019.

_____ *Understanding Dispensational Theology.* Amazon/KDP 2019.

Roberts, Alexander, and James Donaldson. *Ante-Nicene Fathers,* vol. 1, *The Apostolic Fathers, Justin Martyr, Irenaeus.* 1885, Reprinted, Peabody, MA: Hendrickson Publishers, 1995.

_____. *Ante-Nicene Fathers.* Vol. 3. *Latin Christianity: Its Founder,*

Tertullian, I. Apologetic; II. Anti-Marcion; III. Ethical. 1885, Reprinted, Peabody, MA: Hendrickson Publishers, 1995.

Robertson, A. T. *Word Pictures in the New Testament.* Vol. 6. Nashville, TN: Broadman Press, 1932.

Ryrie, Charles C. *Dispensationalism.* Chicago, IL: Moody Press, 1995.

Schaff, Philip. *The Creeds of Christendom.* 1931. Reprinted, Grand Rapids, MI: Baker Book House, 1983.

_____. *Nicene and Post-Nicene Fathers, First Series.* Vol. 7. Augustin: Homilies on the Gospel of John, Homilies on the First Epistle of John, Soliloquies. 1888. Reprinted, Peabody, MA: Hendrickson Publishers, 1999.

Schaff, Philip and Henry Wace. *Nicene and Post-Nicene Fathers. Second Series.* Vol. 14, *The Seven Ecumenical Councils.* 1900. Reprinted, Peabody, MA: Hendrickson Publishers, 1999.

Schurer, Emil. *A History of the Jewish People in the Time of Christ.* 1890. Reprinted, Peabody, MA: Hendrickson Publishers, 2020.

Shedd, W. G. T. *Dogmatic Theology.* 1863. 3 vols. Reprinted, Nashville, TN: Thomas Nelson Publishers, 1980.

_____. *The Doctrine of Endless Punishment.* 1885. Reprinted, Carlisle, PA: Banner of Truth Trust, 1986.

Silva, Moisés. Revision Editor. *New International Dictionary of New Testament Theology and Exegesis.* Grand Rapids, MI: Zondervan, 2014.

Stewart, Kenneth J. *Ten Myths About Calvinism.* Downers Grove, IL: InterVarsity Press, 2011.

Stewart, S.D.F. *The Christian Doctrine of Immortality.* 1895. Reprinted from the 5th ed., 1907, Miami, FL: Hardpress Publishing, n.d.

Thomas, G. Michael. *The Extent of the Atonement.* 1997. Reprinted Eugene, OR: Wipf and Stock Publishers, 2006.

Venning, Ralph. *The Sinfulness of Sin.* 1669. Reprinted, Carlisle, PA: Banner of Truth Trust, 1965.

Westcott, B. F. *The Epistles of St. John.* 1883. 3rd ed. 1892. Reprinted, Grand Rapids, MI: William B. Eerdmans Publishing, 1974.

Wuest, Kenneth S. *Word Studies From the Greek New Testament for the English Reader.* Vol. 2. Article, "In These Last Days," 1954. Reprinted, Grand Rapids, MI: Eerdmans Publishing,1978.

Sources

Zodhiates, Spiros. *The Complete Word Study Dictionary: New Testament*. Revised. Chattanooga, TN: AMG Publishers, 1993.

www.ingramcontent.com/pod-product-compliance
Lightning Source LLC
Chambersburg PA
CBHW051946090426
42741CB00008B/1289